*Lesley Chea...*

# DOING TIME

# DOING TIME
## FEMINIST THEORY AND POSTMODERN CULTURE

### RITA FELSKI

**NEW YORK UNIVERSITY PRESS**
NEW YORK AND LONDON

**NEW YORK UNIVERSITY PRESS**
New York and London

Library of Congress Cataloging-in-Publication Data
Felski, Rita, 1956–
Doing time : feminist theory and postmodern culture / by Rita Felski.
p.   cm. — (Cultural front)
Includes bibliographical references and index.
ISBN 0-8147-2706-9 (cloth : alk. paper) —
ISBN 0-8147-2707-7 (pbk. : alk. paper)
1. Feminist theory. 2. Postmodernism.   I. Title.  II. Cultural front (Series)
HQ1190 .F416 2000
305.42'01—dc21                    00-008898

New York University Press books are printed on acid-free paper
and their binding materials are chosen for strength and durability.

Manufactured in the United States of America
10 9 8 7 6 5 4 3 2 1

# CONTENTS

# ACKNOWLEDGMENTS

I would like to thank Michael Bérubé and Eric Zinner for supporting this project. I am also grateful to my anonymous reader for alerting me to problems in my argument that needed fixing. Individuals who helped me write specific chapters are credited at the end of each chapter. Heather Love provided invaluable help in preparing the final manuscript. Above all, I owe an enormous debt to Allan Megill for his kindness, wisdom, scholarship, and infinite patience.

Most of the chapters in this book have been published previously. In most cases they have been revised, sometimes substantially. I would like to thank *PMLA, New Formations, Women: A Cultural Review, Signs: Journal of Women in Culture and Society, New Literary History, Continuum, Cultural Critique,* and Penn State University Press for permission to reprint. Full details of the original publication are given at the end of each chapter.

# INTRODUCTION
## TIMELY MEDITATIONS

**D**o we live in the same time or different times? This simple question goes to the heart of recent cultural theory and politics. Debates about universals versus particulars and shared worlds versus incommensurable worlds are also arguments about our embeddedness in history and time. If I think of myself as existing in the same time as others, does this commit me to a belief in universal history? Is it possible to carve up the continuum of time into segments, to talk meaningfully about men's time and women's time, Western time and non-Western time? How can we explain the fact that individuals and groups may perceive time very differently and yet seem, in crucial respects, to inhabit the same time? What are the stakes in either affirming or denying the contemporaneity and coevalness of others?

Most of the following essays wrestle with these questions. My intellectual life got into gear only when I stumbled across the work of the Frankfurt School, and I suspect that my thinking remains permanently marked by this encounter. As a result, I cannot help but take to heart Fredric Jameson's often cited injunction to "always historicize." But I do not subscribe to a Marxist understanding of history, nor am I always persuaded by Jameson's dazzling speculations on the aesthetics and politics of postmodern culture. Moreover, I often feel frustrated by Marxist discussions of the modern and postmodern that relegate women to a solitary footnote or, indeed, that fail to acknowledge them at all. To expound on the politics of contemporary culture while ignoring the seismic impact of feminism, perhaps the most influential social movement of the last thirty years, is either foolhardy, myopic, or perverse. The invocation of history in the singular is often a code word for business as usual: left-wing scholarship that remains oblivious or resolutely impervious to alternative visions of what counts as history.

While Jameson and other Marxist scholars want to explain postmodernism historically, another group of writers thinks of postmodernism as synonymous with the demise of historical time. The idea of history, they argue, is firmly glued to modernist conceptions of truth and a naive view of time as evolution and progress. History presumes a confident knowledge of what really happened in the past and an imperious urge to organize the chaotic flux of time into a single streamlined story. In short, we can think of history as a modern mirage, an ephemeral fantasy spun out of words that tries to pass itself off as an objective account of how things really are. Postmodern thought shatters this apparently stable ground and radically alters our way of thinking about time. One of the most distinctive features of postmodernism, in this account, is its challenge to linear logic. Time loses its arrow; it no longer has a coherent goal or direction. We are no longer propelled into the future by the purposeful forward march of events. Instead, we find ourselves adrift, floating aimlessly in a sea of temporal fragments and random moments.

How friendly is this "postmodern" view of time to the interests of women and other disenfranchised groups? Less than one might think. Some writers imagine that a posthistorical consciousness is politically desirable because it is open to diverse perspectives and multiple viewpoints. Postmodernism simply *is* the culture of difference, freeing us from the tyranny of a single, universal time. In actual fact, this liberation is less dramatic than it seems. To think of the postmodern present as enacting a break with linear time is to assign difference a very limited space of operation within a conventional philosophy of history. In other words, difference loses much of its power by being seen in epochal terms. It is the crowning moment in a sequence of stages that leads inexorably from the dreary uniformity of the premodern and the modern to the dazzling plurality of the postmodern era. Women, people of color, and other disenfranchised groups are portrayed as suddenly bursting onto the historical stage, as if they had no prior existence as social subjects and human agents. Otherness is recognized only in the context of the present and subsumed within a familiar story of evolution from sameness to difference, from the one to the many.

How, then, can we do more adequate justice to the question of difference? How can we take into account the messy variety of human lives, activities, and experiences as they affect the full compass and breadth of historical time? An alternative response is to think of difference as vertical rather than horizontal, slicing across time rather than being enclosed within a particular period or epoch. In this view, individual groups have their own distinct histories, rhythms, and temporalities quite apart from traditional forms of periodization. History is not one broad river, but a number of distinct and separate streams, each moving at its own pace and tempo. As a result, terms such as "modern" and "postmodern" lose their universal reach; rather, they are merely the *idées fixes* of white male theorists, of little use in talking about the temporality of others. Women qua women, for example, have a unique relationship to time outside conventional, male-centered forms. Feminine difference pervades the entirety of history rather than being confined to a particular epoch. In this chapter I look briefly at attempts in feminist theory to develop the idea of "women's time." How coherent and plausible is this concept? In questioning the assumption of a radical difference between "masculine" and "feminine" temporality, I draw on relevant debates in anthropology about the cultural relativity of time.

Finally, I consider Ernst Bloch's idea of *ungleichzeitige Gleichzeitigkeit*, or synchronous nonsynchronicity. I find Bloch's elaboration of this concept ultimately unsatisfying because it remains too closely tied to an evolutionary framework. Yet in spite of its ungainliness, Bloch's phrase strikes me as the most promising way of approaching the cultural politics of time. Quite simply, it acknowledges that we inhabit both the same time and different times: individuals coexist at the same historical moment, yet often make sense of this moment in strikingly disparate ways. Women can neither be subsumed within conventional periods nor segregated within a separate "women's time." This idea of sameness and difference in the experience of time is a leitmotif in the following essays, which grapple with the varied and often confusing meanings of modernity and postmodernity from a feminist perspective.

I should stress that this book does not take sides on the merits of the modern over the postmodern, or vice versa. It has become routine for writers in various fields to voice their disagreements about epistemological, ethical, or political issues by staging a standoff between modernists and postmodernists. Modernists are presented as heroic defenders of the Enlightenment and postmodernists as irresponsible, apolitical relativists. Alternatively, postmodernists are hip, savvy thinkers alert to difference and ambiguity, and modernists are dour stick-in-the-muds clinging to anachronistic ideas about objectivity and truth. The use of historical terms to signal praise or abuse in this way is a waste of everyone's time; wielded as slogans, they polarize debate and often obscure the specific philosophical, political, or aesthetic issues that are at stake.[1]

Feminist theory is by no means free of such skirmishes. Things have changed since 1988, when Meaghan Morris mourned the lack of serious engagement between feminism and postmodernism.[2] There is now a substantial and mounting literature on this question. Because postmodernism has become such a baggy and bloated idea, embracing a huge and disparate array of texts, theories, and cultural phenomena, there is not much common ground in this scholarship. Discussions of feminism and postmodernism can involve almost anything, from cyborgs to Cindy Sherman, metaphysics to Madonna, decor to Derrida, shopping to *The Simpsons*. Before going any further, then, I want to describe the particular terrain I stake out in this book.

Like the writing on postmodernism generally, much of the writing on feminism and the postmodern falls into three distinct groupings. First, there are feminist scholars who are interested in postmodernism as a philosophical and theoretical terrain, albeit one with important political ramifications. They often tackle themes such as realism versus antirealism, the status of the subject, universality versus difference, the legitimacy of normative claims, and so on. The usual suspects rounded up for discussion are Derrida, Lacan, Foucault, Kristeva, Irigaray, Lyotard, and similar thinkers. Much of the ensuing argument then revolves around whether feminism should or should not be considered postmodern. Is feminism a child of modernity in a postmodern age? Or does feminism radically subvert the tradition of the Enlightenment?[3]

Some of this work has made valuable contributions to feminist theory. However, there is a real problem in using "postmodern" to describe the work of authors such as Foucault and Derrida who do not talk about postmodernism and who are, for the most part, deeply suspicious of the term (even Lyotard, the most obvious French candidate for inclusion, spent much of his subsequent career qualifying what he wrote in *The Postmodern Condition*). French intellectuals have lined up in droves to distance themselves from what they see as the bizarre English-speaking obsession with postmodernism. This makes the frequent use of postmodernism as a synonym for poststructuralism even more puzzling. A relatively neutral term for some influential philosophical trends is thereby transformed into an adjective with a much more ambitious historical reach. It becomes easy to imagine that specific scholarly debates are an accurate mirror of seismic shifts in our cultural condition, to assume that postmodernism is a reality rather than a particular way of talking about reality. Much poststructuralist thought, by contrast, explicitly rejects this kind of historical thinking and periodizing logic.[4]

There is a second large body of feminist work that looks at postmodernism as a label for certain forms and styles of literature and art. Here again, scholars disagree, often vehemently, about the value of the term in helping us make sense of contemporary trends. For example, is the postmodern novel a boy's game of irony and wordplay, remote from the concerns of most women? Or is women's writing at the very heart of the postmodern? Is Doris Lessing postmodern? What about Kathy Acker? Or Toni Morrison?[5]

How persuasively these questions are answered depends on how the key terms are defined. In some cases, postmodernism is taken to mean a distinct style or form, consisting of pastiche, double coding, open-endedness, playfulness, bricolage, fragmentation, and so on. The case for postmodernism as a distinctively new style has some plausibility in architecture and perhaps the visual arts, but is less persuasive when made by literary critics. Attempts to define postmodern literature in purely formal terms usually overlook the history of modernism or present a highly simplified and foreshortened version of it. If we take modernism to mean not just Anglo-American high modernism but the full span of early-twentieth-century experimentation, including the anarchic anti-art of Dada, surrealism, and other avant-garde movements, it becomes hard to identify any stylistic feature of postmodern literature that is not already present somewhere in modernism.[6]

This is not to say that the 1990s are the same as the 1930s or that Thomas Pynchon and Kathy Acker (to take two names often associated with literary postmodernism) are merely the slavish epigones of Woolf or Faulkner. Rather, it is to suggest that the historical differences may have as much to do with sensibility, theme, worldview, and changing perceptions of the role and function of art as with any radical formal breakthrough. And to broach this question is to be pulled willy-nilly into the third set of debates about feminism and postmodernism. Here the postmodern broadens out to become a label for a general historical and cultural condition. Is postmodernism our "mode of life," "the way we live now"?[7] What are the distinctive features of a postmodern culture? How well does the word encapsulate the images, ideas, beliefs, currents of thought, and ways of "being in the world" of our time? Feminist scholars have often tackled this question by focusing on specific cultural phenomena, such as science and technology, film and visual culture, changing conceptions of sexed bodies, or even feminism itself. These phenomena serve as both cause and symptom of the postmodern, signs of an epochal change that is radically reshaping the fabric of everyday life and our sense of what it means to be male or female.[8]

In one sense my writing is closest in spirit to this last group. While the following essays touch on both poststructuralist theory and aesthetics, they do so in the context of puzzling over the meaning of postmodernism as a label for a general condition. However, while some feminist scholars take it for granted that we inhabit a postmodern moment, I am less confident. In fact, the question of periodization is one of my main interests. What does it mean to say that we live in a postmodern era and how has this idea been fleshed out in recent scholarship? What is to be gained and what is to be lost by describing particular institutions, practices, beliefs, and ways of life as either modern or postmodern? What attitudes about history and time are conveyed by these terms? And how useful or useless are they for feminist theory?

In fact, these questions also arise in commentaries on postmodernism as theory and as aesthetic style, simply because such commentaries almost always smuggle in a historical thesis. In the middle of reading about epistemology or parsing a line by Don de Lillo, we are suddenly confronted with a claim about the repressive logic of Western history or a treatise on the simulacrum as a key to the meaning of postmodern culture. The urge to generalize about the postmodern is almost irresistible. Several of the following essays thus tackle head-on a cluster of themes that lie at the heart of almost all accounts of postmodernism: time, history, and periodization. I turn a somewhat jaundiced and skeptical eye on a ubiquitous vocabulary of crisis, rupture, and ending: postmodernism as the end of history, the end of art, the end of philosophy, the end of sex.

There are two other ideas that connect the following essays. The first deals with the relative merits of "big pictures" (a term I borrow from Richard Rorty) versus "getting specific" (the title of a recent book by Shane Phelan).[9] In some respects, there is a clear shrinking of intellectual and political ambition in current scholarly writing. Authors tend to be more modest about their claims, less likely to claim that they can deliver a "theory of everything," more eager to proclaim the virtues of particularity and difference. But we should not assume that there has been a wholesale retreat from big pictures. Those who see postmodernism as synonymous with the specific, the local, and the different are overgeneralizing. Indeed, as I show in a number of these essays, the urge toward a synoptic vision is hard to resist. Chop off one large claim about the world and another one appears, hydra-like, in its place. We may not generalize about the same kinds of things that the Victorians did, but we generalize nonetheless. In a number of these essays I offer a qualified defense of the desire for big pictures as a persistent and valuable rather than outmoded desire.

Conversely, if some discussions of postmodernism are too fixated on the particular for my taste, others are distressingly global. Part of the problem is that postmodernism is often seen to flatten and neutralize all distinctions in a promiscuous free-for-all. The aestheticization of politics and the politicization of aesthetics are taken to mean that art and politics are now one. This problem is compounded by the fact that postmodernism is a term that has expanded to include almost every possible field and endeavor; we now have postmodern sociology, postmodern history, and postmodern philosophy, as well as postmodern architecture, postmodern literature, postmodern music, and the like. As a result, it is very easy to construct false analogies across different spheres and to imagine that postmodernism means the same thing in all of them. For example, an early article of mine on feminism and postmodernism (reprinted in chapter 9) suggested that feminism should treat postmodern theories of philosophy and social criticism with some caution. Yet I have seen this article cited as evidence of a certain discomfort with postmodern literature (I am, for the record, a great fan of Jeanette Winterson). The shattering of hierarchies in literature does not mean the same thing as the shattering of hierarchies in philosophy, or in the realm of practical politics: these things take place in different, though related, sites. The best evidence against a postmodern dissolution of all boundaries is the very different and often conflicting meanings of postmodernism in specific fields and disciplines.[10]

Second, my own approach to feminism and postmodernism is defined by what is probably a rather weird mix of critical theory and cultural studies (my second formative encounter). Cultural studies has often been reproached for being ahistorical and interested only in the present. Conversely, cultural critics are often highly skeptical about the claims of critical theory and the sweeping historical narratives of the Frankfurt School tradition.[11] My own work does not engage in the detailed analysis of everyday objects and practices that defines some forms of cultural studies. I remain unabashedly interested in philosophical concepts and big pictures. But I do think that the insights of cultural studies can help us achieve a more pluridimensional model of history. It allows us to modify grand claims about the modern and the postmodern by looking at what is going on in specific sites and contexts. It can help us to avoid *Zeitgeist* thinking about the modern and the postmodern. (This is not to say that everyone who does cultural studies avoids this trap. Baudrillard has a lot to answer for.) The various institutions, cultures, and ways of life that make up the modern or the postmodern cannot be boiled down to a single compact idea or a unitary philosophical or political essence. Hence, it makes little sense to talk about feminism being "for" or "against" the modern or the postmodern.

One can, of course, simply shrug one's shoulders and argue that the whole game is not worth the candle, as in one recent discussion of the "lesbian post-modern." In fact, the relationship between sexuality and postmodernism has received a fair amount of attention. Because some prominent poststructuralists are also queer theorists, much of this writing deals with broad theoretical issues. What are the specific links between dominant Western ways of knowing and the heterosexual imperative? What commonalities are there between the self-constitution of gay, lesbian, or queer subjects and "postmodern" theory? Another much-trafficked area of inquiry explores the possible intersections between postmodern and lesbian aesthetics. The works of writers such as Jeanette Winterson, Gloria Anzaldúa, and Nicole Brossard, as well as key predecessors such as Monique Wittig and Gertrude Stein, have inspired much reflection on the links between sexuality and writing, between lesbian themes and fragmented, playful, textual forms.[12] Some of the most recent discussions of the lesbian postmodern extend out to the realm of popular culture, consumerism, and everyday life. Such discussions are leading, according to one critic, to a "wholesale repudiation of femininity and the female body. In its place we now find a semiotic fascination with cyborgs, female-to-male-transsexuals and Barbie."[13]

However, Judith Roof is one scholar who suggests that the whole debate is uninteresting. She expresses a strong skepticism about the idea of "any essential link between ways of life or identities defined by sexual orientation and a set of diverging philosophies about the condition of knowledge, consumer culture and aesthetic practices."[14] Roof astutely identifies some of the problems of linking a "subversive" lesbianism to a "subversive" postmodernism; the supposed shattering of norms that defines the postmodern becomes the new truth of a lesbian identity that is fixed in its very ambiguity, fluidity, and decenteredness. All differences, contradictions, and tensions between aesthetics, politics, and sexual practices are hence elided. Roof is more interested in avoiding the authorizing power of the concept of postmodern. In spite of its apparent rebelliousness, she suggests that this term is fundamentally conservative, enforcing a traditional model of dialectical history and an Oedipal genealogy.

The concept of postmodernism has also received a mixed response among feminist scholars concerned with issues of race and ethnicity. The term "postmodern ethnicity" has been coined by writers interested in exploring the hybrid and contradictory nature of ethnic identity and its estrangement from any notion of an authentic origin. "Postmodern ethnicity," writes Ien Ang, "can no longer be experienced as naturally based upon tradition and ancestry; rather, it is experienced as a provisional and partial site of identity which must be constantly (re)invented and (re)negotiated."[15] Some scholars of postcolonialism have also found postmodernism to be a valuable diagnostic term in questioning the heritage of modernity and analyzing new forms of transnational and global interconnection. For example, Inderpal Grewal and Caren Kaplan discard an aesthetic definition of the term for a political and social one, claiming that "postmodernism exists precisely because of anticolonial critiques" and "opposition to Western hegemony."[16]

However, bell hooks noted in 1990 that very few African American intellectuals were writing about postmodernism. She directs her criticism at a field that "talks the most about heterogeneity, the decentered subject," yet "still directs its critical voice primarily to a specialized audience that shares a common language rooted in the very master narratives it claims to challenge."[17] While hooks welcomes the questioning of an essential black identity, she suggests that postmodernism will become useful only if there is increased dialogue between white and black scholars as well as a more sustained attempt to link the work of the academy to everyday life.

In this context, cultural studies is useful in helping us see that postmodernism is not just a way of talking about culture but also a form of culture. In other words, postmodern themes permeate our environment and help shape it. Some recent criticisms of postmodernism take the tack of dismissing it as a category mistake, a comedy of philosophical errors that needs to be rectified by a turn to better, more rigorous forms of theory.[18] The problem with arguing this way is that postmodernism is not just a series of intellectual propositions but also a panorama of stories, images, and metaphors. These rhetorical figures have been enormously seductive. As overarching symbolic systems, they are not open to proof or disproof in any normal sense. However, we can qualify their power and authority by pointing out that they are not the only stories and metaphors in town.

It may be tempting to dismiss postmodernism as a trendy, arcane form of faculty-club culture, of no possible use or interest to the world outside the academic ivory tower.[19] But this does not seem right. It is certainly true that academic ideas do not always march neatly in step with the rest of society. Discussions of postmodernism often suffer in moving too hastily from the condition of an intellectual and cultural minority to the world as a whole. Still, postmodernism is one of the most successful and widely circulated ideas to come out of the academy. Many postmodern themes filter via circuitous routes into newspapers, movies, TV shows, advertising, science fiction novels, fanzines, and many other popular forms. Postmodern readings of MTV were followed by an MTV show called "Postmodern Videos." The recent Hollywood blockbuster movie *The Matrix* contained sly references to postmodern ideas and the work of Jean Baudrillard. Postmodernism thus helps create its own reality, by fashioning audiences who are encouraged to interpret the world in a postmodern way. "Can

INTRODUCTION: TIMELY MEDITATIONS

post-modernity be a myth," asks Krishan Kumar, "if so many people believe, or can be persuaded that they are living in such a condition?"[20]

My own approach to the modern and postmodern is less concerned with the question of whether they are true (as compared to what?) than whether they are useful. Historical terms, by definition, are not objective, God-given realities but humanly created concepts that are open to questioning and change. For example, I remain agnostic as to the ultimate value of the distinction between the modern and the postmodern. At some points in the book, I find theories of postmodernism helpful in trying to pin down some of the most striking and distinctive features of the present era. Other essays stress the continuity between past and present and argue that our own period is best understood as a moment within modernity. In each case, the decision is made on pragmatic grounds. What do these terms allow us to see more clearly? What do they obscure? How are they helpful to feminism? And how can feminist theory help to unsettle the concepts of the modern and postmodern, which often congeal into absolute, unchallengeable truths?

## GETTING RID OF HISTORY

I want to elaborate on my worries about common accounts of postmodernism by looking at Elizabeth Deeds Ermarth's *Sequel to History: Postmodernism and the Crisis of Representational Time*. Ermarth's book is widely cited and also relies on assumptions that appear in other recent writing. It is thus a good example of a particular way of thinking about the imbrication of time and history. The modern era, in Ermarth's definition, extends from the Renaissance to the turn of the twentieth century, and embraces a relatively coherent and unified set of beliefs about the self, reality, and time. Above all, it is synonymous with the cultural sovereignty of the idea of history. History, according to Ermarth, always involves dialectics, teleology, transcendence, and claims to neutrality. Historical time, she suggests, links the past to the future and thus creates the illusion that there are overarching laws of development governing temporal processes. Furthermore, it is a cultural absolute, shaping the logic of diverse fields of modern life from physics to politics to narrative. Modern historical consciousness thinks of time as a neutral, homogeneous medium, where all relationships can be explained in terms of a common horizon. History thus involves a perpetual transcendence of the concrete. "By emphasizing what is linear, developmental and mediate, historical thinking by definition involves transcendence of a kind that trivializes the specific detail and finite moment."[21] History is linked, therefore, to fantasies of omniscience, neutrality, and sameness; it denies real differences by assuming their common existence within a temporal medium that unifies and ultimately transcends all such differences.

Postmodernism, by contrast, does away with this notion of history. For Ermarth, postmodernism means the experimental fiction of the 1950s and 1960s (Robbe-Grillet, Nabokov, Cortázar), as well as the ideas of such poststructuralist thinkers as Derrida, Kristeva, and Foucault. What unites these various writers, she argues, is their recognition of the primary importance of language and a consequent demotion of history. No longer an unproblematic grounding for human affairs, history is revealed as nothing more than a fragile and ephemeral fiction. Postmodern literature, in particular, undermines any sense of the coherence, linearity, or collective experience of time. Its form is one of rhythm and repetition; it offers to the reader a collection of fragments, of specific, finite moments and intensities that have no stable or systematic connection. While Ermarth claims to be rejecting any notion of truth or representation, she nevertheless seems to believe that this formlessness comes closer to capturing the "real" nature of time.

Ermarth is stern and uncompromising in her rejection of history. She is impatient with those scholars who want to find new ways of thinking about history, insisting that "one cannot oppose history to foundationalism because history *is* foundationalism."[22] In her account, history is not an ambiguous term open to diverse and conflicting interpretations, but an outdated piece of metaphysical baggage. Given this vehemence, it is surprising that Ermarth's own work relies so heavily on not just historical but also historicist arguments. We can see the specter of Hegel hovering over many passages of her writing.

First, Ermarth takes for granted the reality of an epochal sequence of stages: the medieval, the modern, and the postmodern (this sequence is presumably limited to the history of the West, though Ermarth never explicitly addresses this issue). Such a description obviously relies heavily on the very idea of linear coherence that it wants to refute. Ermarth's paradoxical claim that historical thinking is a "thing of the past" reinforces this sense of an inexorable temporal sequence. It is a central axiom of historicism that ideas arise within, and are confined to, a particular stage of the historical process (the past is superseded and outdated by the present).

Each of these historical stages, furthermore, is a relatively unified and coherent whole. For example, Ermarth speaks of modern culture as a discourse that stretches from the fifteenth to the late nineteenth century and comprises a single, distinctive cluster of features. This too is classic Hegelian thinking, which grasps entire centuries as the expression of a single central idea. Within such a framework, homogeneity and sameness become all-important, and dissident or contradictory historical currents are banished to the sidelines of analysis. Painting with such a broad brush inevitably results in the blurring of important distinctions. For example, dialectical thinking and realist narrative, two quintessential features of modern thought targeted by Ermarth, certainly permeate the consciousness of the nineteenth century but will not help us make sense of the cultural climate of Renaissance Europe. One possible conclusion is that homogeneity, rather than being a defining feature of modern history, is produced by the framework through which that history is interpreted.

Finally, this series of stages is progressive in bringing us closer to the truth (in this case, of course, the "postmodern" truth that there is no truth). The scales have fallen from our eyes; we have transcended the errors of the past, with its naïve belief in history, reality, and the subject. Postmodernism ushers in a distinctively new and subversive aesthetic that will help to eradicate outmoded forms of thought. In its heartfelt conviction that the present involves an overcoming of past illusions and its championing of new knowledge over old, this is a quintessentially modern rather than postmodern argument. Rather than subverting the logic of periodization, teleology, and transcendence, Ermarth's argument is deeply embroiled in it.

This form of antihistorical historicism is by no means limited to Ermarth's work. On the contrary, it can be glimpsed in many discussions of postmodernism that tell big historical stories about the demise of historical consciousness and thereby testify to the continuing power of the very modes of thought that they are trying to disprove. One problem is that writers often fail to distinguish between the different meanings of the word they are condemning. "History" is a rich and resonant term that embraces a wide range of meanings, some of which seem more expendable than others. For example, not many people nowadays think of history as chugging inexorably down a single track to a particular destination. This idea forms part of the baggage of nineteenth-century developmental historicism that now seems inappropriate, indeed quaint to our eyes. Nor, for the most part, do we think of history as a dialectical interplay of opposing forces in the manner of Hegelian and Marxist philosophy.

But the meanings of history extend well beyond such specific examples of historicist consciousness. They include other usages that cannot be discarded so easily. For example, people often turn to history to stress temporal difference rather than continuity, to draw attention to the otherness of times before our own. Appealing to history can mean something like "let us try to remain open to the strangeness and unpredictability of the past rather than assuming that it simply mirrors or foreshadows our own concerns." Instead of always erasing the concrete and specific, as Ermarth suggests, history can also express a laborious struggle to give it due recognition. It can alert us to the temporal gulf between past and present, the irredeemably remote and foreign nature of the past. In other words, the modern sense of historical time includes a recognition of ruptures and breaks as well as an affirmation of continuity.

Another key element of historical consciousness is irreversibility: the idea of time as moving from past to future and not vice versa. This sense of the irreversible nature of time is a fundamental aspect of everyday experience: we grow older rather than younger, just as our cars get rustier rather than shinier. Our sense of time is marked by profound asymmetry, embodied in the contrast between the completed nature of the past and the openness of the future. This is not to deny that we always interpret the past from the standpoint of the present, so that its meaning is constantly in flux, always open to new acts of deciphering. But although we constantly rewrite the past, we cannot redo or undo the past, alter the outcome of historical processes, step into past time in order to change what actually happened. This sense of the irretrievable nature of the past is a historical insight, yet it is not one that is easily discarded as erroneous.

Thus "history" includes a wide range of diverse, loosely connected, and sometimes competing ideas. It may refer to a belief in the objective portrayal of what actually happened, large philosophical stories of temporal progress or decline, a recognition of the irreversibility of time, an elaborate armature of teleological concepts, a sense of the past's remoteness from the present. Some of these ideas are anachronistic, but others continue to shape our understanding of the world at a very deep level. History is not easily banished from our repertoire of useful tools to think with. Indeed, the very use of a term such as "anachronistic" and the accompanying sense that the world of the nineteenth century is no longer our world simply underscore the tenacious and intractable grip of historical modes of thought.

What about the political stakes of defining postmodernism as the end of history? Ermarth presents this idea as if it were in harmony with the concerns of new social movements such as feminism. Yet the very status of the modern/postmodern distinction has been questioned by some recent scholars, including feminists. Such a distinction assumes that we have all passed through a series of historical stages in more or less the same way and at the same time. However, if different groups have experienced modernity in distinctive and uneven ways, the question of periodization becomes much more complicated. As I show in more detail in chapter 2, new scholarship is changing our sense of what modernity is and consequently modifying some of the ways we distinguish between the modern and the postmodern.

Ermarth and other like-minded scholars want to claim that our sense of time has undergone a profound transformation. The ordered, chronological time of the modern era has splintered into a chaotic heap of temporal shards. Yet this big, sweeping story of epochal change cannot capture the unevenness of history and time. It exaggerates the fragmented, chaotic nature of present time (clock time, timetables, and other forms of regulated, "objective" time have not yet disappeared from our lives), while denying the temporal complexity of the past. Preoccupied with establishing the differences *between* epochs, such a story cannot begin to explore the historical differences that exist *within* epochs.

Of course, not all scholars are so keen to anchor postmodernism historically. For example, Diane Elam puts forward an alternative view of postmodernism as subverting all forms of chronology and periodization. "Postmodernism is not a new, more depressing narrative but rather the coexistence of multiple and mutually exclusive narrative possibilities without a point of abstraction from which we might survey them."[23] I am sympathetic to Elam's troubling of temporality and her desire to explore the coexistence of multiple times. The problem is that Elam turns her view into a normative definition of postmodernism. She insists repeatedly that postmodernism is not X but Y; postmodernism is not a stage in historical time but the mutual coexistence of multiple times.

But what exactly is postmodernism? Elam, like many other scholars, talks about postmodernism as if it were an object in the world, an unambiguous phenomenon whose essential properties can be listed and described. Yet postmodernism is not a discrete reality, but a series of perspectives. Postmodernism is nothing more than the totality of discourses on postmodernism. And many—I would argue most—of those discourses do make large historical claims. They are saturated in temporality and narrative.

At one point, Elam expresses an uneasy recognition that postmodernism is not quite what she would like it to be. She distinguishes between popular forms of postmodernism and academic postmodernism. The former are still in thrall to historical and linear thinking, thus turning postmodernism into a new version of modernism. The latter, however, is a sophisticated and ironic interrogation of time and chronology.[24] But this account will not work as an empirical description of the field. As Steven Connor points out, the first use of postmodernism was to talk about historical changes in specific art forms, for example, the style that followed modernism in architecture. Since then, postmodernism has become common academic shorthand for a general historical condition or a popular synonym for "contemporary." Ermarth's book is by no means atypical in this regard.

Hence when Elam writes that "postmodernism is X," what she really means is, "postmodernism *should* be X." But it is hard to see why she is so adamant about retaining the term for her ironic questioning of temporality given the insurmountable historical connotations of "post." Furthermore, if a historical definition of postmodernism is problematic, an ahistorical one is surely even more so. To talk of postmodern Chaucer, postmodern Shakespeare, or even postmodern Walter Scott strikes me as misguided. It flattens out major differences between the way these writers perceived the world and the way we make sense of it now. To respect the difference of the past is not necessarily to resort to simplistic schemas and big historical stories.

## WOMEN'S TIME?

Feminist scholars have also questioned conventional forms of periodization. Since Joan Kelly first asked the question, "Did women have a Renaissance?" they have shown that the past often looks very different when viewed from a feminist perspective. Once a single gender no longer has exclusive rights to represent the path of history, everything, it seems, is up for grabs. How should we divide time into periods and where should we draw the boundaries? To put it bluntly, times that are good for men have often been bad for women, and vice versa. The peaks and valleys of historical time may appear in very different places, depending on who is looking and whose fortunes are being tracked across the centuries.

This thesis is well illustrated in the new scholarship on the European fin de siècle. Traditionally, literary scholars have often regarded the dandy as the period's emblematic figure. While hardly typical (few men aspired to such a role), he was nevertheless an evocative symbol of a particular cultural sensibility. The dandy's studied elegance and cultivated ennui bespoke a crisis of contemporary manhood, as Victorian ideals of rugged virility gave way to ironic posing, gender reversal, and a sense of historical belatedness. Indeed, decadence and the fin de siècle have come to be seen as more or less synonymous terms. But feminist scholars focusing on representations of the New Woman have uncovered a very different cultural and historical mood during the same period. Gazing firmly into the future rather than nostalgically into the past, moving boldly into public space rather than withdrawing into ornate interiors, seizing hold of new opportunities to advance her own self-development and the cause of women, the New Woman was a powerful symbol of modernity, change, and the future. A shift in perspective leads to a very different view of the temporal culture of the fin de siècle.

Similar contrasts appear in the present. The meaning of our present time is often crystallized in a melancholic sense of decline and loss. Postmodernity simply is the end of the line, the place where the dazzling promises and utopian dreams of the modern are exposed as tawdry and hollow. This sensibility is eloquently conveyed in Andreas Huyssen's description of our current fin de siècle as a "twilight condition," marked by a surrender of hope, the disappearance of the future, and a general waning of historical consciousness. Yet Huyssen also remains alert to conflicting currents within the present rather than assuming an abrupt termination of historical and future-oriented thought. For example, feminist scholars, whatever their views on the subject of postmodernism, are unlikely to look back wistfully to an earlier stage of modernity. For women who are only now beginning to assume a major role in the public sphere, it makes little sense to think of our time as one of loss, melancholia, and belatedness.[25]

Clearly, men and women may make sense of historical processes in different ways. Does this observation justify the bolder claim that the sexes inhabit different temporal worlds? Do female lives, experiences, and bodies conform to distinctive modalities and rhythms? This idea is explored by Julia Kristeva in her inquiry into women's relationship to time. She suggests that the struggles of first-wave suffragettes and existential feminists "aspired to gain a place in linear time as the time of project and history."[26] For Kristeva, this aspiration is synonymous with the demands of a feminism that champions equality rather than difference. The vision of time as "project, teleology, linear and prospective unfolding" is linked to the universalizing logic of modernity and the ideology of the nation-state. When they enter historical time, women consent to the erasure of their specific identities as sexed subjects.

Conversely, the new generation of feminists that appears after 1968 refuses this conception of linear time and its related ideas about politics and history. Instead, in trying to give voice to female difference, it aligns itself with an alternative vision of time grounded in the archaic, the mythical, and the cyclical. Such a temporality, it is claimed, expresses the distinctive psychic and bodily experiences of women. Kristeva, while reluctant to endorse any belief in essential female difference, nevertheless suggests that women's affinity with space and their distance from becoming and history are confirmed by the investigations of psychoanalytical thought.

> As for time, female subjectivity would seem to provide a specific measure that essentially retains *repetition* and *eternity* from among the multiple modalities of time known through the history of civilizations. On the one hand, there are cycles, gestation, the eternal recurrence of a biological rhythm which conforms to that of nature and imposes a temporality whose stereotyping may shock, but whose regularity and unison with what is experienced as extrasubjective time, cosmic time, occasion vertiginous visions and unnameable *jouissance*. On the other hand, and perhaps as a consequence, there is the massive presence of a monumental temporality, without cleavage or escape, which has so little to do with linear time (which passes) that the very word "temporality" hardly fits.[27]

The idea of time, as Kristeva's article makes clear, includes but also goes beyond history as it is conventionally understood. Indeed, time is a concept of

enormous complexity, including questions of measurement, rhythm, synchro-
nization, sequence, tempo and intensity. It spans the personal and the public,
work and leisure, the instantaneous and the eternal, intimate relations and
global structures, everyday life and conditions of extremity. It exists at many
different levels and is experienced in radically divergent ways. In an excellent
book on the social meanings of time, Barbara Adams writes,

> Time is multifaceted: it is involved in physical processes and social
> conventions, in the abstract relations of mathematics and concrete re-
> lations between people. We measure it in clock-time units and by celes-
> tial motion, with the aid of recurrent events and through changes in
> our bodies. We utilize it as a medium of exchange for goods, services or
> payment. We use it as a resource of nature, of society, of people and of
> institutions . . . time for us is clearly not exhausted by the clock-time
> measure.[28]

In thinking about how gender affects the experience of time, I want to propose a tentative distinction between three temporal levels: everyday time, life
time, and large-scale time (history and myth). Such a distinction is largely
heuristic: in our lives these levels constantly intermingle and merge together. In
a detailed phenomenological account of a few seconds sitting in an aircraft that
is about to take off, Adams shows that a single moment may contain many different time references and time measurements and embrace the past, present,
and future.

First, there is the realm of *everyday time*, or the phenomenological sense of
time. This is the way we experience time on a day-to-day basis. Do we perceive
time to be passing quickly or slowly, moving in fits and starts or according to
the regular rhythm of the clock? Is our daily sense of time most strongly influenced by the relentless, impersonal regularities of clocks and timetables, by the
frenzied, flickering pace of television and media culture, or by the subterranean
flow of natural bodily rhythms? How are these experiences affected by our existence as embodied and sexed subjects with differing social roles? Do we feel
ourselves to be controlled by time or controlling time, does time flow in a certain direction or does it seem repetitive and cyclical?

Second, there is the level I call *life time*. This is the way we make sense of our
identities by endowing them with a temporal *Gestalt*. It is the process of understanding one's life as a project that encompasses and connects the random segments of daily experience. It is the creation of oneself as an autobiographical
subject and the act of reflecting on one's existence and finitude. This aspect of
the culture of time has received considerable attention from feminist scholars of

**17**

autobiography, who have explored the different ways women and men have imbued their lives with shape and meaning.

Finally, there is *large-scale time*, the ways we think about the long-term processes of time that transcend the limits of our personal existence. These larger time frames allow us to talk about shared pasts and collective futures and to fashion larger narratives around group identities such as nation, religion, or ethnicity. Indeed, the creation and survival of social communities rely heavily on the telling of such narratives.[29] These stories may take different forms, from triumphal stories of social struggle or spiritual progress to melancholic reflections on an inexorable decline from a lost golden age. Sometimes the shape of time is seen as essentially circular rather than moving upward or downward. As Kristeva suggests, this vision of repetitive, mythic time has often been linked to female reproductive capacities. Women are seen to be anchored in an eternal biological cycle of death and birth that transcends the contingencies of historical time.

While much has been written on women and history, the broader question of women's relationship to time has hardly been touched on. One relevant book is a collection of essays entitled *Taking Our Time: Feminist Perspectives on Temporality*. In most of the chapters, time is thought of as falling into two main types, namely, "phallocentrically structured, forward moving time" and "gynocentric, recurrent time."[30] The introduction, for example, claims that linear time is inimical to "cyclical time, the realm of nature and of women." According to the editor, conventional philosophies of time based on movement toward death are of little relevance to women, for whom birth has temporal and ontological priority. Another contributor suggests that mythic time is felt most intensely during pregnancy, birth, and lactation, at which moments women feel themselves to be partaking of an eternal cycle of biological reproduction.

There is something very familiar about this division between linear and cyclical time. It is also the way we often distinguish between industrial and agricultural societies. It is a truism that non-Western cultures experience time differently from the West. This thesis has received empirical support from such studies as Clifford Geertz's fieldwork in Bali. According to Geertz, Balinese culture is characterized by a condition of pure simultaneity that strongly downplays any sense of temporal duration or linear development. Time is, in a sense, immobilized. Geertz marshals several examples to substantiate this thesis. He examines the distinctive features of the Balinese calendar, the lack of a dramatic climax in theatrical performances, and the depersonalizing concept of personhood in Balinese culture, which minimizes the significance of biological aging and death. As a result, Balinese social life takes place in a motionless present. The Balinese exist outside historical time.[31]

Geertz's seemingly persuasive thesis is, however, questioned by Maurice Bloch, who points out that it relies on a highly selective reading of Balinese culture. Geertz focuses on those ritual dimensions of Balinese life that are closely linked to sacred objects and practices. He ignores or treats as secondary those elements of the local culture that do not fit this rubric and that rely on a chronological, linear view of time. These elements include many aspects of mundane practical life, as well as the domain of both local and national politics. Comparing the sacred, ritual aspects of Balinese culture to the practical, instrumental aspects of Western societies thus gives a misleading view of both. In each case, the part is made to stand for the whole. Noting that it is a "recurrent professional malpractice of anthropologists to exaggerate the exotic nature of other cultures," Bloch warns against reading specific elements of a culture as symbolic of an entire way of life.[32]

Bloch's warning is echoed and extended by Akhil Gupta in an acerbic account of popular views of Eastern and Western time. Gupta sums up the pertinent clichés as follows: "whereas time in industrial capitalism becomes abstract, homogeneous, empty, linear, and progressive, shorn of 'nature's rhythms', and unconnected to the task at hand, historical and cultural Others construe time as concrete, cyclical, closely connected to nature, and experience it in the context of specific tasks."[33] The rest of his essay is devoted to dismantling these propositions. What about the parallels, Gupta asks, between the daily cycles of Nuer shepherds and those of urban commuters, or between the seasonal patterns of Indian agricultural laborers and Minnesota construction workers? On the one hand, Western culture, in spite of its strong reliance on linear time, is also saturated with time cycles, from the boom-bust rhythms of economics to the annual rites of Christmas, Hannukah, and Thanksgiving, to the small-scale routines of everyday life. On the other hand, the non-Western world cannot simply be seen as dwelling in archaic, non-linear time. Gupta cites the example of Indian villages, "where work is primarily agricultural, where many men wear watches, where radio programs, buses, and trains work on schedules made up in abstract time (or at least are supposed to), where reincarnation and transmigration occurring across incredibly large temporal units are considered a commonplace feature of everyday life."[34] How can one make sense of such a confusing mélange of times? Surely not by opposing linear and cyclical time as the essential and mutually exclusive principles of East and West.

Barbara Adams has recently undertaken what is perhaps the most thorough dismantling of the linear/cyclical opposition. She notes that both cyclical and linear time are integral to social life. All cultures rely on repetition and ritual, although we sometimes lose sight of the vital role of cyclical time in modern Western societies. Conversely, no culture, however archaic, exists in an eternal

INTRODUCTION: TIMELY MEDITATIONS

present of endlessly recurring sameness. Human societies are always subject to temporal processes of change and decay. Repetition always involves variation; it takes place within rather than outside the irreversibility of time. In other words, linear and cyclical times are always mutually implicated and interdependent. Adams concludes that "all social processes display aspects of linearity and cyclicality. . . . whether we 'see' linearity or cyclicality depends fundamentally on the framework of observation and interpretation."[35]

This sounds exactly right. For example, those who believe that linear time is masculine and cyclical time feminine usually point to the dramatic contrast between the grand narratives of male historical time and the repetitive everyday time of women. This difference then serves as evidence of a vast gendered gulf in temporal experience. Here is an instance of the problem noted by Maurice Bloch: one facet of cultural experience is taken to be exemplary and representative of an entire (gendered) way of life. The part is taken for the whole.

If, however, the daily lives of women are compared to the daily lives of men, the contrast is much more muted. The realm of everyday life simply *is* repetitive, being largely defined by monotony, routine, and habit. It is the realm of the eternal daily round, of what the French call "métro, boulot, dodo" (metro, work, sleep). The grey-suited commuter waiting for the 6:30 train or the male sports fan glued to the television every Saturday is as much a creature of routine as is any woman. As I argue in chapter 3, the perception that cyclical time is a uniquely female province is highly misleading.

Such a perception arises from the fact that cyclical time is often seen as natural time, and hence the sphere of women. Yet there is nothing particularly natural about the routines through which most people in the West organize their lives: Burger King at 6 P.M., *Friends* at 8, a weekly trip to Walmart, the church, or the mall. Of course, the idea that cyclical time is natural does contain an important grain of truth. We know that human bodies are programmed to eat, sleep, and get rid of waste at regular intervals and do not cope well with major alterations to these rhythms (think, for example, of the well-documented disorientation of workers required to work irregular shifts). There are clear limits to the adaptability of human bodily rhythms. Yet the organization of such physical needs within everyday life is always an affair of culture, not nature.

Rather than being elemental creatures attuned to natural rhythms, many women nowadays are, if anything, even more preoccupied with time measurement than men. Caught between the conflicting demands of home and work, often juggling child care and frantic about their lack of time, it is women who are clock watchers, who obsess about appointments and deadlines, who view time as a precious commodity to hoard or to spend.[36] Because women's work at home is unpaid and hence is not translatable into exchange value, scholars have sometimes assumed that it remains outside the modern time economy. Yet the regulation of time pervades all aspects of everyday life and is no longer limited to those engaged in paid work. The housewife who places her cake in the oven for exactly thirty-five minutes, writes down her appointments in her daily planner, and makes sure that she gives her children several hours of quality time each day is as much a creature of modern time measurement as is any male worker.

If the everyday time of women and men reveals many parallels as well as differences, much the same is true of life time. Traditionally men (or rather, white men of the middle class) were encouraged to think of their lives in linear terms. A man's life was a project; ideally, it would lead toward the goal of individual and public achievement through a series of well-defined stages. Subject to a father's and then a husband's tutelage, their lives interrupted by constant childbearing, women did not for the most part have the luxury of imagining a self-directed future. Their lives consisted of a series of fragments, not a carefully choreographed upward ascent.

It would be wrong, however, to conclude that women never think of their lives in developmental terms and to oppose female formlessness to male linearity. Think, for example, of a contemporary phenomenon such as the self-help manual, with its heavy reliance on the language of personal growth. This genre is aimed primarily at women and speaks eloquently and at length about psychological development, life passages, personal goals. It presents female lives as a movement through a series of stages toward ever greater self-knowledge. As the spread of therapeutic ideas encourages individuals to assess the meaning of their lives in terms of internal growth as well as external success, so women are knitted ever more deeply into the rhetoric of self-development and are encouraged to view their lives as a meaningful and coherent story.

Finally, there is the relation between gender and large-scale narratives of time. It is surely false to assume that women are essentially at odds with such narratives. On the contrary, they have often been passionate believers in national progress, racial uplift, women's growing freedom, and many other big historical stories. Furthermore, such stories are not always iniquitous. Meaghan Morris points out that "rhetorics of evolution, elevation, advancement, 'upward mobility,' and cohesively linear time have served with as much tenacity to articulate the aspirations of radicals, reformers and dissenters as they have to validate and channel colonial power."[37] So too, stories of progress have worked for as well as against the interests of women. More generally, feminism is clearly indebted to forms of historical thinking made possible by modernity. We can see this heritage in its conviction that the past does not define the present, and that women have the capacity to affect their own destiny. Feminism defines itself in a critical relationship to the past, and aspires to a better future. Feminism is, in other words, a *project*, requiring a purposeful and hopeful relationship toward future time.

There are thus many important commonalities, as well as differences, in male and female relations to time. Furthermore, all experience of time is multi-leveled, complex, and heterogeneous. Consequently, it is hard to argue for a distinctive "women's time" without oversimplifying the links between gender and temporality. Similar problems arise in trying to draw a hard-and-fast distinction between modern and postmodern time. Writers sometimes zero in on what they see as quintessentially postmodern phenomena, such as the ubiquitous spread of computer and cyberculture, or the disorienting experience of drowning in consumerism at the mall, or the knowing pastiche of past styles in much contemporary art. These phenomena are then read as symptoms of a new temporal culture that is bleached of authentic historical knowledge and marked by schizophrenia, amnesia and a sense of eternal present.

Now it is clear that our sense of time is no longer that of the nineteenth century. We inhabit a world of dizzying technological change and fast-moving information; our lives are saturated with glossy media images that can flatten historical differences into a jumbled and incoherent simultaneity. We can point to the accelerated, frenetic tempo of everyday consumer culture and to our consequent sense of distance from even the very recent past. But we also inhabit a world that is still rich in big historical schemas, narrative constructions of self, sedimented daily routines, and other supposedly modern or premodern forms of time. Furthermore, specific groups and regions often experience changes in their modes of temporality in varying and markedly uneven ways. Writers often move far too hastily from the analysis of a specific cultural artifact—a novel, a film, a snippet of popular science—to a global theory of the postmodern. Again, the part is taken for the whole.[38]

Perhaps the most forceful critic of the idea that different groups inhabit different times is Johannes Fabian. Fabian's *Time and the Other* is a sustained attack on the belief that time is relative across cultures. This belief, he notes, results in a persistent tendency to place the object of anthropological study in a time other than that of the anthropologist. Individual cultures are seen as fenced off from each other, each experiencing its own time. Fabian finds this relativism deeply troubling because it denies the interconnections between cultural systems. Instead, he argues for coevalness, the simultaneous existence of different cultures. Rather than espousing a notion of temporal relativism, we need to attend to "the radical contemporaneity of mankind."[39] There is only one time, he insists, not a multiplicity of times.

As Fabian recognizes, however, this thesis poses its own problems, since it implies a certain sameness of temporal experience. Fabian wants, rightly, to impart a recognition of the contemporaneity of others. Even if specific cultures have very different ways of understanding time, nevertheless the members of those cultures inhabit, in one sense, the same time. Their differing ways of measuring time do not prevent them from existing in the same temporal plane, any more than people from cultures that draw maps differently are thereby precluded from finding themselves in the same place. We need to have a way of talking about this coevalness. Otherwise, it would be impossible to make sense of cross-cultural interaction, the flows of objects, information, and people from one place to another, our sense of coexistence with others, our mutual dependence on the material world for our existence. If at some future moment a comet comes crashing into the earth, we will all be killed at more or less the same time.

Yet in another sense, of course, time *is* relative to specific cultures and groups. We make sense of it differently, imagine its passing in myriad ways, fashion wildly divergent pasts and futures for ourselves. Our temporal scripts vary dramatically. Thus an approaching comet will be seen by some as a terrible portent of the coming apocalypse and the end of time, by others as nothing more than a potential natural disaster. We need to insist that temporal coevalness does not prevent individuals and cultures from experiencing time in very different ways: Elliot Jacques captures the distinction nicely.

> No two men living *at* the same time live *in* the same time. Each one, living at the same moment, has his own personal time perspective, his own living linkage with past and future, the content of which, and the scale of which, are as different between one person and another as are their appearance, their fingerprints, their characters, their desires, their very being.[40]

This distinction between living *at* the same time and *in* the same time is crucial.

## SYNCHRONOUS NONSYNCHRONICITY

"Not all people exist in the same Now. They do so only externally, through the fact that they can be seen today. But they are thereby not yet living at the same time with the others."[41] In *Heritage of Our Time* (1935) Ernst Bloch grapples with precisely this question of sameness and difference in the experience of time. Bloch is trying to make sense of fascism, to understand why so many people were susceptible to the appeal of Nazi rhetoric. He is also in dialogue with a Marxist tradition that imagines history as propelled forward by synchronous contradictions, such as the conflict between the proletariat and the bourgeoisie.

As a result, however, Marxists have paid scant attention to expressions of social unrest that do not fit this particular view of historical change.

Bloch notes that Germany is the classic land of nonsynchronism, of unsurmounted remnants of older forms of being and consciousness. Its late and rapid experience of modernization marked its national culture in distinctive ways; semifeudal attitudes and attachments to premodern forms of life have stubbornly persisted in the midst of dramatic historical change. According to Bloch, German farmers, young people, and the lower middle class found the rhetoric of fascism appealing precisely because of their ambivalent attitude to modernity. The life of peasants and farmers, for example, continued to follow premodern rhythms, while the lower middle class found in fascism an outlet for their own distrust and fear of the new. Time, Bloch suggests, cannot be imagined as a smooth sequence of stages. Instead, earlier times and uncompleted pasts continue to haunt the present. It is in this context that he introduces his idea of synchronous nonsynchronicity, as a way of explaining how groups that coexist in time may nevertheless experience time very differently.

Bloch's work is a bold attempt to rethink our sense of time and to disrupt the idea of history as a smooth developmental sequence. He wants to show how sedimented layers of past time continue to shape contemporary experience, how in the very act of experiencing the Now we constantly brush up against the all too solid ghosts of the past. The present is always haunted by the history it seeks to transcend. At the same time Bloch's discussion cannot wrench itself free of the presuppositions of evolutionary thought. Even as he points to the multiple and varied experiences of time, he ranks these experiences according to a transcendent ideal of historical progress. Certain groups, such as the working class, are described as embodying the most advanced stage of historical consciousness. Other groups, such as the lower middle class, lag behind in an earlier stage of development (see my discussion of this issue in chapter 1). To experience a dissonant relationship to the forward-looking gaze of modernity is thus, for Bloch, synonymous with a condition of retardation. It is to be backward, to remain moored in past time.

Bloch's work allows us to grasp more clearly the problems that arise in accounting for both historical regularities and historical variations. Is it possible to talk about both temporal difference and temporal sameness without succumbing to the reductive pull of an evolutionary framework? How do we account for the fact that individuals live at the same time, but not necessarily in the same time? Can we trace out the disjunctive and uneven temporalities of particular groups without implying that some of these groups are more advanced or backward than others? Such questions seem crucial to any project of reworking, rather than simply discarding, the concept of historical time.

One helpful guide in thinking about these questions is Homi Bhabha. Much of Bhabha's work tries to rethink the modern in such a way that the time of the non-Western world is neither seen as belated nor simply subsumed and rendered invisible within a single universal frame. His suggestive, if somewhat opaque, discussion of time lag points to the disjunctive temporalities of modernity. "Each repetition of the time of modernity is different, specific to its historical and cultural conditions of enunciation."[42] By invoking the idea of modernity to talk about the cultures of the non-Western world, Bhabha wants to make it clear that they are not autonomous, separate, self-defined entities. Rather, they have been powerfully shaped by the global changes carried out in the name of modernization.

Yet at the same time, Bhabha insists on differences within the time of the modern. Apparently similar ideas may acquire quite diverse meanings and have unpredictable effects as they circulate through different cultural and geopolitical spaces. A set of beliefs that appears outdated in one milieu may seem newly resonant and powerful in another. The translation of modern ideas into a particular habitus and way of life often brings with it unexpected changes of register and meaning. Thus the unseating of the white bourgeois male as subject of history brings with it a fracturing or splitting of a previously unified historical narrative, a recognition of the ambivalent temporalities within the modern itself.

The following essays address, in various ways, these disjunctive temporalities. I am interested in thinking about how the modern and postmodern both influence and are complicated by questions of gender. As is surely obvious by now, I do not think that feminism can afford to discard these categories. The idea of the modern, and to a lesser extent that of the postmodern, serves as a useful shorthand for identifying clusters of historical phenomena and mutually interacting social forces that have had a powerful impact on women's lives. For example, it is impossible to explain the emergence of feminism via the ahistorical male-female polarity embodied in the psychosexual theme of sexual difference (see chapter 5). Such features of Western modernity as capitalism and the Enlightenment are not quintessentially male creations inimical to the concerns of women. Rather, they are inherently ambiguous historical phenomena whose contradictions helped to inspire the birth of feminism.

Historical periods are not homogeneous and self-contained blocks of time governed by a single unifying spirit. They are not woven into the weft of an objectively given reality but are created, often belatedly and hesitantly, by those struggling to make sense of the passing of time. But the fact that periods are socially created should not lead us to conclude that they are false. It is far more implausible to think of the past as nothing more than a heap of random, unconnected temporal fragments. At any given moment, there are cross-linkages and connections, patterns of mutual influence, shared perspectives within and across specific contexts. Some of these patterns are relatively stable, persisting over years, decades, or even centuries. As Siegfried Kracauer argues, it is in this sense that we must think of a historical period: not as a unified entity with a spirit of its own but as a "precarious conglomerate of tendencies, aspirations, and activities."[43]

Precisely for this reason, our understanding of periods is always changing. One of the achievements of feminism has been to provide illuminating new interpretations of past time. For example, it is now obvious to many scholars that the history of modernity is intimately linked to changing conceptions of the body and sexuality, the important role of women in commodity culture, and the gender-specific meanings of emotion, affect, and the private sphere. Thirty years ago, this was obvious to almost no one. Such cultural phenomena were simply not seen, because there was no framework at hand to render them meaningful or interesting.

It is in this spirit, then, that we need to approach the question of gender and temporal difference, by exploring the dense entanglements and disjunctures within and between specific male and female experiences of history and time. This is a project that is empirical as well as theoretical and hence that is continually open to revision as we run up against the unpredictability of the world and are forced to modify or relinquish our original assumptions. Women are neither avatars of the mythic and the archaic nor a revolutionary vanguard leading the way toward a radiant future washed free of all inequity. Rather, women's relationship to modern time is as uneven and contradictory as modernity itself.

To question the grand narratives of evolutionism is not, I should stress, to abandon all comparative historical judgment. For example, it is indisputably the case that women acquired certain political and legal rights—such as the right to vote—later than men. In this sense, women's access to specific forms of modern subjecthood is indeed belated. But this is not because women were languishing in an earlier stage of development. On the contrary, the idea of separate spheres that served to justify women's exclusion from public life was itself a distinctively modern idea. As scholars now recognize, a central aspect of modernity is the importance accorded to interiority and authentic feeling as guides to human conduct. In this context, it is possible for Nancy Armstrong to claim that the middle-class woman of the eighteenth century was in fact the first modern subject.[44] In other words, the question of whether men or women are deemed to be the more modern sex depends entirely on how the modern is defined.

The apparently frothy novels of Judith Krantz provide an opportunity for exploring the complexities of gender and periodization. As I argue in chapter 4, we can see in Krantz's novels, and in contemporary popular culture more generally, the female appropriation of a traditionally male narrative of *Bildung* that links personal development to success in the public world. This is a form of repetition with a difference, of course; the fact that it is a female protagonist who is striving toward public power and achievement leads to some significant modifications in the genre. Nevertheless, the popularity of the "money, sex, and power" novel and similar genres confirms that women are now being offered a fantasy of unlimited self-development and triumphant individualism that was previously available only to men. This is one telling instance of women's belated insertion into a modern cultural narrative that was previously the province of one sex.

Yet at the same time, the novels of Krantz also sketch out a distinctively postmodern world of celebrity, style, and glamour in which women are the quintessential denizens and subjects. They are creatures of consumer culture, attuned to the significance of subtle yet crucial changes in style and fashion, skillful performers of both masculine and feminine roles, adept in navigating the complexities of a media-oriented world. Rather than latecomers to postmodern culture, they are its quintessential representatives, primed for the society of the spectacle by their long-standing familiarity with performance and masquerade. Are women, then, on the side of the modern or the postmodern? Krantz's novels reveal the impossibility of a simple answer to this question by pointing to the complexity and unevenness of women's positioning in historical time.

The rhetorical stance underlying most of the following essays is best summarized as "yes, but . . ." *Yes,* of course current debates around modernism and postmodernism are relevant to scholars of gender, *but* looking at things from a feminist angle may also put them in a different light. For example, in chapter 7 I reflect on the role of contemporary intellectuals, while in chapter 8 I look at the question of aesthetics and the autonomy of art. Both of these fields are distinct, relatively autonomous worlds with their own complex histories, vocabularies, conventions, and modes of perception. As ever more women enter these spheres, their work is shaped by and indebted to those traditions.

At the same time, however, some of the sweeping statements about postmodernism are much less persuasive when women enter the picture. For example, the claim that the postmodern era signals an end to political art simply does not make sense in the context of feminist art history. Women entered art in significant numbers on the coattails of the women's movement and often saw their work as an attempt to bring together artistic and political concerns. While female artists are not magically exempt from the postmodern theme of the death of the avant-garde, women's art may be paving the way for a rather different vision of the relationship between art and politics. Similarly, my discussion of the so-called crisis of intellectuals in the postmodern era notes the scant attention paid to the recent phenomenon of the feminist intellectual. Recent work on the relationship between intellectuals and social movements usually ignores the feminist scholars who are simultaneously, if often awkwardly, positioned in both spheres.

I want to conclude with some comments on the following essay, which differs from the others in looking at class. This essay takes the place of the autobiographical sketch that scholars nowadays often feel obliged to deliver to their readers. It arose out of my recognition that at a phenomenological level, class has always been more important to my everyday sense of self than gender. I *feel* myself to be a classed subject more often and more intensely than I feel myself to be a gendered one. Yet the language of Marxist class analysis has proved an impossibly clumsy and coarse-grained tool for describing the nuances of that self-perception. Furthermore, the romance of marginality that swirls around discussions of race and gender has made it difficult to engage, except derisively, with the experience of class mobility. This essay thus developed, slowly and painfully, out of an attempt to comprehend the reasons for the awkwardness of lower-middle-class subjectivity.

In retrospect, however, I now see important connections between this excursus on class and the questions I raise about gender. The awkward status of the lower middle class is closely linked to modern ideas about history and time. At various moments, both the working class and the intelligentsia have been seen as a revolutionary force that will sweep away the inequities of the present and fashion a better world. But the lower middle class has never functioned as a symbol of utopian hopes and the embodiment of the new. Rather, from Marx's time until our own, the petite bourgeoisie figures, persistently and repeatedly, as the symbol of backwardness. It is the class that holds back the wheel of history; its politics are reactionary, its aesthetics regressive. The animus directed at the lower middle class is profoundly saturated by historical—and historicist—assumptions about who counts as an authentically modern subject.

This is, then, the leitmotif that links many of the following essays. Who gets to represent the modern or the postmodern and who does not? Why are some social groups and cultural forms seen as authentically of their time and others doomed to lag behind, moored in an earlier era? Why are our cultural perceptions and fantasies about gender, race, and class so closely tied to historical and temporal schemes? To ask such questions is not to abandon the terrain of historical understanding but rather to reclaim it. The failures of history, I suggest, can become visible only from the standpoint of a more adequate history.

## NOTES

Thanks to Allan Megill and Robyn Wiegman for reading a first draft of this chapter, and to Michael Bérubé and Heather Love for useful information.

1. For an incisive analysis of the formulaic rhetorical moves underlying most discussions of postmodernism, see John Frow, "What Was Postmodernism?" in *Time and Commodity Culture: Essays in Cultural Theory and Postmodernity* (Oxford: Oxford University Press, 1997).

2. Meaghan Morris, *The Pirate's Fiancée: Feminism, Reading, Postmodernism* (London: Verso, 1988).

3. See, inter alia, Alison Assiter, *Enlightened Women: Modernist Feminism in a Postmodern Age* (London: Routledge, 1996); Seyla Benhabib, *Situating the Self: Gender, Community and Postmodernism in Contemporary Ethics* (New York: Routledge, 1992); Seyla Benhabib, Judith Butler, Drucilla Cornell, and Nancy Fraser, *Feminist Contentions: A Philosophical Exchange* (New York: Routledge, 1995); Susan Hekman, *Gender and Knowledge: Elements of a Postmodern Feminism* (Cambridge: Polity, 1990); Somer Brodribb, *Nothing Mat(t)ers: A Feminist Critique of Postmodernism* (Melbourne: Spinifex, 1992); Jane Flax, *Thinking Fragments: Psychoanalysis, Feminism and Postmodernism in the Contemporary West* (Berkeley: University of California Press, 1991), and *Disputed Subjects: Essays on Psychoanalysis, Politics and Philosophy* (New York: Routledge, 1993); Linda Nicholson, *The Play of Reason: From the Modern to the Postmodern* (Ithaca: Cornell University Press, 1999); and most of the essays in *Feminism/Postmodernism*, ed. Linda Nicholson (New York: Routledge, 1990).

4. According to Niall Lucy, the differences go far deeper, such that the two terms should never be used synonymously. "For poststructuralism, the concept of structure always already contains sufficient 'give' (or 'tolerance') to provide a little room for manoeuvre, while for postmodernism a concept of structure as fully closed and present to itself is an essential requirement for the concept of a playfully open and unruly (or 'structureless') structure." In other words, postmodernism relies on a metaphysics of presence in its "totalizing negation of such allegedly fully presentable concepts as criticism, realism, science and the work," whereas poststructuralism recognizes that all such concepts are always internally unstable. See Niall Lucy, *Postmodern Literary Theory: An Introduction* (Oxford: Basil Blackwell, 1997), 102.

5. See, inter alia, Patricia Waugh, *Feminine Fictions: Revisiting the Postmodern* (London: Routledge, 1989); Linda Hutcheon, *A Politics of Postmodernism* (London: Routledge, 1989); Magali Cornier Michael, *Feminism and the Postmodern Impulse: Post–World War II Fiction* (Albany: State University of New York Press, 1996); Molly Hite, *The Other Side of the Story: Structures and Strategies of Contemporary Feminist Narratives* (Ithaca: Cornell University Press, 1989).

6. See, e.g., Steven Connor, "Postmodernism and Literature," in *Postmodernist Culture: An Introduction to Theories of the Contemporary*, 2nd ed. (Oxford: Basil Blackwell, 1997); Susan Suleiman, "Feminism and Postmodernism: In Lieu of an Ending," in *Subversive Intent: Gender, Politics and the Avant-Garde* (Cambridge: Harvard University Press, 1990).

7. Jennifer Wicke and Margaret Ferguson, "Introduction: Feminism and Postmodernism, or The Way We Live Now," *Feminism and Postmodernism* (Durham: Duke University Press, 1994).

8. See, e.g., Donna Haraway, "A Manifesto for Cyborgs: Science, Technology and Socialist Feminism in the 1980s," in Nicholson, *Feminism/Postmodernism*; Anne Friedberg, *Window Shopping: Cinema and the Postmodern* (Berkeley: University of California Press, 1993).

9. Richard Rorty, "Introduction: Pragmatism and Philosophy," in *Consequences of Pragmatism* (Minneapolis: University of Minnesota Press, 1982), xl (I discuss the relevant quotation in chapter 7); Shane Phelan, *Getting Specific: Postmodern Lesbian Politics* (Minneapolis: University of Minnesota Press, 1994).

10. The best survey of this confusing diversity remains Connor's *Postmodernist Culture*.

11. See Meaghan Morris, "Introduction: History in Cultural Studies," in *Too Soon, Too Late: History in Popular Culture* (Bloomington: Indiana University Press, 1998), for a suggestive exploration of these questions.

12. On "postmodern" theory and lesbian politics, see, e.g., Phelan, *Getting Specific: Postmodern Lesbian Politics* and, for a very different view, Suzanna Danuta Walters, "From Here to Queer: Radical Feminism, Postmodernism and the Lesbian Menace (Or Why Can't a Woman Be More Like a Fag?)," *Signs: Journal of Women in Culture and Society* 21, 4 (1996): 830-69. On lesbian postmodern aesthetics, see Penelope Engelbrecht, "'Lifting Belly Is a Language': The Postmodern Lesbian Subject," *Feminist Studies* 16, 1 (1990): 85-114. For both, as well as articles locating the lesbian in the culture of postmodernity, see Laura Doan, ed., *The Lesbian Postmodern* (New York: Columbia University Press, 1994).

13. Dana Heller, "Purposes: An Introduction," *Cross-Purposes: Lesbians, Feminists and the Limits of Alliance*, ed. Dana Heller (Bloomington: Indiana University Press, 1997), 13. For a strong rejection of postmodernism as a threat to lesbian identity, see Susan J. Wolfe and Julia Penelope, "Sexual Identity/Textual Politics: Lesbian Decompositions," in *Sexual Practice, Textual Theory: Lesbian Cultural Criticism*, ed. Susan J. Wolfe and Julia Penelope (Cambridge: Blackwell, 1993).

14. Judith Roof, "Lesbians and Lyotard: Legitimation and the Politics of the Name," in Doan, *The Lesbian Postmodern*, 47.

15. Ien Ang, "On Not Speaking Chinese: Postmodern Ethnicity and the Politics of Diaspora," *New Formations* 24 (1994): 18. See also Ellen McCracken,

*New Latina Narrative: The Feminist Space of Postmodern Ethnicity* (Tucson: University of Arizona Press, 1999).

16. Inderpal Grewal and Caren Kaplan, "Introduction: Transnational Feminist Practices and Questions of Postmodernity," in *Scattered Hegemonies: Postmodernist and Transnational Feminist Practices* (Minneapolis: University of Minnesota Press, 1994), 4.

17. bell hooks, "Postmodern Blackness," in *Yearning: Race, Gender and Cultural Politics* (Boston: South End Press, 1990), 25.

18. See, e.g., M. J. Devaney, *"Since at Least Plato"... and Other Postmodernist Myths* (London: Macmillan, 1997) for a deft skewering of the theoretical errors in many accounts of postmodernism.

19. I take the term "faculty-club culture" from Peter Berger, "In the Faculty Club," *Times Literary Supplement,* August 20, 1999, 8.

20. Krishan Kumar, *From Post-Industrial to Post-Modern Society: New Theories of the Contemporary World* (Oxford: Basil Blackwell, 1995), 4. Terry Eagleton's response to Kumar's question would be a firm yes. See *The Illusions of Postmodernism* (Oxford: Basil Blackwell, 1996). On the idea that postmodernism creates its own audience, see also Mike Featherstone, *Consumer Culture and Postmodernism* (London: Sage, 1991), 11.

21. Elizabeth Deeds Ermarth, *Sequel to History: Postmodernism and the Crisis of Representational Time* (Princeton: Princeton University Press, 1992), 31.

22. Ermarth, *Sequel to History,* 55.

23. Diane Elam, *Romancing the Postmodern* (London: Routledge, 1992), 13.

24. Elam, *Romancing the Postmodern,* 10.

25. Andreas Huyssen, *Twilight Memories: Marking Time in a Culture of Amnesia* (New York: Routledge, 1995).

26. Julia Kristeva, "Women's Time," in *Feminist Theory: A Critique of Ideology,* ed. Nannerl O. Keohane, Michelle Z. Rosaldo, and Barbara C. Gelpi (Chicago: University of Chicago Press, 1982), 36.

27. Kristeva, "Women's Time," 34.

28. Barbara Adams, *Time Watch: The Social Analysis of Time* (Cambridge: Polity, 1995), 20.

29. See David Carr, *Time, Narrative and History* (Bloomington: Indiana University Press, 1986).

30. Frieda Johles Forman, ed., *Taking Our Time: Feminist Perspectives on Temporality* (Oxford: Pergamon, 1989), xii.

31. Clifford Geertz, *The Interpretation of Cultures* (New York: Basic Books, 1973).

32. Maurice Bloch, "The Past and Present in the Future," *Man* 12, 2 (1977): 285.

33. Akhil Gupta, "The Reincarnation of Souls and the Rebirth of Commodities: Representations of Time in 'East' and 'West'," *Cultural Critique* 22 (1992): 196.

34. Gupta, "Reincarnation of Souls," 202.

35. Adams, *Time Watch,* 38.

36. See Arlie Russell Hochschild, *The Time Bind: When Work Becomes Home and Home Becomes Work* (New York: Henry Holt, 1997).

37. Morris, "Introduction," 11.

38. For a bracing critique of this tendency and of careless analogies in postmodern theory generally, see Devaney, *"Since at Least Plato."*

39. Johannes Fabian, *Time and the Other: How Anthropology Makes Its Object* (New York: Columbia University Press, 1983), xi.

40. Elliot Jacques, "The Enigma of Time," in *The Sociology of Time,* ed. John Hassard (London: Macmillan, 1990), 21.

41. Ernst Bloch, *Heritage of Our Time* (Cambridge: Polity, 1991), 97.

42. Homi Bhabha, *The Location of Culture* (New York: Routledge, 1994), 241.

43. Siegfried Kracauer, *History: The Last Things before the Last* (Princeton, NJ: Markus Wiener, 1995), 66.

44. Nancy Armstrong, *Desire and Domestic Fiction: A Political History of the Novel* (Oxford: Oxford University Press, 1987).

# 1

# NOTHING TO DECLARE

## IDENTITY, SHAME, AND THE LOWER MIDDLE CLASS

t is a striking fact of scholarly life that talking about oneself has become a virtue. The culture of confession, once limited to self-help manuals, therapy groups, and talk shows, has gradually penetrated the walls of the academy. For critics who are disenchanted with the spread of theory or who simply want to explore different kinds of scholarly writing, autobiography can be an appealing alternative. Getting personal can take a wide variety of forms, from a terse vignette prefacing a conventional piece of scholarly writing to a full-blown striptease by an academic superstar. Often it is accompanied by an ethical imperative. I am doing this, the author implies, and you should do it too.

What authorizes the discourse of personal criticism? Why is writing about oneself deemed important or interesting? Sometimes the answer is fame. In a culture of celebrity the private life of a prominent scholar appeals to our curiosity and becomes worthy of our attention. Alternatively, the therapeutic or the political value of autobiographical criticism comes to the fore. Writing about oneself is presented, with varying degrees of intellectual sophistication, as an act of catharsis or a means to self-knowledge. It is also clearly indebted to the "politics of recognition" informing new social movements grounded in group identities.[1] Feminists, in particular, have often been at the vanguard of personal criticism, arguing that traditional forms of academic language need to be replaced by a more personal voice.

As someone who has never wanted to write about herself, I began to wonder about the reasons for this reticence. Of course, no trend is without its critics, and a number of writers, including some feminists, have expressed reservations about the value of self-disclosure as an intellectual or political strategy.[2] There is a sustained questioning of confession within poststructuralist theory, as well as a flourishing body of autobiographical writing informed by such theory. But neither defenders nor critics of autobiography have gone far in exploring the various social conditions that may affect the desire to speak or remain silent about the self. I want to pursue one aspect of this question by examining some of the meanings of class in relation to contemporary academic culture.

More specifically, I am interested in the lower middle class, my own social origin. Being lower-middle-class is a singularly boring identity, possessing none of the radical chic that is sometimes ascribed to working-class roots. In fact, the lower middle class has typically been an object of scorn among intellectuals, blamed for everything from exceedingly bad taste to the rise of Hitler. Yet as older forms of class polarization and class identification begin to dissolve, the lives of ever more individuals in the industrialized West are defined by occupations, lifestyles, and attitudes traditionally associated with the lower middle class.

At the same time, lower-middle-classness is not so much an identity as a nonidentity: "the one class you do *not* belong to, and are not proud of at all, is the lower middle class. No one ever describes himself as belonging to the lower middle classes."[3] What, then, is one to make of this widespread yet indeterminate, important yet underanalyzed class stratum? In what ways is the inbetweenness of the lower middle class at odds not only with the identity politics of gender and race but also with traditional ways of thinking about class?

My response to these questions is intended to be exploratory rather than conclusive. It forgoes some of the usual approaches to class in focusing on the psychic as well as the social, semiotics as much as economics. It is interested as much in literary and cultural representations of the lower middle class as in the objective reality of this class formation. And it is fully cognizant of the paradoxes involved in a semiautobiographical reflection on the problems of writing autobiographically.

## ON CLASS

There is a noticeable silence about class in much contemporary cultural theory. This is certainly true of my own field, feminism, which has been galvanized and transformed by issues of race but has yet to deal substantially with the current realities of class. While feminist critics sometimes give a cursory nod toward the importance of class differences, it is rarely acknowledged that class is a complex and contested idea, the present subject of wide-ranging intellectual and political debates.[4]

Thus the most basic questions of class—how many classes are there? how should they be defined? what are their functions?—are being rethought in social theory. Most writers agree that the traditional Marxist view of class as a polarized struggle between bourgeoisie and proletariat is of little use in the contemporary Western context. Not only has there been a dramatic decline in the industrial working class as a result of technological changes and shifts in the global division of labor, but also a range of new class formations has become prominent. These include a fragmented array of middle classes characterized by diverse political and cultural allegiances, along with a so-called underclass defined by long-term unemployment and poverty. Furthermore, class theorists have become increasingly interested in consumption as well as production. Clearly, work continues to play a major role in shaping social status and life chances, but class distinctions are also shaped by consumption practices and lifestyle patterns that do not bear any simple relation to the basic division between capital and labor.[5]

An obvious resource is the British tradition of cultural studies. Literary critics such as Raymond Williams and social historians such as E. P. Thompson have done much to illuminate the symbolic and cultural meanings of class. Yet class for British cultural studies has almost always meant the working class, and a historically specific form of English male working-class life that is of little help in looking at other classes or other contexts. Contemporary work in cultural studies is often cognizant of this fact, yet there is relatively little interest in exploring the current demographics of class divisions and class groupings.[6] Instead, the task of investigating the complex historical articulations of class and culture is addressed, if at all, through a dualistic theory of the body.

The source here is usually the work of Bakhtin, frequently mediated by Peter Stallybrass and Allon White's influential discussion of carnival in *The Politics and Poetics of Transgression*.[7] However, while Stallybrass and White focus on the middle-class *perception* that the lower classes are little more than pure body, some cultural critics seem to endorse this perception as fact. John Fiske, for example, grounds his account of popular culture in a notion of unruly and resistive bodies. Whereas the bourgeoisie is identified with discipline, hygiene, and repression, popular pleasures, by contrast, "are experienced or expressed through the body."[8] This claim underpins Fiske's analysis of "offensive bodies and carnival pleasures" as essential features of working-class or, more generally, popular culture. Lawrence Grossberg, while more conscious of the dangers of essentializing popular culture, also claims that "the popular is that which is always inscribed upon the body: tears, laughter, spine-chilling, screams, fright, erections, etc."[9] Such examples can easily be multiplied, and their frequency in cultural studies suggests that a form of compensation may be at work. Only too conscious of the charges of aridity and abstraction often leveled at intellectual work, cultural critics eagerly ally themselves with the image of a vital, sensual, popular body. A similar response is evident in the recent academic fascination with "white trash" as a subversive symbol of vulgarity, excess and bad taste.[10]

Such arguments are open to question from several perspectives. Thinking of "bourgeois ideology" as synonymous with a repression of pleasure and of the body does not much help one make sense of the historical complexities of Victorian culture. It is far from clear that such a thesis is directly relevant to late-twentieth-century consumer capitalism, which has embraced pleasure and instant gratification with a vengeance. Conversely, equating popular culture with the demands of the body ignores an important tradition of respectability in working-class life. Frugality, decency, and self-discipline, rather than enthusiasm for Dionysian orgies, have often been the core values of the poor. Such values have their own cultural distinctiveness as forms of life and cannot be understood as simply bourgeois norms imposed from above. Working-class women, in particular, often have a powerful interest and investment in respectability, as a means of distancing themselves from sexualized images of lower-class women's bodies.[11]

Furthermore, opposing a repressed and repressive bourgeoisie to an unruly, pleasure-driven working class leaves little room for exploring the various class fractions that fall outside this opposition. The lower middle class is one such example of a messy, contradictory amalgam of symbolic practices, structures of feeling, and forms of life. It usually includes both the traditional petite bourgeoisie of shop owners, small businesspeople, and farmers and the "new" lower middle class of salaried employees such as clerical workers, technicians, and secretaries. Such positions pay little more and often less than blue-collar industrial jobs. The lower middle class often feels itself to be culturally superior to the working class, however, while lacking the cultural capital and the earning power of the professional-managerial class. How does this contradictory positioning complicate the relations between culture and class? How helpful are the traditional accounts of the petite bourgeoisie? And what do these accounts tell us about intellectuals' own class anxieties?

A useful place to begin is with the work of one of the most astute commentators on the complex relations between culture and class. George Orwell's early fiction is devoted to a ruthlessly detailed portrayal of the English lower middle class of the 1930s, showing how a particular economic position is translated into the textures, practices, and emotions of everyday life. The same landscape reappears in novel after novel, enfolding and stifling its inhabitants in the death grip of mingy decency. It is a world of identical, small, semidetached houses stretching into infinity, all equipped with stucco fronts, privet hedges, green front doors, and showy nameplates. Orwell's characters are not waving but drowning in the accumulated detritus of lower-middle-class life: stewed pears, portable radios, false teeth, lace curtains, hire-purchase furniture, teapots, manicure sets, life insurance policies. This material culture is profoundly expressive, attesting not only to economic status but also to a complex blend of moral values and structures of feeling: respectability, frugality, social aspirations. These are epitomized in the image of the drab, indestructible aspidistra displayed in every parlor window, the ubiquitous symbol of the pathos and triumphs of lower-middle-class life.

As portrayed by Orwell, the lower middle class is driven by the fear of shame, tortured by a constant struggle to keep up appearances on a low income. One manifestation of this status anxiety is a craven respect for high culture accompanied by almost complete ignorance of its content. George Bowling, the insurance salesman hero of *Coming Up for Air*, reminisces about a childhood spent in a household without books. His parents disapproved of his reading comics; they "thought I ought to read something 'improving' but didn't know enough about books to be sure which books were 'improving.'"[12] Culture is an empty but potent signifier, a talisman that offers the promise, however opaque, of entry into a higher world. A similar mentality creates the customers for the "fourth-rate private schools" exhaustively described in *A Clergyman's Daughter*. These are parents "too poor to afford the fees of a decent school and too proud to send their children to the council schools,"[13] eager to purchase a veneer of superior education and distinction yet profoundly suspicious of unfamiliar teaching practices.

Baffled if deferential before the mysteries of high culture the lower middle class is simultaneously barred by its ethos from participating in rowdier forms of popular pleasure. As portrayed by Orwell, it inhabits a world that is almost completely lacking in spontaneity, sensuality, or pleasure. This peculiar joylessness is most vividly embodied in his female characters: the disapproving landlady of *Keep the Aspidistra Flying*, the repressed drudge Dorothy in *A Clergyman's Daughter*, and the miserable Hilda in *Coming Up for Air*, "a depressed, lifeless, middle-aged frump" eternally brooding over gas bills, school fees, and the price of butter.[14] Permanent anxiety about money and keeping up appearances conspire to create a gray, cringing mentality composed equally of conformity and bitterness. The lower middle class has completely internalized the strictures of authority; it is the ultimate example of psychic self-regulation, a class that has built the bars of its own prison:

> We're all respectable householders—that's to say Tories, yes-men and bumsuckers. . . . We're all bought, and what's more we're bought with our own money. Everyone of those poor downtrodden bastards, sweating his guts out to pay twice the proper price for a brick doll's house that's called Belle Vue because there's no view and the bell doesn't work—every one of those poor suckers would die on the field of battle to save his country from Bolshevism.[15]

Aspects of Orwell's portrayal of the textures of English lower-middle-class life are perceptive, yet his vision is also a curiously monochromatic one. Orwell's relentless focus on petit bourgeois vulgarity and small-mindedness often brings to mind the high-handed denunciations of mass culture emanating from the Frankfurt School. While *Keep the Aspidistra Flying* concludes with a final epiphany, whereby the erstwhile rebel Gordon Comstock comes to recognize the vitality, honor, and decency that dwell in suburban souls, this conversion is largely unmotivated and singularly unconvincing.

How typical is Orwell's attitude? Critics have devoted much attention to the hostile view of mass culture espoused by many modern artists and intellectuals. Yet less has been said about the specific class dynamics at the heart of this conflict. Often it is simply assumed that the modernist disdain for the masses continues and extends the Victorian bourgeoisie's fear of the working class. But, as John Carey has argued, the horror of the mass in modernism is often a horror of a newly visible and expanding lower middle class.[16] The social threat, in England at least, now lies less in the revolting proletariat than in the consuming petite bourgeoisie. The growth of white-collar workers brings with it a rapid expansion of the suburbs; writers mourn the irrevocable loss of the English countryside as it recedes before a spreading wasteland of villas and bungalows. This spatial encroachment is echoed by a cultural encroachment; the literate lower middle class, rather than the less educated industrial workers, are the primary consumers of the new best-selling novels and popular magazines excoriated by Q. D. Leavis and others. Even worse are the social aspirations of those clerks and shop assistants eager to improve themselves through exposure to great books. The conservative social critic T. W. H. Crosland fulminates against the suburban habit of buying cheap reprints of canonical works: "the rush for low-priced classics has been a mean, discreditable suburban rush."[17] For Crosland, this is simply another example of the quintessential feature of the lower middle class: its propensity toward cheap ostentation.

As Carey points out, E. M. Forster's *Howards End* is a particularly telling exploration of the embarrassment of lower-middle-class cultural aspirations. For the insurance clerk Leonard Bast, a chance encounter with the idealistic and intellectual Schlegel sisters offers the hope of access to a genteel culture to which he has always aspired. Yet for the two sisters, his fumbling references to music or books are a constant reminder of his lack of genuine education, an index merely of "vague aspirations, mental dishonesty, the familiarity with the outsides of books."[18] Bast's laborious repartee and evident class insecurities mark him as a petit bourgeois aspirant toward a culture that can be authentically inhabited only by those who experience it from birth. It is precisely because Bast's class is not so far removed from the Schlegels' own, because he stands "at the extreme verge of gentility,"[19] that his manner appears so excruciatingly jarring and false. Bast is attractive to the sisters only when his cultural aspirations drop away and he can be seen to represent the authentic sublimity of the Common Man.

Similarly, the "young man carbuncular" of T. S. Eliot's *Waste Land* is an estate agent's clerk characterized by his "assurance" and a "bold stare." While he may not command the wealth of the self-made "Bradford millionaire" to whom he is compared, the clerk shares the same upstart confidence and refusal to know his place in the traditional class order. Such literary representations voice not simply the undiluted snobbery and class condescension suggested by Carey but also more ambivalent attitudes. The lower middle class is irredeemably other yet uncomfortably close, a mirror in which aspects of the intellectual's own life and destiny are reflected. The office worker trudging to the railway station to catch the 8:20 train comes to serve as a resonant symbol of the modern dehumanized self, with its docile internalization of rules and regulations, table manners and timetables. It is no coincidence that Gregor Samsa, mysteriously transformed into an unspecified insect in *The Metamorphosis*, is a conscientious traveling salesman anxious that he will be late for work. In Kafka's work, petit bourgeois clerks and commercial travelers are no longer despicable others but powerful allegories of the constrained and compromised modern soul.

How has the lower middle class fared in more recent fiction? Hanif Kureishi's coming-of-age novel *The Buddha of Suburbia*, published in 1990, is usually interpreted through the lens of postcolonial theory, but it is also a novel about the shifting meanings of class in the 1960s and 1970s. The narrator's father is a "badly paid and insignificant" clerk in the British civil service,[20] and his mother is a sales assistant in a shoe store. Lower-middle-classness is still a "cage of umbrellas and steely regularity,"[21] marked by respectability, rigidity, and gray routine. There are the same guilt about money, anxiety about status, and fear of the neighbors' disapproval: the narrator wryly notes, "my mother could never hang out the washing in the garden without combing her hair."[22] The social life of the lower middle class is almost nonexistent, as the ubiquitous English pub is considered vulgar, working-class, and hence out of bounds. "No one went out, there was nowhere to go, and Dad never socialized with anyone from the office . . . Mum and Dad went to the pictures maybe once a year, and Dad always fell asleep; once they went to the theatre to see *West Side Story*."[23] In many ways, the petit bourgeois structures of feeling mapped out in *The Buddha of Suburbia* are remarkably similar to those described by Orwell almost fifty years earlier.

Yet the face of lower-middle-class life is also undergoing a transformation. Kureishi's narrator, Karim Amin, is the child of an Indian father and English mother, "a funny kind of Englishman, a new breed as it were, having emerged from two old histories."[24] He is also bisexual and he exhibits no anxiety or guilt as he embarks on a series of affairs with men and women. The sexual mores of suburbia are changing; the divorce of the narrator's parents and his father's affair with the socially ambitious Eva help precipitate Karim's own personal and social transformation. Furthermore, the new ideologies and lifestyles disseminated by the mass media are blurring the rigid distinctions between classes. The countercultures of the 1960s and 1970s are infiltrating the orderly homes of the lower middle class. Buddhism is emerging as a fad among the progressive adults in the suburbs, while the sounds of the Clash echo in teenage bedrooms around the country.

*The Buddha of Suburbia* is a story about the permeability of class divisions and the new possibilities of social mobility in postwar Britain. Karim eventually becomes a successful actor, escaping his suburban origins for a bohemian metropolitan world of artists and upper-middle-class intellectuals. But the novel also traces the tenacity and continuing power of class distinctions, as Kureishi's hero is constantly confronted with the differences between his background and that of his new friends. "What infuriated me—what made me loathe both them and myself—was their confidence and knowledge. The easy talk of art, theatre, architecture, travel; the languages, the vocabulary, knowing the way round a whole culture—it was invaluable and irreplaceable capital."[25]

Karim's cultural dislocation forces him to become a sort of class detective, hypersensitive to the complex and often confusing codes of class distinction. His new friends dress down, adopt working-class accents, and cultivate a local street sweeper, Heater, as an authentic voice of the proletariat. "Heater was the only working-class person that most of them had met. So he became a sort of symbol for the masses and consequently received tickets to first nights and to the parties afterwards, having a busier social life than Cecil Beaton."[26] Heater politely reciprocates by performing working-class life for his friends, talking about "knife fights, Glasgow poverty and general loucheness and violence"[27] before feeling free to broach the subjects that really interest him, Beethoven's late quartets and a textual problem in Huysmans.

Such instances of cross-class identification underscore the tenacity of class distinctions, the profound divisions between those who aspire upward and those whose status and cultural capital allow them to go slumming. Karim and his suburban friends are desperate to escape to London, lured by the fantasy of a glamorous, bohemian, metropolitan world. The intellectuals and artists who inhabit that culture have their own fantasy of an authentic, gritty, working-class existence. But the lower middle class is no one's fantasy and no one's desire; it has no exchange value in the cultural marketplace. Thus Karim gradually learns to cover over his traces and hide his origins; like Eva, he seeks "to scour that suburban stigma" right off the body.[28] On the one hand, he is driven by his ambition and his loathing of the past; on the other hand, his new identity remains "a second language, consciously acquired,"[29] perpetually reminding him of the class differences that he seeks to transcend.

## SHAME AND SOCIAL MOBILITY

Kureishi's novel raises broader questions about class identity and its relation to social mobility. When we look at class through the theoretical frameworks of recent years, a host of new and interesting questions appear. What, for example, is the ontological status of class as a marker of personhood? How stable or indeterminate is it? As a signifier, class seems to be different from race and gender, which often inescapably mark identity. One can change one's class in a way that one cannot, for the most part, change one's sex or race. Social mobility, either upward or downward, is an increasingly common experience in the industrialized West. This permeability of class boundaries affects the nature of class identities and class interests.[30]

Is class origin, then, more analogous to sexuality as a marker of identity that can be disguised and hidden from others? A person from a lower-class background who has acquired education and money might be said to pass as middle- or upper-class in the same way as a gay man or lesbian can pass as straight. Yet this analogy does not seem right either. The example of sexual passing suggests a strong disjuncture between a felt identity and an act of impersonation, yet this does not seem to be true of class, at least not in the same way. For example, if one has become upper-middle-class as a result of social mobility, then one really *is* upper-middle class—class being, in one sense, nothing more than the sum of its material manifestations: the Ann Klein suits and goat cheese soufflés, the high-definition TV and laptop computer, the postmodern novels and the holidays in Tuscany.

Does the possibility of moving up or down the class hierarchy imply, then, that class has a contingency not shared by other forms of identity? If we think of class in purely economic and sociological terms, the answer is yes. But if class also has cultural and psychological dimensions, the issue becomes more complicated. In an important autobiographical work, *Landscape for a Good Woman*, Carolyn Steedman portrays class identity as a structure of feeling, a complex psychological matrix acquired in childhood. Whereas Marxism has conventionally linked class consciousness to labor and the workplace, Steedman shows how it is ingrained from an early age in the psychological rhythms and flows of the mother-child relationship. Using her own life as a case study, she challenges romantic feminist views of the mother-daughter bond, revealing how class-based attitudes of fatalism, resentment, envy, and shame are inexorably transmitted from the working-class mother to her child.[31]

In spite of Steedman's movement out of the working class, she remains haunted by psychic markings from her childhood, conscious of the gulf between her background and that of her upper-middle-class friends. Yet she cannot simply celebrate her origins; indeed, they stand for a material and psychic impoverishment she is glad to have escaped. The sentimental myths of working-class life propagated by British cultural historians are largely irrelevant, presenting heroic images of the male proletariat while dismissing working-class women's yearnings for consumer goods and their romantic dreams of "marrying up." Lower-class origins, in other words, cannot provide a source of positive identity; hence Steedman's final insistence on the need to consign her story to the dark. But class has a powerful negative role, its psychic effects blocking any automatic sense of affiliation with women from different backgrounds. *Landscape for a Good Woman* is one of the few books to explore analytically the entangled emotions accompanying class mobility, and one of even fewer to consider its gender dimensions.[32]

Shame, one of the structures of feeling invoked in Steedman's book, may provide an important clue to the connections between class identity and social mobility. Until recently, it was often claimed that Western societies were guilt cultures rather than shame cultures, and researchers focused most of their attention on the analysis of guilt. There is now an upsurge of interest in shame as a cultural and psychological phenomenon of continuing relevance. The distinction between shame and guilt can be schematically defined as follows. Guilt is a sense of inner badness caused by a transgression of moral values; shame, by contrast, is a sense of failure or lack in the eyes of others. It has less to do with infractions of morality than with infractions of social codes and a consequent fear of exposure, embarrassment, and humiliation.

Shame, then, is fundamentally connected to everyday sociability. This emotion comprises a painful experience of self-consciousness, resulting from a sudden recognition of a discrepancy between one's behavior and that of one's peers. Shame can often be triggered by a seemingly unimportant event. Helen Lynd writes, "It is the very triviality of the cause—an awkward gesture, a gaucherie in dress or table manners, 'an untimely joke,' always 'a source of bitter regret', a gift or witticism that falls flat, an expressed naivete in taste, a mispronounced word, ignorance of some unimportant detail that everyone else surprisingly knows—that helps to give shame its unbearable character."[33] Furthermore, our shame is often doubled by our recognition of its trivial cause; "we are ashamed because of the original episode and ashamed because we feel so deeply about something so slight that a sensible person would not pay any attention to it."[34]

Some social conditions are thus more likely than others to induce a sense of shame. The child of immigrant parents, Lynd suggests, is often acutely embarrassed by their different manners and customs, by the public exposure of their uncertain and unseemly behavior in an alien land. Similarly, those who are poor often experience shame when their poverty is exposed before the eyes of others. Shame, in other words, rises out of a discrepancy between certain norms and values and others perceived as superior. The opportunities for experiencing shame increase dramatically with geographic and social mobility, which provide an infinite array of chances for failure, for betraying by word or gesture that one does not belong in one's new environment.

Shame is thus a relevant concept for analyzing a range of experiences of dislocation, including those of class.[35] Pierre Bourdieu, one of the few sociologists of culture to document the habitus of the petite bourgeoisie, notes its particularly strong investment in education as a means to social mobility. Many of this class's traditional values—hard work, deferred gratification, respect for culture—are closely linked to educational aspirations. Furthermore, because of its acute anxiety about status, it is hypersensitive to the most minute signs of class distinction. What happens, then, when individuals from such a background find themselves in an academic milieu that disdains lower-middle-class cultural values? How do they negotiate the tension between their old and their new class positions?

My own history, for example, includes experiences of both ethnic difference—growing up in an eastern European family in England in the 1960s—and a lower-middle-class upbringing. The effects of ethnicity, however, were largely overridden by those of class. Anxious to safeguard their tenuous social status, my parents subscribed to a classic petit bourgeois ethos of insularity, respectability, and minding one's own business that had little in common with the glowing vision of folkloric community often associated with ethnic difference. Their values, in fact, did not differ greatly from those of their English neighbors: discipline, propriety, and the importance of keeping up appearances.

Thus my memories of English lower-middle-class culture in the 1960s and 1970s dovetail with Orwell's and Kureishi's descriptions. The prevailing ethos was an anxious display of refinement on a low income: an immaculately mown lawn, a carefully presented collection of knickknacks and ornaments in a rarely visited front room, starched and fastidiously arranged lace curtains. These and similar items signaled cleanliness, respectability, and distance from the perceived grubbiness and disorder of working-class life. It was a world largely without books, music, or knowledge of art; nevertheless it affirmed, from a respectful remove, the vital importance of education and the improving value of culture. The major exception was modern art, which was dismissed as an elaborate fraud perpetrated on a naive public by longhaired, left-wing subversives. The purpose of culture was not to dwell on the unpleasant or distasteful aspects of life but to be positive, educational, and morally uplifting.

It is this perceived combination of aesthetic naïveté, cultural pretension, and moral rectitude that has made the lower middle class an object of amusement and scorn for the intelligentsia. The problem posed by the lower middle class, as Helen Chappell points out, is that it crosses the line of conventional class boundaries.[36] It nurtures aspirations that distance it from stereotypes of working-class identity and that in turn appear pretentious and banal to those higher up the social ladder. Lacking the ironic and self-critical dimensions of high culture and any connections to an organic tradition of working-class community, the culture of the lower middle class is viewed as singularly inauthentic and uniquely conservative.[37]

In fact, most writers on class have roundly endorsed Marx's claim that the petits bourgeois "are reactionary, for they try to roll back the wheel of history."[38] Petit bourgeois has become an all-purpose term of abuse that is routinely applied to any form of conservative or backward thinking. To be lower middle class is to refuse the challenge of modernity, to remain moored in past time. In a survey of the historical literature, David Blackbourn writes,

> It has become customary for historians to stress the reactionary political potential of the lower middle class. Both the pre-industrial, independent lower middle class and the modern white-collar class have been cast as the natural prey of the extreme Right, the easily alarmed

and defenseless victims of demagogues who have played successfully on the "classic" lower middle-class weaknesses of economic insecurity, status anxiety, parochialism and conservative social morality. The susceptibility of the lower middle class to anti-modernist appeals has also become axiomatic.[39]

Thus much of the scholarly writing about the lower middle class is devoted to analyzing its role in the emergence of fascism and in Hitler's rise to power. Theories of lower-middle-class status anxiety were applied to the United States in the 1950s to explain right-wing political movements and McCarthyism.[40] More recently, commentators have attributed the success of Thatcherism to the gradual embourgeoisement of the British working class, which abandoned its traditional values and embraced an individualistic and consumer-oriented ethos.

On an aesthetic level, the lower middle class attracts even more scorn. It is despised by everyone: by the defenders of elite culture for its irredeemably bad taste (kitsch is often seen as quintessentially petit bourgeois) and by radicals for its moral and artistic conservatism and its reverence for high culture. Herbert Gans, for example, notes that the culture of the lower middle class is largely defined by a preference for romantically inflected realism and explicit moral values in art.[41] Pierre Bourdieu emphasizes the gap between recognition and knowledge, between the petite bourgeoisie's respect for high art and its ignorance of the prevailing styles and codes of interpretation. Thus the bohemian and avant-garde elements of modern art and criticism remain largely incomprehensible to individuals from a petit bourgeois cultural milieu. "Self-made men, they cannot have the familiar relationship to culture which authorizes the liberties and audacities of those who are linked to it by birth."[42]

According to Bourdieu, this division between the lower middle class and the intelligentsia arises from a difference of styles rather than of objects of consumption. Any particular element of petit bourgeois culture, from historical romances to garden gnomes, is always open to appropriation by fashionable intellectuals in "one of those taste-makers' coups which are capable of rehabilitating the most discredited object."[43] But the fundamental distinctions between these class groupings—irony versus earnestness, cultural knowledge versus cultural ignorance—remain constant. The petit bourgeois must remain ignorant not because of any specific lack of knowledge, but because "legitimate culture ceases to be what it is as soon as he appropriates it."[44]

The boundaries between intellectual and petit bourgeois culture are not always as impermeable as Bourdieu indicates. This is particularly true in a country such as the United States, where a vast, internally stratified college system and significant regional diversity combine to create a much less cohesive professoriat than in France. The issue is further complicated by the recent growth of part-time and temporary academic workers with high cultural capital but relatively low status and income, whose class position remains ambiguous. Clearly, the financial rewards, occupational autonomy, and social prestige of tertiary-level teaching can vary dramatically both within and across institutions. Nevertheless, Bourdieu is correct insofar as the public face of the humanities, as exemplified in its most highly regarded institutions and its dominant frameworks and methods of interpretation, is deeply disdainful of petit bourgeois values. Within the elaborate minuet of distinction, the intelligentsia may choose to align itself with the culture of the most oppressed but must constantly differentiate itself from the culture closest to it.[45]

## A NEGATIVE IDENTITY

It has become clear, I hope, why lower-middle-classness is a singularly uncool identity that is unlikely to attract much support or enthusiasm in intellectual life. Petit bourgeois subjects have nothing to declare: their class origins cannot be assimilated into a discourse of progressive identity politics. As John Hartley points out, the lower middle class is "the social class with the lowest reputation in the entire history of class theory, the social class that attracts no love, support, advocacy or self-conscious organization . . . the class for whom it seems hardest (certainly it's very rare!) to claim pride of membership."[46] Is it any wonder that individuals of lower-middle-class origins remain silent about their background, preferring camouflage over confession?

What is particularly interesting about the lower middle class is that it does not constitute a class "for itself." In other words, individuals who fit the sociological criteria of lower-middle-classness do not usually form a group consciousness around that status. Instead, they simply think of themselves as being middle-class. In this sense lower-middle-classness is a negative rather than positive identity. It is a category usually applied from outside, by those of higher social status, or retrospectively, by those who once belonged to the lower middle class and have since moved beyond it. In both these cases, it becomes an object of irony, humor, or scorn rather than a term around which people rally and with which they identify.

Identifications, in other words, need to be clearly distinguished from identities. Social status, position, and life chances are shaped by multiple factors, but only under certain conditions do some of these factors become willed points of affiliation and public affirmation. In this context I have tried to elucidate the peculiar status of the petit bourgeois subject in relation to contemporary cultural politics. My aim is not to present the lower middle class as another victimized group whose culture deserves recognition, but rather to suggest that it points to the limits of a politics based on the celebration of group difference.

Several issues are at stake here. First, there is an important and inevitable tension between class analysis and the logic of identity politics, because class is essentially, rather than contingently, a hierarchical concept. Any form of class politics is ultimately concerned with overcoming or at least lessening class differences, not with affirming and celebrating them.[47] Second, class does not have the same status as race or gender in debates over equal representation in academic culture, simply because that culture inescapably alters the class identities of those who inhabit it. As Elazar Barkan succinctly notes, "while women, ethnic and racial minorities or homosexuals do not change their identity because of academic gentrification, the poor cannot help it."[48] Scholarly writing about lower-class life is produced by individuals who are distanced from that life in important respects. Finally, the distinctive features of the lower middle class, I have suggested, do not lend themselves to the cross-class desire and identification that have sometimes shaped the intelligentsia's vision of the working class. The petite bourgeoisie is peculiarly resistant to the romance of marginality.

Because the lower middle class does not generate an identity politics, however, does not mean that it cannot become a serious object of analysis in cultural studies. Indeed, everything still remains to be said about the lower middle class. If the collapse of the Marxian grand narrative implies that a single class can no longer be hailed as the revolutionary subject of history and modernity, it is also no longer possible to dismiss another entire class as the symbol of reactionary thinking and retrograde desires. The changing forms and diverse manifestations of lower-middle-class culture require much more thoughtful investigation.

Here, national differences play an important role. For example, the minute details of class distinction are not etched with the same sharp-edged precision or registered with the same acuity in the United States as they are in England. Still, it would be foolish to conclude that class analysis is irrelevant or inappropriate in the United States. Arno J. Mayer, for example, offers the intriguing thesis that the United States is a quintessentially lower-middle-class nation. In the first half of the nineteenth century, the country was primarily composed of independent small producers and property owners. While this old petite bourgeoisie has largely disappeared, contemporary American society, made up of white-collar workers, has become "a uniquely lower-middle-class nation whose labor force is preeminently nonmanual, modestly salaried and totally dependent."[49]

Mayer's comments underscore both the importance of class analysis and the blurring of class boundaries. The lower middle class has typically stressed such boundaries, anxiously distinguishing its culture and values from those of the industrial working class. Yet many of the traditional distinctions between the lower middle class and the working class are being eroded in a society where white-collar work is increasingly the norm. It is sometimes argued that the lower middle class has been "proletarianized."[50] At the same time, the lower middle class also includes increasing numbers of the downsized and downwardly mobile. Such reluctant refugees from the middle and upper middle classes are often highly educated, and their attitudes and expectations may diverge significantly from those of the traditional petite bourgeoisie.

Christopher Lasch, one of the few intellectuals to praise the American lower middle class, does so from a position of nostalgia. He claims that its distinctive culture of patriotism, loyalty, and moral conservatism is rapidly disappearing, losing ground to the phony, liberal, and cosmopolitan values of the professional-managerial class.[51] Yet perhaps lower-middle-class culture is not so much disappearing as taking new forms. For example, much scholarly writing on the lower middle class presents it as provincial, narrow-minded, even racist. How is this thesis complicated by the growing influx of migrant groups, who often create small family businesses or work in white-collar occupations? To what extent do such migrant groups adopt traditional Western petit bourgeois attitudes and to what extent are they transforming them? How does racial and ethnic difference modify conventional understandings of class?

The relation between gender and the lower middle class is also a complex one, which I can only touch on. The lower middle class is strongly feminized in two ways. First, it contains large numbers of women, who are disproportionally represented in white-collar jobs and secretarial work. Divorce can also have an important effect on class status, causing women from middle- or upper-middle-class households to slide into the genteel poverty of the lower middle class. Second, many of the values and attitudes traditionally associated with the lower middle class are also identified with women: domesticity, prudery, aspirations toward refinement. (*Keeping Up Appearances*, a long-running British sitcom, plays on the comic possibilities of this type of feminine gentility.) Whereas the working class is represented through images of a virile proletariat in left rhetoric, the lower middle class is often gendered female, associated with the triumph of suburban values and the symbolic castration of men. This theme is eloquently summarized by the hero of *Keep the Aspidistra Flying*: "every man you can see has got some blasted woman hanging around his neck like a mermaid, dragging him down and down—down to some beastly semidetached villa in Putney, with hire-purchase furniture and a portable radio and an aspidistra."[52]

Yet these gender associations are also shifting significantly. The sexual revolution, Gans notes, has had a major, if uneven, influence on lower-middle-class culture, such that conservative sexual attitudes are no longer ubiquitous. Rather, traditionalists who hark back to the moral values of the 1950s now intermingle with avid consumers of Judith Krantz and *Cosmopolitan.* "Today, lower-middle culture appears to be increasingly fragmented: differences among traditional, conventional and progressive factions seem to be sharper than in other taste cultures."[53] This view is echoed by Bourdieu, who notes the varied and often contradictory dimensions of this rapidly changing class fraction, which includes both the upwardly and the downwardly mobile. Thus the "new" petite bourgeoisie includes employees in such areas as sales, marketing, and advertising who often reject traditional sexual morality, are attracted to therapy, feminism, New Age religions, and the like, and have abandoned asceticism in favor of a more hedonistic and expressive lifestyle heavily reliant on credit.[54] The diverse class origins, attitudes, and lifestyles of the contemporary lower middle class make it increasingly difficult to deduce its ideology and politics from its economic location.

Furthermore, petit bourgeois values of hard work and individual achievement are increasingly disseminated to daughters as well as sons; the investment in education as a means to social mobility is no longer limited to one gender. Yet women from the lower middle class who pursue such aspirations are sometimes chastised for being too ambitious and "masculine." This was a common response to Margaret Thatcher, whose politics were routinely explained with joking references to her petit bourgeois origins as a grocer's daughter and her excessively male persona. Yet to idealize feminine traits is to remain oblivious to the intense pressures of class on gender; the vision of a nurturing, noncompetitive femininity presumes a certain distance from the grubby reality of economic hierarchies.

The difficulties that stand in the way of developing a nuanced account of the lower middle class are clearly visible in Stuart Hall's sophisticated work on English popular culture. Hall presents this work as a critique of the complacency and dogmatism of traditional left politics, which has failed, he argues, to pay sufficient attention to the changing social fabric of Western industrialized cultures and to the reasons for Thatcherism's success among the electorate. Hall makes an eloquent case for attending to the profound reshaping of the classes in contemporary British society, arguing that this "recomposition is transforming the material basis, the occupational boundaries, the gender and ethnic composition, the political cultures and the social imagery of 'class.'"[55]

Yet in spite of these admonitions, the only legitimate class subject acknowledged by Hall remains the working class, and his use of the term *petit bourgeois* is invariably accompanied by such pejorative adjectives as virulent, regressive, and reactionary. In this regard, Hall remains captive to the Marxist grand narrative that

49

perceives the lower middle class as an unfortunate anachronism on the path to socialism. Yet the lower middle class is not disappearing but expanding; it is not static, but gradually changing in response to various social influences, from new information technologies to feminism. Angie McRobbie, for example, points to the "new politics of work" in Britain as exemplified in the growth of self-employment and small businesses among artists, designers, computer experts, and the like, whose social attitudes are often progressive but whose economic status is unambiguously petit bourgeois.[56]

Interestingly, in a recent interview Hall describes his father as belonging to the "coloured lower middle class" of Jamaica and notes that his own identity was formed through an explicit rejection of his parents' class-based aspirations and desires.[57] Hall's harsh attitude toward his class background echoes the theme that I have been tracing: the intense, often visceral sense of alienation from their origins frequently felt by intellectuals from lower-middle-class backgrounds. Such alienation is not necessarily to be lamented. Indeed, I have suggested that there are genuine, perhaps irresolvable antagonisms between the cultural values of the intelligentsia and those of the traditional lower middle class. My argument has explored some of the reasons for this antagonism instead of claiming to overcome it. I want to avoid the upbeat ending of the self-discovery plot, where negative stereotypes are triumphantly discarded so that an authentic identity can be reclaimed.

Nevertheless, it is surely time for scholars to think more carefully about their portrayal of the petite bourgeoisie. It is the ultimate act of bad faith among left intellectuals to want the working class to remain poor but pure, untainted by consumer culture and social aspirations. The issues raised by the "problem" of the lower middle class—issues relating to changing forms of employment, desires for social mobility, aspirations for one's children—are more pertinent to much of the population in the industrialized West than is the Left's residual fantasy of an organic working class. If cultural studies is really interested in the majority culture, it needs to take such issues on board. Rather than exemplify an anachronistic or outmoded class formation, an irrelevant backwater on the road to modernity, the petite bourgeoisie may offer an important key to the contemporary meanings of class.

## NOTES

This essay was originally published in *PMLA* 115, 1 (2000). Reprinted by permission of the copyright owner, The Modern Language Association of America. I would like to thank Stephen Arata, Michael Bérubé, Sara Blair, Kim Chabot Davis, Jonathan Flatley, Susan Fraiman, Nancy Fraser, Melissa Kennedy, Eric Lott, Janet

Lyon, Allan Megill, and Jennifer Wicke. I benefited from the thoughtful and engaged responses of audiences at the University of Illinois, Urbana-Champaign, Oregon State University, Reed College, and the Space Between Conference at SUNY New Paltz.

1. On the politics of recognition, see Nancy Fraser, *Justice Interruptus: Critical Reflections on the "Postsocialist" Condition* (New York: Routledge, 1997).
2. For a range of perspectives on personal criticism, see H. Aram Veeser, ed., *Confessions of the Critics* (New York: Routledge, 1996).
3. Helen Chappell, "Below the Scampi Belt," *New Society* 8 (October 1991): 51.
4. I am aware, of course, of an important early body of work that tried to integrate Marxist and feminist perspectives. I should also acknowledge those feminist scholars who have approached questions of culture through class, including Lilian S. Robinson, *Sex, Class and Culture* (Bloomington: Indiana University Press, 1978): Donna Haraway, "A Manifesto for Cyborgs: Science, Technology and Socialist Feminism in the 1980s," in *Feminism/Postmodernism*, ed. Linda Nicholson (New York: Routledge, 1990); and Teresa Ebert, *Ludic Feminism and After: Postmodernism, Desire and Labor in Late Capitalism* (Ann Arbor: University of Michigan Press, 1996). I stand by my claim, however, that there is remarkably little knowledge among feminist literary and cultural critics of the rethinking of class that is currently going on in sociology and social theory.
5. There is a vast body of literature on this topic, which is usually divided into neo-Marxist and neo-Weberian schools. For a useful overview, see Rosemary Crompton, *Class and Stratification: An Introduction to Current Debates* (Cambridge: Polity, 1993); and Nicholas Abercrombie and John Urry, *Capital, Labour and the Middle Classes* (London: Allen and Unwin, 1983).
6. One exception is John Frow, *Cultural Studies and Cultural Value* (Oxford: Oxford University Press, 1995). See also Stuart Hall *The Hard Road to Renewal: Thatcherism and the Crisis of the Left* (London: Verso, 1988), discussed in more detail below.
7. Peter Stallybrass and Allon White, *The Politics and Poetics of Transgression* (Ithaca: Cornell University Press, 1986).
8. John Fiske, *Understanding Popular Culture* (New York: Routledge, 1989).
9. Lawrence Grossberg, "The Formations of Cultural Studies: An American in Birmingham," in *Relocating Cultural Studies: Developments in Theory and Research*, ed. Valda Blundell, John Shepherd, and Ian Taylor (London: Routledge, 1993), 63.
10. A number of essays in Matt Wray and Annalee Newitz, eds., *White Trash* (New York: Routledge, 1997) fall into this trap, though there are some exceptions, such as Allan Bérubé's thoughtful essay.
11. See Beverley Skeggs, *Formations of Class and Gender* (London: Sage, 1997).

12. George Orwell, *The Penguin Complete Novels of George Orwell* (Harmondsworth: Penguin, 1976), 482.
13. Orwell, *Complete Novels*, 393.
14. Orwell, *Complete Novels*, 511.
15. Orwell, *Complete Novels*, 437.
16. John Carey, *The Intellectuals and the Masses: Pride and Prejudice amongst the Intelligentsia, 1880–1939* (London: Faber and Faber, 1992).
17. T. W. H. Crosland, *The Suburbans* (London: John Long, 1902), 188.
18. E. M. Forster, *Howards End* (New York: Bantam, 1985), 90.
19. Forster, *Howards End*, 34.
20. Hanif Kureishi, *The Buddha of Suburbia* (New York: Viking, 1990), 7.
21. Kureishi, *Buddha of Suburbia*, 26.
22. Kureishi, *Buddha of Suburbia*, 188.
23. Kureishi, *Buddha of Suburbia*, 46.
24. Kureishi, *Buddha of Suburbia*, 3.
25. Kureishi, *Buddha of Suburbia*, 177.
26. Kureishi, *Buddha of Suburbia*, 175.
27. Kureishi, *Buddha of Suburbia*, 176.
28. Kureishi, *Buddha of Suburbia*, 134.
29. Kureishi, *Buddha of Suburbia*, 178.
30. Erik Olin Wright, *Class Counts: Comparative Studies in Class Analysis* (Cambridge: Cambridge University Press, 1997), 534–35.
31. Carolyn Steedman, *Landscape for a Good Woman: A Story of Two Lives* (London: Virago, 1985).
32. On this issue, see also Annette Kuhn, *Family Secrets: Acts of Memory and Imagination* (London: Verso, 1995).
33. Helen Merrell Lynd, *On Shame and the Search for Identity* (New York: Harcourt, Brace, 1958), 40.
34. Lynd, *On Shame*, 42.
35. For an interesting elaboration of shame in British working-class culture, see Pamela Fox, *Class Fictions: Shame and Resistance in the British Working-Class Novel, 1890–1945* (Durham: Duke University Press, 1994).
36. Chappell, "Below the Scampi Belt."
37. Of course, the idealization of the working class is also, as I have indicated, not without problems. In *Daddy's Girl: Young Girls and Popular Culture* (Cambridge: Harvard University Press, 1997), Valerie Walkerdine complains about how the British Left has exoticized the working class, subjecting it "to the most minute of gazes but always to look for signs of something" (5). For a discussion of the rather different meanings of working-class origins in American academia, see C. L. Barney Dews and Carolyn Leste Law, *This Fine Place So Far from Home: Voices of Academics from the Working Class* (Philadelphia: Temple University Press, 1995).
38. Karl Marx and Friedrich Engels, "Manifesto of the Communist Party," in

*Basic Writings on Politics and Philosophy*, ed. Lewis S. Feuer (London: Fontana, 1969), 59.

39. David Blackbourn, "The *Mittelstand* in German Society and Politics, 1871–1914," *Social History* 2 (1977): 409. This thesis has been challenged by some historians; for an overview of the debates, see Richard F. Hamilton, *The Social Misconstruction of Reality: Validity and Verification in the Scholarly Community* (New Haven: Yale University Press, 1996). For a useful discussion of the lower middle class in England, see Geoffrey Crossick, "The Emergence of the Lower Middle Class in Britain: A Discussion," in *The Lower Middle Class in Britain, 1870–1914*, ed. Geoffrey Crossick (London: Croom Helm, 1977).

40. See Val Burris, "The Discovery of the New Middle Classes," in *The New Middle Classes: Life-Styles, Status Claims, and Political Orientations*, ed. Arthur J. Vidich (New York: New York University Press, 1995).

41. Herbert Gans, *Popular Culture and High Culture: An Analysis and Evaluation of Taste* (New York: Basic Books, 1974), 87.

42. Pierre Bourdieu, *Distinction: A Social Critique of the Judgment of Taste* (Cambridge: Harvard University Press, 1984), 331.

43. Bourdieu, *Distinction*, 327.

44. Bourdieu, *Distinction*, 327.

45. For a recent investigation of this phenomenon, see Janice Radway, *A Feeling for Books: The Book-of-the-Month Club, Literary Taste and Middle-Class Desire* (Chapel Hill: University of North Carolina Press, 1997).

46. John Hartley, *Popular Reality: Journalism, Modernity, Popular Culture* (London: Arnold, 1996), 161.

47. This question is addressed from different perspectives in Fraser, *Justice Interruptus*; Diane Coole, "Is Class a Difference That Makes a Difference?" *Radical Philosophy*, no. 77 (1996): 17–25; and John Guillory, *Cultural Capital* (Chicago: University of Chicago Press, 1993).

48. Elazar Barkan, "History and Cultural Studies," in *History and . . . : Histories within the Human Sciences*, ed. Ralph Cohen and Michael S. Roth (Charlottesville: University Press of Virginia, 1995), 362.

49. Arno Mayer, "The Lower Middle Class as Historical Problem," *Journal of Modern History* 47, 3 (1975): 422.

50. Harold Braverman, *Labor and Monopoly Capital: The Degradation of Work in the Twentieth Century* (New York: Monthly Review Press, 1974).

51. Christopher Lasch, *The True and Only Heaven: Progress and Its Critics* (New York: Norton, 1991).

52. Orwell, *Complete Novels*, 649.

53. Gans, *Popular Culture and High Culture*, 88.

54. Bourdieu, *Distinction*, 354–71.

55. Hall, *Hard Road to Renewal*, 5.

56. Angie McRobbie, "Looking Back at New Times and Its Critics," in *Stuart*

*Hall: Critical Dialogues in Cultural Studies*, ed. David Morley and Kuan-Hsing Chen (London: Routledge, 1996), 258.

57. Kuan-Hsing Chen, "The Formation of a Diasporic Intellectual: An Interview with Stuart Hall," in Morley and Chen, *Stuart Hall: Critical Dialogues in Cultural Studies*, 485–90.

# 2

# NEW CULTURAL THEORIES
# OF MODERNITY

**M**odernity is back with a vengeance. People are reflecting anew on the protean meanings of the modern, on its ambiguous legacies and current realities. While only a few years ago, everyone was fixated on postmodernism, we are now going back to that enigmatic phenomenon that precedes the "post." The significance of modernity is clearly not yet exhausted. Yet this return is also a beginning, as scholars tackle well-worn ideas and calcified debates from new angles. As a result, our view of modernity is changing dramatically. The modern is not what it used to be.

This rethinking of the modern is happening on various fronts. In this chapter I will look at a handful of recently published books that reveal suggestive affinities: Paul Gilroy's *The Black Atlantic: Modernity and Double Consciousness,*

Arjun Appadurai's *Modernity at Large*, Henning Bech's *When Men Meet: Homosexuality and Modernity*, and Janet Lyon's *Manifestoes: Provocations of the Modern*, as well as my own book *The Gender of Modernity*. All these books range across the competing definitions of modernity in different fields. They know about agreements and disagreements between those who see modernity as an uncompleted philosophical project, a global socioeconomic system, a distinctive array of aesthetic techniques, or a specific phenomenological reality. To give one example, Janet Lyon's survey of the manifesto as a guide to the unresolved contradictions of modernity draws on debates about the public sphere, avant-garde art, modern forms of universalism, and the gendered meanings of political rhetoric since the French Revolution. While scholarship on modernism and modernity has often developed along separate and parallel tracks, scholars in such fields as sociology, anthropology, and literary criticism are now striving to create genuinely cross-disciplinary perspectives on the modern.

There are three main causes for this new work. One is the dramatic upsurge of interest in the idea of culture across a broad spectrum of disciplines. Think, for example, of the new cultural history, the growth of cultural sociology, the influence of new historicism on the study of literature, and the rapid expansion of cultural studies itself as a new discipline or anti-discipline. Culture is not, of course, a new idea, but its meanings have shifted profoundly in recent times. The established view of culture, spelled out most clearly in the annals of anthropology, assumed a certain unity, internal coherence, and continuity. Culture was the relatively stable symbolic system through which individuals were socialized and integrated into their respective worlds. By contrast, contemporary scholars often view culture as a much more unstable affair. It is a loose-knit ensemble of interconnected yet divergent behaviors, perceptions, and ways of life, which are rich in ambiguity and contradiction rather than simply serving the interests of social reproduction.

The specific value of the culture concept for interdisciplinary approaches to modernity lies in helping to bridge a persistent divide between the study of art and the study of society. To study culture is to study everything that signifies; the modern world is no longer an objective system peopled by more or less rational agents but is permeated through and through by diverse and competing practices of interpretation. The structures of social life cannot be separated from the layerings of symbolic meaning in which they are embedded. Arjun Appadurai writes of his analysis of contemporary social systems, "these are not objectively given relations that look the same from every angle of vision . . . but deeply perspectival constructs, inflected by the historical, linguistic and political situatedness of different sorts of actors."[1] However, it is important to realize that "actors" for Appadurai are multinational corporations and nation-states as well as individual human beings. By linking cultural analysis to theories of modernity, scholars make it clear that they do not see culture as a redemptive sphere that floats free of the grubby realities of money and power.

A second important reason for revising modernity is the rich efflorescence of writing on the history of women, people of color, gays and lesbians, and other disenfranchised groups. Popular forms of modernization theory have traditionally told a cheerful and uncomplicated story of history as progress, in which ever more groups would come to benefit from the fruits of Western development. Irritated by the complacency and smugness of this view, scholars of marginalized groups often responded by stressing the oppressive nature of the modern as both a historical reality and a philosophical ideal. The story of the modern world, they claimed, was a story by and about white men, who had erased all other voices and replaced real differences with a fantasy of sameness. Modernity was thus not a concept that could speak to the experiences, hopes, and desires of the oppressed.

In hindsight, some of the weaknesses of this response are apparent. It is one thing to point out that Western development contains many painful stories of exploitation and suffering; it is quite another to claim that the experience of modernity has been calamitous for all but a privileged few. Living in the modern world has been a deeply contradictory experience for people from many different backgrounds; these contradictions are emblazoned on the bodies of the powerless as well as the powerful. When scholars claimed that modernity was white male history and that other groups had played no part in its unfolding, they were echoing the willful blindness to difference that had marred traditional approaches to the past. To think seriously about the desires, hopes, and actions of such groups in the making of the modern world was to open the door to alternative ways of thinking about history. Now peopled by previously invisible figures, by suffragettes and shoppers, actresses and rap artists, Indian cricketers and gay *flâneurs*, the landscape of modernity is a more interesting and less familiar place.

There is, I would argue, a crucial link between the turn to cultural theories of modernity and the desire to write the histories of those traditionally absent from history. The interest in redefining the modern calls for new frameworks that are more hospitable to such analyses. The study of culture provides one such framework. Until recently, the most influential ways of thinking about modernity came out of two main intellectual traditions: sociology and criticism of literature and art. Each of these traditions has given us a specific picture of what it means to be modern.

Within sociology, those who did not accept the optimistic view of modernization sketched out above were often willing to subscribe to a darker vision of

NEW CULTURAL THEORIES OF MODERNITY

history grounded in a selective reading of Marx and Weber. They saw the modern as synonymous with the rise of bureaucracy and capitalism, the unchecked expansion of technology and industrialization, the loss of overarching meaning, and the profound alienation of human beings. In this world view, which was underwritten by the influential work of the Frankfurt School and echoed in the more paranoid moments of poststructuralism, modern individuals are dwarfed by institutional structures and systems of power, subject to ever greater forms of surveillance and control. Women and people of color clearly did not play much of a role in the creation of such systems and structures. To rely on the conventional sociological account of modernity is thus to go along with the view that these groups were absent from modernity, existing only as its silent victims and others.

The other main framework for making sense of the modern has been an aesthetic one, found in literary and art criticism. Here, modernity is approached through the great works of aesthetic modernism: Joyce's exuberant verbal experiments, Picasso's splintered forms and figures, Woolf's deft rendering of unconscious murmurings, the anarchic eruptions of Dada and surrealism. The modern world revealed by such works of art is a far more chaotic and mysterious place. The discourse on aesthetic modernism dwells on the experience of rupture and ambiguity rather than order and control. It speaks of the chaotic workings of the unconscious, the fragmentation of the self, the unreliability of language, the confused nature of perception. The modern is an experience of crisis and groundlessness that is simultaneously exhilarating and terrifying. The polyglot languages, skewed forms, and fragmented images of modern literature and art offer an authentic window into the nature and meaning of modern experience.

This view of the modern is also a very influential one. The exhaustive and scrupulous attention given to the great works of literary and artistic modernism in schools, museums, books, and journals has guaranteed its widespread dissemination in our culture. Yet it is also a partial view. To equate the experience of the modern with the aesthetics of high modernism is to leave out much that has been historically important in modern life: everyday rhythms and regularities, the continuing appeal of realist and sentimental forms of cultural expression, the stubborn persistence of religion and other metaphysical systems. The canon of modern art, mostly fashioned out of the desires, ambitions, and experiences of an urban intellectual elite, was not necessarily a reliable guide to all aspects of modern experience. And here too, while an occasional black or female modernist artist has been allowed into the canon, they remain exceptional figures, defined in terms of their marginal status.

The new theories of modernity are important because they allow scholars to engage seriously with the role of nonelite groups in the formation of the modern world. Reading the modern through the concept of culture makes such groups central rather than tangential. It directs our attention to everyday practices, popular forms of cultural expression, and the rich but often overlooked textures of daily experience. It reminds us that the rich brew of ideas, images, and stories that defines the modern world is not simply imposed from above on a docile populace but is constantly re-created through forms of negotiation and critical response. In this sense, while nonelite groups have not been the primary architects of modernity, their desires, beliefs, and acts have helped to shape the contours of the modern world.

Henning Bech, for example, charts the connections between homosexuality and modernity, claiming that many distinctive aspects of modern urban culture, such as the ubiquity of surfaces, the power of the gaze and the anonymous encounter, are closely connected to the history of sexuality and the development of a specific homosexual "mode of being." Paul Gilroy shows that the formal hybridity of black popular music offers a key to understanding the ambiguous nature of modern temporality as a complex blend of innovation and tradition. And my own discussion of the female consumer highlights her importance to discourses of modernity as both a historical reality and a resonant mythic figure. In these, as in other similar examples, we can see how the history of modernity is formed through the cultural images and lived experiences of race, gender, and sexuality.

Viewing the modern through the lens of culture thus brings into sight a dazzling array of phenomena that have been ignored or given scant attention in conventional scholarship: popular novels, fashion, film, shopping, journalism, interior decor, music, architecture, and the like. All these help to make up the everyday experiences of modernity and are central, in particular, to the histories of ordinary individuals. We are indebted to the new cultural historians who are excavating the everyday and often ephemeral experiences of modern life: styles of advertising, forms of interior design, changing concepts of identity and selfhood as expressed in everything from bureaucratic forms to tombstones. It is often the most banal, prosaic, and taken-for-granted aspects of everyday life that powerfully evoke the strangeness of the recent past. A cultural approach to the modern also invites us to reflect critically on the history of scholarly knowledge itself. Such disciplines as sexology, sociology, and psychology have played an influential role in shaping our understanding of what counts as modern. They do not simply describe modern culture, they have also helped to create it.

Of course, approaching the modern through the concept of culture is not a completely new idea. Important and influential predecessors that come to mind include Walter Benjamin, Marshall Berman, Stephen Kern, and many others.

What *is* different is the desire to rethink the meaning of modern culture through the interests, struggles, and perspectives of those often seen as languishing outside historical time. It is this shift in perspective that is altering our sense of what the modern means.[2]

Furthermore, cultural studies is an odd hybrid of sociology and literary criticism, and the new cultural approaches to modernity should not be seen as simply discarding these other forms of knowledge. For example, the works of high modernism and the avant-garde are major markers of modern consciousness, their resonances powerful and wide-reaching. Hence, much of the scholarship on modern art remains enormously useful. However, cultural theorists are likely to see art as part of a continuum of responses to the maelstrom of modernity rather than a uniquely subversive or redemptive sphere of endeavor. Similarly, sociological perspectives on bureaucracy and capitalism influence this new work. However, as I argue in more detail below, cultural theorists see the relations between institutions and everyday life as more dynamic and interactive than do many sociologists. They are alert to the various constraints that mold human lives but do not see modern culture as merely a pallid reflection of the sovereign power of capitalism, bureaucracy, and the nation-state.

Finally, there is a third important context that needs mentioning. Clearly, the new interest in modernity has been sparked by the widespread debates around postmodernism in the 1970s and 1980s. Many, though not all, of these debates defined the postmodern against the modern. Modernity stood for the logic of assimilation and the tyranny of sameness, the domination of "grand narrative," the belief in the redemptive power of great art. The postmodern era, by contrast, involved a breakdown of foundational truths, an exhilarating liberation of difference and multiplicity and a blurring of boundaries between high art and popular culture. The postmodern, in this account, was seen as coming after and redeeming the modern, by transforming it into its opposite. For defenders of the Enlightenment, by contrast, the discourse on postmodernism was a symptom of cultural crisis, a lapse into irony, relativism, and nihilism.

With hindsight, however, such strong distinctions between the modern and the postmodern seem less compelling. Scholars in diverse fields have pointed out that a culture of consumption has informed the *longue durée* of modernity, that the new social movements are not all that new but have a long history, and that the philosophies and worldviews of modernity are more contradictory than postmodern theories have often allowed. As a result, the postmodern critique of historical totalization is now being directed at the idea of postmodernism itself. Writers are coming to think of our own time as one moment within the long history of modernity rather than as a radical break with that history.

In contrast to the subtitle of a recent book, *From the Modern to the Postmod-*

*ern*, I thus offer an alternative slogan, "from the postmodern to the modern."[3] We may need to go backward rather than forward, to rethink our relationship to past time rather than assume we have transcended it. Redefining the modern means rethinking our sense of history and time, continuity and rupture, revolution and tradition. Janet Lyon observes, "modernity is not a seamless temporal entity characterized by period, progress, and development, though its narratives often prefer that plotline. It is, instead, subject to the very discontinuities of time that its narratives seek to disguise: different 'times' co-exist within the same discrete historical moment, just as surely as homologous 'times' exist across centuries."[4]

The rest of this chapter explores the implications of this insight. I organize my discussion around five theses that define new cultural approaches to modernity. I do not wish to minimize the difference in content, methodology, and concerns among the works I discuss. They do not, in any sense, exemplify a single school or body of thought. Nor, I hope, do I simply project my own scholarly views about the modern onto the work of others. All the books I examine, however, seek to reframe the modern through the concept of culture and the histories of those who have not been recognized as full political subjects. As such they exemplify a sea change in approaches to modernity.

## MODERNITY DOES NOT EQUAL SAMENESS

Clearly, there are many ways modernity does cause much of the world to become more and more alike. Its philosophical claim to represent universal values is echoed at a material level in the relentless diffusion of Western—and above all American—products and ideas. Modernity draws everything into a single capitalist system of exchange and subjects it to the laws of the market. It is the arena of mass production and mass reproduction; identical commodities, images, and texts are sent spiraling around the globe from a central source. It creates bureaucratic structures governed by rules and regulations, which often leave little room for spontaneity and improvisation. It is, finally, linked to a history of imperialism and the ardent desire of the West to impose its culture and values on the rest of the world. Spatial differences are leveled and vast distances bridged, as surprisingly similar objects, ideas, and types of speech crop up in very different contexts.

Yet modern subjects never inhabit a single, unified world; rather, they live in multiple worlds. An interest in this phenomenon unites the new cultural approaches to modernity. Paul Gilroy, for example, questions the view that modernity "affects everyone in a uniform and essentially similar way," seeking to explore "the variations and discontinuities in modern experience."[5] How are these discontinuities evident? First, the shape of individual lives is obviously

NEW CULTURAL THEORIES OF MODERNITY

formed by the demographics of specific identities. While they may both inhabit a system of capitalist rationalization, the daily lives of a black female factory worker and a white male CEO are worlds apart. These contrasts are intensified if we take the transnational dimensions of the modern into account and think seriously about the contemporaneity of the non-Western world. Modernity does not erase differences, but undoes and redoes them in complicated ways, creating dramatic variations in human experience. It is a mistake, for example, to think of sexual or racial hierarchies as anachronistic residues that reveal the lingering power of premodern ways of thought. Such divisions have been central to the development of the modern; they are not primordial remnants of an irrational past, but an integral part of the history of the Enlightenment.[6]

For example, Janet Lyon traces the genealogy of the manifesto as a key to the unresolved contradictions of modernity. The manifesto is a document that appeals to democratic ideals even as it protests their present failure; it encodes universalist claims yet also expresses an impetus toward radical individualism and particularism. "Modernism's signal crisis—how to negotiate between radical individualism and forms of representation—found its expression in the paradoxes of the manifesto, the form that is at once political and aesthetic, rational and irrational, angry and restrained."[7] From the time of the French Revolution, the history of the manifesto reveals women's difficult relation to the militant, utopian, future-oriented discourse of modern radicalism. These difficulties persist and intensify as revolution shifts from politics to aesthetics in the early twentieth century. In many of the founding texts of modernist aesthetics, women come to embody a regressive force. Femininity is the realm of tradition, oppressive domesticity, and messy emotions against which the male avant-garde defines its own radical, forward-looking purity.

Modern plurality, as Lyon's work makes clear, is not simply a question of the varying standpoints and experiences of individual subjects. Modern societies are also differentiated at a structural level; they contain distinct cultural domains with their own histories, vocabularies, and practices. Such spheres as science, law, politics, religion, and art are interconnected yet also relatively independent, offering differing ways of engaging with and making sense of the world. These cultural domains often cut across hierarchies of race, gender, and class in complicated ways. For example, attempting to make sense of the specific histories of art, science, or law by invoking a general concept such as patriarchy does not take us very far. It remains too coarse-grained to explain the important differences between these spheres, or the reasons for these differences. Why, for example, has art been more interested in gender ambiguity and the idea of the feminine than, say, the law, and how does this relate to the history, positioning, and ethos of art and artists in modern Western societies? Masculinity is not a unified, internally coherent identity, and the various expressions of a male-dominated culture reveal important differences.

Conversely, the forms of expression essayed by women are themselves filtered through the specifics of institution, discourse, and genre. For example, in my own work on gender and modernity I contrast three forms of "women's culture"—political rhetoric, avant-garde art, and popular fiction—as a way of exploring the diversity of cultural expression even among white women of the middle class. I suggest that the relations between the feminine and the modern cannot be understood in terms of a global narrative of exclusion and absence. Rather, women persistently appear and reappear across the uneven and often contradictory discourses that make up the self-understanding of modernity. There is no single aesthetic or political definition of the feminine that can sum up what it means to be a woman in modernity.

Increasingly, individuals partake of multiple worlds that rely on quite different vocabularies, assumptions, and modes of self-presentation. Imagine, for example, the very different behaviors of a student in the course of a single day, as she attends an aerobics class, goes to church, takes part in an academic discussion on e-mail, and goes to a bar in the hope of finding a sexual partner. This point is explored by Anthony Giddens in his discussion of the "pluralization of life worlds," the fact that everyday life often consists of a series of distinct segments that may bear little relationship to each other.[8] Furthermore, this plurality also extends over time; individuals may change their cultural allegiances at various points in their life history and adopt or reject various identity "scripts."

Of course, the freedom to make such choices is powerfully affected by material conditions. It is in the West, above all, that the world is increasingly imagined as a supermarket of lifestyle choices. But Appadurai points out that even the humblest individuals in non-Western societies now participate, imaginatively if not actually, in multiple alternative worlds. The reasons for this lie in the various scripts, images and fantasies disseminated by the mass media around the globe. As a result, life experiences are increasingly perceived as contingent rather than natural, framed by the injunction "it could be otherwise."

We need, as Appadurai suggests, to attend to "disjuncture and difference" in the experience of modernity. Much of Appadurai's work addresses this issue in a transnational context, presenting a sustained critique of the claim that globalization equals sameness. He distinguishes, for example, between five kinds of global cultural flow: those involving money, machinery, people, images and ideas. Rather than moving in smooth harmony, or being controlled by a single underlying cause such as capitalism or technology, these different social levels are marked by unpredictable interactions and disjunctures. As a result,

NEW CULTURAL THEORIES OF MODERNITY

globalization is by no means the same as sameness or the emergence of a single coherent world system.

Furthermore, these levels of global exchange become meaningful only in the specific milieus in which their effects are felt and lived. The time of the modern is unevenly realized across geopolitical space. Appadurai fleshes out this insight by reflecting at some length on the dense entanglement of the global and the local, showing how specific groups take up and use the resources of modernity in different ways. For example, his analysis of Indian cricket shows how an imperial gentleman's sport was gradually fashioned into a distinctively indigenous cultural product and form of entertainment. Yet Appadurai also warns against a romantic view of the local as a pure form of identity: "groups are no longer tightly territorialized, spatially bounded, historically unselfconscious, or culturally homogeneous."[9] The local is formed in constant dialogue with the global. Those committed to fashioning specific, place-bound identities, affirming the value of local, tribal or national communities, cannot hope to shake themselves free of external influence. The local is not the site of pure difference.

## THE DISENFRANCHISED ARE NOT JUST VICTIMS OR OTHERS OF MODERNITY

As I noted earlier, scholars have developed powerful tools for diagnosing the pathologies of modernity. Feminists have stressed the power of the private/public division, arguing that Western history could present itself as synonymous with universal reason only by pushing out of sight the lives, experiences, and bodies of half of humanity. Scholars of race are piecing together the details of a long history of slavery and colonization, claiming that the brutalization and murder of people of color were often justified by appeals to Enlightenment ideals and scientific theories of racial inferiority. Historians of sexuality have shown how sexual desires and practices have been subject to elaborate procedures of normalization and control.

This charting of modernity's painful history has sometimes led to a view of oppressed groups as lacking all power to act, as silenced victims and invisible others in a world not of their making. By contrast, recent scholarship positions these groups squarely within the modern by acknowledging and embracing the ambivalence of modernity itself. This is not just a philosophical point; the argument, familiar from Habermas and others, that the critique of the Enlightenment draws on the assumptions of the Enlightenment to make that critique. It is also an argument about the cultural experience of modernity, about everyday encounters with technology, urban space, consumer culture, and the mass media. While such facets of modern life have been decried as deeply alienating, they also help to fuel expressions of refusal and dissent. Modernity goes all the way down; it forms the psyches of its most passionate critics as well as its supporters.

For example, Wendy Parkins's history of the suffragette movement traces its complex relation to the liberal ideal of the public sphere as well as to a distinctively modern culture of consumption. The "aestheticization of politics" that is often condemned by the Left was a crucial part of women's struggles for emancipation, actualized in dazzling forms of spectacle, fashion, and display.[10] Janet Lyon shows how the history of women's anger at the "broken promises of modernity" was often filtered through the rhetoric of the manifesto, a quintessentially modern genre. Women have protested their exclusion from political culture through recourse to a distinctive form marked by absolutist demands, an apocalyptic language of prophecy and war, and the appeal to a collective political identity. Feminist discourse boldly reassigns the gender of the revolutionary subject and reveals the fundamental tensions within the language of universalism. But when it rejects the status quo and exhorts us to imagine a radically other world, it does not depart from the culture of modernity but repeats a quintessentially modern gesture.

Henning Bech makes a strong case for homosexuality as a distinctively modern identity. He points to the weakening of moral norms, the instability and permeability of family structures, urban anonymity, the increasing theatricality of everyday life, and above all the "omnipresent, diffuse sexualization of the city" as allowing new experiences of closeness and distance, freedom and danger.[11] Bech suggests, provocatively, that homosexuals are at the vanguard of modernity, paving the way for a broader cultural transformation. Thus, before others and more than others, homosexuals have experienced the distinctive pleasures and dangers, anxieties and risks of the modern world. Yet at the same time, he claims, the world is becoming more and more "homosexualized," such that the identity of the homosexual will eventually disappear.

In a related move, Paul Gilroy charts the complex borrowings and interminglings between black culture and the aesthetic and philosophical heritage of European and American modernity. Rejecting any notion of separate and incommensurable racial traditions, Gilroy explores the interest of black intellectuals in the work of European philosophers such as Hegel and Sartre as well as their dialogue with other black artists and scholars. *The Black Atlantic* makes a case for the profound importance of cultural interchange and hybridity in the unfolding of the modern world. While insisting on the horrible centrality of racial enslavement to Western history, a centrality unacknowledged in traditional theories of modernity, Gilroy nevertheless insists that black culture and creativity cannot be thought of outside this fraught history.

NEW CULTURAL THEORIES OF MODERNITY

All these texts affirm difference but reject incommensurability. They do not see group identities as internally unified or tightly bounded against the outside world. On the contrary, they are all interested in leakages, borrowings, and translations between and across the various cultures of modernity. Moreover—and this is what distinguishes them from traditional social history—they see modernity as going all the way down. The modern is not an alien, external force bearing down on an organic community of the disempowered. Rather, modernity becomes real at the most intimate and mundane levels of experience and interaction. Its traces can be found in dreams and fantasies, ways of looking, modes of dress, ways of inhabiting one's body. The modern is felt in the very pores of the skin, the rhythm of the heartbeat, the intimate recesses of thought and feeling.

For example, describing his own memories of going to American movies as a young boy in Bombay, Appadurai speaks of the modern as "embodied sensation." Inchoate yearnings, resonant images, tastes, and smells, the talismanic power of certain objects and commodities are psychic markers that connect, through labyrinthine, multi-forked paths, to the material and political structures of the social world. Yet Appadurai does not use his example to drive home a point about the insidious colonization of psychic life by the Western media. Rather, he suggests, the images and scripts of the mass media also enable new possibilities by disrupting the authority and inevitability of what is. "The work of the imagination, viewed in this context, is neither purely emancipatory nor entirely disciplined but is a space of contestation in which individuals and groups seek to annex the global into their own practices of the modern."[12] There are no psychic and cultural enclaves untouched by large-scale processes of change. Acts of refusal and resistance are ignited by the very conditions that they also protest.

## MODERNITY DOES NOT DESTROY SUBJECTIVITY

Traditionally, sociologists think of modernity as made up of large-scale systems such as capitalism, bureaucracy, or the mass media. For Marxists, the alienation involved in selling one's labor and in the transformation of things into commodities permeates and tarnishes all aspects of human existence. Weberians see the spread of bureaucracy as a symbol of widespread processes of rationalization and the pervasive disenchantment of the social world. And for critical theorists such as Adorno and Horkheimer, the unparalleled power of the mass media in the twentieth century heralds a brave new world of standardization and sameness, vacuous entertainment and the promise of endless fun. In these large-scale theories of the modern, power is exercised from the top down; the individual shrinks to an insignificant and powerless speck, dwarfed by the immense power of social systems. (A similar diminution, though couched in a different philosophical vocabulary, can be found in poststructuralist theories of the death of the subject.)

Recent theories of modernity, by contrast, deliberately adjust their focus and zero in from the general to the particular. Viewed from the standpoint of grand theory, individuals merge into an anonymous and helpless mass, but a closer look produces a more differentiated picture. Cultural analysis provides a way of understanding how human beings engage with and make sense of large social structures in their own lives. As a result, some of the generalizations about modernity in traditional social theory become less compelling.

Appadurai, for example, argues that the pivot of his approach to modernity "is not any large-scale project of social engineering . . . but . . . the everyday cultural practice through which the work of the imagination is transformed."[13] While he wants to present a general thesis about the impact of migration and the mass media on contemporary experiences of modernity, Appadurai illustrates his argument through specific examples, such as the rural women who migrate from southern India to work as cabaret dancers in a Bombay nightclub. In his account, the women are not simply passive reflections of global forces, but individuals "putting lives together, fabricating their own characters, using the cinematic and social materials at their disposal."[14] In his analysis of homosexuality and modernity, Bech also "snuggles up to what is quotidian and recognizable, even trivial, for the inhabitants of the life-world."[15] Expressing a certain skepticism about the theories of language popular with many scholars of sexuality, Bech wants to record the complex swirl of behaviors, perceptions, places, and ways of feeling that make up the fabric of daily life. The railway station, the discotheque, the cabdriver, the group of men clustering in front of a shop window to watch sports on television: for Bech, these everyday phenomena are magical images that crystallize certain key aspects of homosexuality and modernity.

Yet it would be a mistake to equate modern culture with the everyday or the popular. It also embraces the academic and the eccentric, the canonical and the avant-garde. Moreover, the divisions between cultural forms are constantly breached. Modern art raids the world of mass culture, scooping up newspaper headlines, advertising images, popular design, fragments from the lyrics of popular songs. In turn, everyday experience is shaped by the trickle-down of the avant-garde, which eventually dissolves into popular styles and taken-for-granted ideas. What distinguishes recent cultural theories of modernity from more established art criticism is a refusal to isolate or romanticize the experimental gesture. Modernism and the avant-garde are one important building block in the edifice of modern culture, not the window into its very soul.

For example, in my own book on the modern, I read the work of Rachilde, the so-called queen of decadence, in relation to questions of gender and the avant-garde, exploring her interest in perversion, performance, transvestism, female sadism, and similar themes. While the recent popularity of such ideas makes it tempting to reclaim Rachilde as a sexual revolutionary, a queer theorist *avant la lettre*, placing her work in the historical context of fin-de-siècle France makes her a less radical, though perhaps a more interesting, figure. Similarly, Paul Gilroy intertwines discussions of Hegel and Ice T, Du Bois and Michael Jackson in his reading of the cultures of the Black Atlantic. Refusing to nominate either high or popular culture as the primary arena of black modernity, Gilroy provides a careful account of a diverse range of artistic and intellectual projects.

Everyone agrees that the consumer is a key symbol of modernity, but there is much less consensus as to what this entails. The idea of "consuming" holds together in tightly compressed form a wide range of meanings and metaphorical associations. These include the economic transaction of buying goods or services; the reception of popular, though not usually elite, texts; and physiological processes of swallowing, devouring, and ingestion. Conventionally, consumerism has often been seen as a sign of human enslavement, or at least stupefaction, and closely linked to the feminine and the irrational. The works I am discussing take a different view. Consumption does not simply march in step with the interests of production or serve as a shorthand for human alienation and spiritual impoverishment. Rather, it involves agency, imagination, and even work. Consumption is the site at which the intricate connections between large-scale social systems and the experiences, desires, and struggles of ordinary individuals are forged.

In his discussion of black popular music, for example, Gilroy argues for an "enhanced understanding of 'consumption' that can illuminate its inner workings," as shaped by "the relationships between rootedness and displacement, locality and dissemination."[16] In implicit dialogue with Adorno's well-known polemic against popular music, Gilroy sees the fractures, juxtapositions, and recombinations of hip-hop as a key to its hybrid aesthetic and racial politics. Instead of endorsing the usual thesis of subcultural resistance followed by massmarket appropriation, Gilroy offers the reader an ironic reversal of this narrative. Thus he argues that "the basic units of commercial consumption in which music is fast frozen and sold have been systematically subverted by the practice of a racial politics that has colonised them."[17] For Bech too, commercially mediated experience is not simply evidence of the alienation of daily life. Superficiality, fetishism, and fragmentation, terms often used to diagnose the malaise of consumer culture, are for Bech more positive phenomena that can offer a temporary liberation from the burden of interiority and the persistent injunction to "be oneself." He writes, "It can be quite fatiguing to be yourself all the time. Superficiality makes possible new forms of pleasure, a new aesthetic creativity and new forms of experience."[18]

In spite of this rather upbeat account of the pleasures of surface and style, cultural theories of modernity do not simply celebrate consumption. Appadurai warns that consumption may be the site of agency, but that agency is not synonymous with freedom. While exploring the active ways people throughout the world appropriate media forms and inflect them with humor, irony, or anger, he also looks at how the temporal rhythms of consumer capitalism shape the intimate recesses of human subjectivity. Particularly suggestive is Appadurai's discussion of "imagined nostalgia" as an increasing powerful structure of feeling, teaching "consumers to miss things they have never lost."[19] This nostalgic mode expresses a response to the speed of change and the acceleration of the fashion cycle; increasingly, we inhabit a mass-mediated culture driven by the aesthetics of ephemerality. Yet Appadurai also points out that consumption is intimately linked to repetition, anchored in the social inertia of bodily practices and the habitual rhythms of daily life. The experience of time in modernity includes both "small cycles, anchored in the techniques of the body, which constitute the core of all durable consumption practices, and . . . the more open-ended historical sequences in which they are embedded."[20] The varying temporalities of the modern and the persistence of repetition in daily life inspire my next thesis.

## THE MODERN IS NOT SYNONYMOUS WITH THE NEW

This sounds like a deeply paradoxical idea because the modern and the new are often seen as synonymous and interchangeable. As Craig Calhoun observes, "modernity is the self-conception of an era idealizing change and especially progress."[21] To be modern is to reject the dead weight of tradition, to respond to the siren call of the new and the now. It is to see oneself as a creature of contingency and flux, no longer beholden to the scripts of the past. Of course, this vision of the present as transitory, fugitive and contingent has often inspired anxious or angry responses from those mistrustful of a capitalist juggernaut that destroys everything in its path and causes all that is solid to melt into air. Nevertheless, the injunction "il faut être de son temps" remains compelling; to be contemporary is both a desire and a duty when the old is synonymous with the obsolete and the outmoded. The new becomes a value in itself, indeed *the* ultimate value in the modern era.

Clearly, this description sums up an essential moment of the ethos and experience of modernity. Nevertheless, it is misleading to think of the modern only as constant change and thus synonymous with a single experience of time. The

NEW CULTURAL THEORIES OF MODERNITY

rhythms of modernity are much more varied: they include repetition as well as innovation, stability as well as flux. There are important strands of continuity within individual lives as well as in the historical processes by which cultures reproduce themselves over time. Scholars of modernity have sometimes been infatuated with the glamour and excitement of constant change (I am thinking here of such works as Marshall Berman's influential *All That Is Solid Melts into Air*). As a result, they have not paid much attention to the myriad facets of modern life that do not conform to this exhilarating vision of authentic newness. There is a great deal of writing on modernity and the city, but much less on modernity and the suburb, much on the avant-garde, but much less on twentieth-century realism and melodrama, much on nihilism and the absurd, but much less on modern forms of religion and spirituality.

There are two levels at which we can think about continuity: the macro-level of culture as a whole and the micro-level of everyday life. Clearly, all societies contain institutions, behaviors, and beliefs that are handed on from one generation to the next: no culture can create itself anew at each moment. In this sense, modernity always contains elements of tradition, defined as the reproduction of values and practices over several generations. When scholars refer to modernity as a "post-traditional" culture, they are appealing to an imaginary ideal rather than an actual reality. Yet elements of tradition are not simply isolated remnants left over from the past, archaic traces frozen in time. Rather, they acquire new meanings in new temporal frames; the seemingly moribund comes back to life, is recharged and reenergized in often unexpected ways and speaks afresh to the concerns of the present. In this sense, as Kwame Gyeke points out, we can speak of the modernity of tradition as well as the tradition of modernity.[22] Scholars of Western modernity, with occasional exceptions such as Walter Benjamin, have paid little attention to this intriguing question. It is in the recent scholarship on Africa, Japan, and other non-Western societies that we can find the most sophisticated explorations of the hybrid temporality of the modern.

Affiliation to the past has also been important to many ethnic and racial minorities as a source of comfort and inspiration in harsh times. Reflecting on the middle passage and the history of slavery, Paul Gilroy speaks to the value of tradition while disagreeing with those who view tradition as a form of primordial authenticity and as modernity's polar opposite. He pushes toward a more complex view of tradition, as "both actively reimagined in the present and transmitted intermittently in eloquent pulses from the past."[23] In other words, traditions are not just static scraps of past time, nor are they simply narcissistic inventions of the present. Even as they bear witness to the otherness of the past, traditions are always dynamic, unstable, and impure.

The stubborn survival of long-established beliefs, symbols, and practices does not affect only ethnic minorities or the non-Western world. For example, Robert Nye argues that the apparently anachronistic idea of honor helps us make sense of modern forms of Western masculinity. Ideals of male honor were originally forged in feudal societies as a way of governing forms of aristocratic combat. This context and indeed the very concept of honor itself seem far removed from contemporary values and ways of life. Yet many of the protocols of the honor code continue to govern everyday forms of sociability and solidarity between men in the professions, sports, and politics. Ideas such as competitiveness, *politesse*, and fair play were carried over from the medieval period into the bourgeois era to become an integral part of the performance of modern masculinity. Here, as in many other examples one might choose, Western modernity is shown to contain multiple traces and residues of the past, to consist of a complex, nonsynchronous blend of the old and the new.[24]

There is another level at which continuity remains central to the experience of modernity. Everyday life, by definition, is the realm of repetition, of what happens day after day. It consists of more or less regular cycles that impose a certain order on our lives. Daily life, furthermore, is the sphere of the mundane and taken-for-granted; it is governed by sedimented patterns of behavior that are often not subject to conscious thought but carried out in a habitual, semiautomatic manner. As I argue in chapter 3, the everyday has often been problematic for scholars of modernity precisely because of its familiarity, its associations with repetition, habit, and the home. How can the world ever become authentically modern when inertia and convention continue to define so much of everyday life? Yet the everyday is also a reminder of the persistent rhythms of human embodiment and the recurring need to carve out patterns of stability and continuity within the maelstrom of change.

Thus the idea of modernity as acceleration and constant change misses much that is important. This is not to deny that individuals in modern societies have faced dramatic experiences of technological, social, and cultural change far beyond anything their ancestors could have imagined. It is, however, to look with skepticism at the polarity of tradition and modernity, defined as a contrast between societies seen as rural, agrarian, prescientific, resistant to change, and bound by a perception of the past and those societies seen as scientific, innovative, future-oriented, culturally dynamic, industrial, and urbanized.[25] This opposition has had pernicious effects on the West's view of non-Western cultures. It also has a powerful impact on the gender dynamics of the modern; woman has been persistently figured as the source of nostalgia and assigned to the role of modernity's other.[26] By contrast, recent scholarship is beginning to explore the uneven times of modernity and the traces of the noncontemporary that

**NEW CULTURAL THEORIES OF MODERNITY**

inhabit the contemporary. So, too, the idea of tradition becomes less clear-cut. As I noted in my introduction, no human society, however stable or apparently static, exists outside history and linear time.

## MODERNITY IS NOT A SELF-EVIDENT IDEA

My final axiom follows logically from what has gone before, but its implications need to be fleshed out. Until recently, many scholars have talked about modernity as if it were a natural kind, an unambiguous object existing in the world. Conventionally, as I've just noted, the modern was defined in opposition to a schematic idea of tradition. In recent times, it is also contrasted with another distinct period known as postmodernity. In a recent debate about the relationship between feminism and postmodernism, Judith Butler questions the terms of this debate and criticizes the recourse to the modern/postmodern distinction as a Hegelian hangover.[27]

I agree with Butler's criticism of the overly casual ways these terms are often employed. In several of the following chapters, I analyze some common ways of distinguishing between the modern and postmodern with a degree of skepticism. Yet Butler's own writings on gender, language, and power bypass historical questions altogether and never explain how the performance of gender and the recognition of gender's performative aspects are affected by broader temporal shifts. In this regard, modernity strikes me as an indispensable concept, yet one that requires a high level of self-consciousness. For example, a survey across disciplines reveals that temporal divisions are at least partly shaped by the internal logic of particular fields. The distinctive qualities attributed to the modern, as well as its actual dates, vary significantly within philosophy, sociology, and literary criticism.[28]

This issue of periodization becomes even more complicated when marginal groups are factored into the writing of history. While many European accounts of the modern and postmodern are disguised polemics for or against a Marxist theory of history, Gilroy argues that conceptions of modernity among American black intellectuals started from quite different premises. "They were founded on the catastrophic rupture of the middle passage rather than the dream of revolutionary transformation."[29] Furthermore, much of the supposed novelty of the postmodern evaporates in the light of certain uncanny repetitions of racial ideology. Reflecting on this point, Gilroy writes, "defenders and critics of modernity seem to be equally unconcerned that the history and expressive culture of the African diaspora, the practice of racial slavery, or the narratives of European imperial conquest may require all simple periodisations of the modern and postmodern to be drastically rethought."[30] Janet Lyon also questions a smoothly sequential concept of history, suggesting that time must be understood as nonsynchronous and multidirectional. She points to the echoes and continuities across historical time, the moments "when 'history' repeats itself, and also, conversely, when seemingly cogent historical moments break into nonsynchronous shards."[31]

Not only the temporal but also the spatial coordinates of the modern are being subject to scrutiny. For example, feminist scholars are questioning the automatic association of modernity with a male-defined public world. Indeed, the interior and domestic spheres associated with women and the feminine have played a central role in the fashioning of distinctively modern subjects. Griselda Pollock, for example, offers a thoughtful reading of the topography of modernity, tracing the different ways nineteenth-century men and women experienced mobility and negotiated public space.[32] At another level, scholars of race are dismantling the concept of the nation-state as the natural boundary of modern societies. Thus Gilroy's coining of the term "Black Atlantic" allows him to explore the various cross-cultural connections within the African diaspora rather than confining the culture of race within national borders. Similarly, Appadurai presents a sustained critique of the "common-sense" of nationalism, arguing that late modernity can be understood only as a global phenomenon formed out of a network of postnational diasporas.[33]

Finally, there is much less agreement about the causes of modernity than there used to be. Is it primarily a product of capitalism? Technology and industrialization? Secularization and new forms of subjectivity? Slavery and imperialism? The division of public and private spheres? All of the above? Scholars are ever more hesitant to explain modernity through recourse to a single unifying theory. Thus a sociologist who takes seriously the new scholarship on culture and difference concludes by admitting that "we cannot solve all puzzles at once with a 'critical theory of modernity.'"[34] The scholars of modern culture whose work I have been discussing endorse this view. Their focus is partial. They aim to capture certain facets of the modern, to record experiences, practices, and repertoires of imagery and thought that have often been left out of the picture. But they do not claim to explain the modern once and for all. It has become clear that there is not one modernity, but many. As one scholar of Japanese culture tartly notes, what has defined itself as universal may in certain respects be deeply parochial.[35]

To some readers, such a conclusion may seem excessively "postmodern," to echo a general sense of relativism and impotence within intellectual life. Admittedly, it does not square with the belief that, given sufficient thought and effort, the logic of modernity can be fully grasped once and for all. Writing about the experiences of the disenfranchised, the new cultural theorists of modernity are acutely aware that there is no universal subject of history. The modern histories

NEW CULTURAL THEORIES OF MODERNITY

experienced by particular groups cannot be smoothly woven into a single story or neatly summarized in a single checklist of features (that my own theses are couched as negative rather than positive statements is symptomatic of this view).

But partiality and plurality are not the same as unbreachable difference, radical fragmentation, or an ethic of "anything goes." The scholars whose work I've been discussing do not share the view of some "postmodern" historians that we should satisfy ourselves with interpreting and rearranging random scraps and heterogeneous fragments of the past. They do not believe that it is no longer permissible to reflect on systemic patterns or to think about the larger meaning of historical processes.[36]

Rather, by invoking the concept of modernity, they signal their interest in thinking about the "big picture," making sense of larger historical patterns without endorsing the idea of a single unified system. Viewing the modern through the lens of race, gender, and sexuality brings to light certain regularities of exclusion and disenfranchisement. It is vital to track these regularities, to document their historical force and their continuing power. The history of modernity is not an innocent or neutral history. But we must not lose sight of the dense textures of individual texts and specific experiences, which often bear witness to the struggles of subordinate groups within and against modern times. To speak only of the eternal sameness of the modern is to render such struggles invisible.

## NOTES

Peter Fritzsche's invitation to discuss "theories of modernity for historians" with the history department at the University of Illinois, Urbana-Champaign, inspired the first draft of this chapter. I am very grateful to him and Sonya Michel and to all those who attended the seminar for their collegiality and intellectual engagement. Thanks also to Krishan Kumar for reading a draft of the chapter.

1. Arjun Appadurai, *Modernity at Large* (Minneapolis: University of Minnesota Press, 1997), 33.

2. Even here, however, there are no absolutely new beginnings. Long before most other feminist critics, Elizabeth Wilson was writing about women as exemplary modern subjects. See *Adorned in Dreams: Fashion and Modernity* (Berkeley: University of California Press, 1985) and *The Sphinx in the City: Urban Life, the Control of Disorder and Women* (London: Virago, 1991). On the absence of women from conventional theories of modernity, see Janet Wolff, *Feminine Sentences: Essays on Women and Culture* (Berkeley: University of California Press, 1990).

3. Linda Nicholson, *The Play of Reason: From the Modern to the Postmodern* (Ithaca: Cornell University Press, 1999).

4. Janet Lyon, *Manifestoes: Provocations of the Modern* (Ithaca: Cornell University Press, 1999), 203.
5. Paul Gilroy, *The Black Atlantic: Modernity and Double Consciousness* (Cambridge: Harvard University Press, 1993), 46.
6. Gilroy, *The Black Atlantic*, 49.
7. Lyon, *Manifestoes*, 5.
8. Anthony Giddens, *Modernity and Self-Identity: Self and Society in the Late Modern Age* (Stanford: Stanford University Press, 1991).
9. Appadurai, *Modernity at Large*, 48.
10. Wendy Parkins, "Taking Liberty's: Suffragettes and the Public Sphere, 1905–1914" (Ph. D. diss., Murdoch University, Australia, 1996).
11. Henning Bech, *When Men Meet: Homosexuality and Modernity* (Chicago: University of Chicago Press, 1998), 118.
12. Appadurai, *Modernity at Large*, 4.
13. Appadurai, *Modernity at Large*, 9.
14. Appadurai, *Modernity at Large*, 63.
15. Bech, *When Men Meet*, 6.
16. Gilroy, *The Black Atlantic*, 105.
17. Gilroy, *The Black Atlantic*, 105.
18. Bech, *When Men Meet*, 213.
19. Appadurai, *Modernity at Large*, 77.
20. Appadurai, *Modernity at Large*, 74.
21. Craig Calhoun, *Critical Social Theory: Culture, History and the Challenge of Difference* (Oxford: Basil Blackwell, 1995), 291.
22. Kwame Gyeke, *Tradition and Modernity: Reflections on the African Experience* (New York: Oxford University Press, 1997), 271.
23. Gilroy, *The Black Atlantic*, 74.
24. Robert Nye, *Masculinity and Male Codes of Honor in Modern France* (Oxford: Oxford University Press, 1993).
25. Gyeke, *Tradition and Modernity*, 217.
26. For an extensive discussion of this theme, see Rita Felski, "On Nostalgia," in *The Gender of Modernity* (Cambridge: Harvard University Press, 1995).
27. Judith Butler, "Contingent Foundations: Feminism and the Question of 'Postmodernism,'" in Seyla Benhabib, Judith Butler, Drucilla Cornell, and Nancy Fraser, *Feminist Contentions: A Philosophical Exchange* (New York: Routledge, 1995).
28. See Felski, *The Gender of Modernity*, 30–36.
29. Gilroy, *The Black Atlantic*, 197. See also Jan Clammer, *Difference and Modernity: Social Theory and Contemporary Japanese Society* (London: Kegan Paul International, 1995), where Clammer argues that the modern/postmodern distinction simply does not make sense in the Japanese context.
30. Gilroy, *The Black Atlantic*, 42.
31. Lyon, *Manifestoes*, 204.

32. Griselda Pollock, "Modernity and the Spaces of the City," in *Vision and Difference: Femininity, Feminism, and Histories of Art* (London: Routledge, 1988).

33. While Appadurai is right to point to the existence of a diverse range of cultural formations outside the nation-state, from local ethnicities to multinational corporations to diasporic structures, his conclusion that the nation-state is obsolete as a historical actor strikes me as premature.

34. Calhoun, *Critical Social Theory*, 290.

35. Clammer, *Difference and Modernity*, 4.

36. See F. R. Ankersmit, "Historiography and Postmodernism," in *The Postmodern History Reader*, ed. Keith Jenkins (London: Routledge, 1997).

# THE INVENTION OF
# EVERYDAY LIFE

*Good chapter*

**E**veryday life is the most self-evident, yet the most puzzling of ideas. It is a key concept in cultural studies and feminism and an important reference point in other scholarly fields, part of a growing interest in micro-analysis and history from below. Yet those who use the term are often reluctant to explain exactly what it means. While doing the research for this chapter, I was struck by how many recent books mention everyday life in the title and how few list everyday life in the index. This reticence is surely intentional; recourse to the everyday often springs from a sense of impatience with academic theories and hairsplitting distinctions. After all, everyday life simply is, indisputably: the essential, taken-for-granted continuum of mundane activities that frames our forays into more esoteric or exotic worlds. It is the ultimate nonnegotiable reality, the unavoidable basis for all other forms of human endeavor. The everyday, writes Guy Debord, "is the measure of all things."[1]

The powerful resonances of such appeals to everyday life are closely connected to its fuzzy, ambiguous meanings. What exactly does it refer to? The entire social world? Particular behaviors and practices? A specific attitude or relationship to one's environment? At first glance, everyday life seems to be everywhere, yet nowhere. Because it has no clear boundaries, it is difficult to identify. Everyday life is synonymous with the habitual, the ordinary, the mundane, yet it is also strangely elusive, that which resists our understanding and escapes our grasp. Like the blurred speck at the edge of one's vision that disappears when looked at directly, the everyday ceases to be everyday when it is subject to critical scrutiny. "The everyday escapes," writes Blanchot, "it belongs to insignificance."[2]

Yet everyday life is also a concept with a long history. Beyond the often cited work of Michel de Certeau, there is an extensive tradition of writing on the everyday. This includes not just the work of Henri Lefebvre, but also of philosophers and sociologists such as Lukács, Heidegger, Heller, Schutz, Goffman, and Habermas among others. The fact that much of this writing has not been taken up in feminism and cultural studies may be partly due to its often abstract philosophical character. Given the current interest in the concrete and the particular, and the enormous variations in human lives across cultural contexts, in what sense is it meaningful to talk about everyday life in general?[3]

As a result of this focus on the particular, however, everyday life is rarely taken under the microscope and scrutinized as a concept. Like any analytical term, it organizes the world according to certain assumptions and criteria. For example, everyday life bears a complicated relationship to the distinction between private and public; it includes domestic activities but also routine forms of work, travel, and leisure. Furthermore, everyday life is not simply interchangeable with the popular: it is not the exclusive property of a particular social class or grouping. Bismarck had an everyday life and so does Madonna. What, then, does the term signify? What are its parameters? To what is it opposed?

Lefebvre argues that everyday life is a distinctively modern phenomenon that only emerged in the nineteenth century. The claim seems counterintuitive, going against the presumed universality of the everyday. There is in fact a long history of writing on daily life extending from ancient Greece to medieval Christianity to the Enlightenment.[4] But it is true that everyday life becomes increasingly important in the nineteenth century as an object of critical reflection and representation in literature and art. What is the cause of this new visibility? Lefebvre points to the impact of capitalism and industrialization on human existence and perception. As bodies are massed together in big cities under modern conditions, so the uniform and repetitive aspects of human lives become more prominent. Similarly, Alvin Gouldner suggests that the rapidly changing fabric of ordinary lives creates a new awareness of the mundane. That which was previously taken for granted becomes visible, in both its new and its traditional, disappearing forms.

Everyday life is also a secular and democratic concept. Secular because it conveys the sense of a world leached of transcendence; the everyday is everyday because it is no longer connected to the miraculous, the magical, or the sacred. (Hence, a recent New Age best-seller is entitled *The Re-Enchantment of Everyday Life*.)[5] Democratic because it recognizes the paramount shared reality of a mundane, material embeddedness in the world. Everyone, from the most famous to the most humble, eats, sleeps, yawns, defecates; no one escapes the reach of the quotidian. Everyday life, in other words, does not only describe the lives of ordinary people, but recognizes that every life contains an element of the ordinary. We are all ultimately anchored in the mundane.

At the same time, some groups, such as women and the working class, are more closely identified with the everyday than others. Everyday life is not just a material by-product of capitalism, as Lefebvre argues, but also a term that is deployed by intellectuals to describe a nonintellectual relationship to the world. For Lukács and Heidegger, for example, the everyday is synonymous with an inauthentic, gray, aesthetically impoverished existence. Lefebvre views it with more ambivalence; everyday life is a sign of current social degradation under capitalism, but it is also connected to bodily and affective rhythms and hence retains a utopian impulse. More recently, for some scholars in cultural studies, history, and related fields, everyday life has emerged as an alternative to theory and an arena of authentic experience. Faced with a legitimation crisis about the value and purpose of humanities scholarship, intellectuals have often found an alibi in the turn to the ordinary. Everyday life, in other words, is rarely viewed with neutrality. The concept is marked by a rich history of hostility, envy, and desire, expressing both nostalgia for the concrete and disdain for a life lacking in critical self-reflection.

Yet as a term, everyday life remains strangely amorphous. As Lefebvre notes, it is often defined negatively, as the residue left over after various specialized activities are abstracted. One of these activities is philosophy. Conventionally, scholars have opposed everyday life to critical reflection and speculation. It is synonymous with the "natural attitude" rather than the "theoretical attitude," with the realm of common sense and taken-for-grantedness rather than hardheaded skepticism.[6] A second influential distinction is between the everyday and the aesthetic. This distinction is addressed in Alice Walker's well-known story "Everyday Use," which turns on the differing attitudes of two daughters to some old family quilts. For one daughter they are simply useful objects in her daily life, while for her college-educated sister they have become examples of authentic folk art, to be hung on the wall and admired.[7] To contemplate something as art is to remove it, at least temporarily, from the pragmatic needs and demands of the quotidian. Finally, everyday life is typically distinguished from the exceptional moment: the battle, the catastrophe, the extraordinary deed. The distinctiveness of the everyday lies in its lack of distinction and differentiation; it is the air one breathes, the taken-for-granted backdrop, the common-sensical basis of all human activities. "The heroic life," writes Mike Featherstone, "is the sphere of danger, violence and the courting of risk whereas everyday life is the sphere of women, reproduction and care."[8]

As Featherstone's statement makes clear, gender has been an important factor in conceptions of everyday life. Lefebvre, like some other theorists, regards women as the quintessential representatives and victims of the quotidian. "Everyday life weighs heaviest on women," he writes. "Some are bogged down by its peculiar cloying substance, while others escape into make-believe. . . . They are the subject of everyday life and its victims."[9] Women, like everyday life, have often been defined by negation. Their realm has not been that of war, art, philosophy, scientific endeavor, high office. What else is left to a woman but everyday life, the realm of the insignificant, invisible yet indispensable?

Such a negative view of the quotidian is, however, open to criticism. Both feminism and cultural studies have questioned the view that the everyday exists only as something to be transcended, as the realm of monotony, emptiness, and dull compulsion. Furthermore, such a division between the everyday and the non-everyday slides imperceptibly into a ranking of persons: those exemplary individuals able to escape the quotidian through philosophy, high art, or heroism versus the rest of humanity. Recent scholarship has argued, by contrast, that critical thinking is not simply the province of philosophers, that aesthetic experience need not be severed from everyday life, and that there are other forms of heroism besides war or Oedipal conflict.

Is it possible to think about the everyday in ways that do not simply treat it as negative or residual? A driving impulse behind some cultural studies scholarship has been the desire to invert this perception and to invest the everyday with supreme value and significance. In particular, de Certeau's *Practice of Everyday Life* has inspired numerous readings of daily life as synonymous with acts of resistance and subversion. Yet this new account of the everyday often loses sight of the mundane, taken-for-granted, routine qualities that seem so central to its definition—the very everydayness of the everyday. By contrast, the phenomenological and sociological writing on everyday life focuses explicitly on this very question. From a reading of the work of Lefebvre, Heller, and Schutz, I want to piece together an alternative definition of everyday life grounded in three key facets: time, space, and modality. The temporality of the everyday, I suggest, is that of repetition, the spatial ordering of the everyday is anchored in a sense of home, and the characteristic mode of experiencing the everyday is that of habit.

This vision of the everyday is interesting for several reasons. First, as I've suggested, it differs markedly from the way everyday life is conceptualized in contemporary cultural studies, where writers often rhapsodize about subversion, indeterminacy, nomadism, and the like. I would like to explore these differences and to bring the various traditions of scholarship on everyday life into a more explicit dialogue. Second, the association of the everyday with repetition, home, and habit often involves assumptions about gender and women's relationship to the modern world. These assumptions become most explicit in Lefebvre's sociological and Marxist-oriented account of everyday life. While I have found many of his insights useful, I want to question his view that the habitual, home-centered aspects of daily life are outside, and in some sense antithetical to, the experience of an authentic modernity.

## REPETITION

Everyday life is above all a temporal term. As such, it conveys the fact of repetition; it refers not to the singular or unique but to that which happens "day after day." The activities of sleeping, eating, and working conform to regular diurnal rhythms that are in turn embedded within larger cycles of repetition: the weekend, the annual holiday, the start of a new semester. For Lefebvre, this cyclical structure of everyday life is its quintessential feature, a source of both fascination and puzzlement. "In the study of the everyday," he writes, "we discover the great problem of repetition, one of the most difficult problems facing us."[10] Repetition is a problem, or as he says elsewhere, a riddle, because it is fundamentally at odds with the modern drive toward progress and accumulation.

Lefebvre returns repeatedly to this apparent contradiction between linear and cyclical time. Linear time is the forward-moving, abstract time of modern industrial society; everyday life, on the other hand, is characterized by natural circadian rhythms, which, according to Lefebvre, have changed little over the centuries.[11] These daily rhythms complicate the self-understanding of modernity as permanent progress. If everyday life is not completely outside history, it nevertheless serves as a retardation device, slowing down the dynamic of historical change. Lefebvre resorts at several points to the concept of uneven development as a way of explaining this lack of synchronicity. Because of its reliance on cyclical time, everyday life is *belated*; it lags behind the historical possibilities of modernity.

Time, writes Johannes Fabian, "is a carrier of significance, a form through which we define the content of relations between the Self and the Other."[12] In other words, time is not just a measurement but a metaphor, dense in cultural meanings. Conventionally, the distinction between "time's arrow" and "time's cycle" is also a distinction between masculine and feminine. Indeed, all models of historical transformation—whether linear or cataclysmic, evolutionary or revolutionary—have been conventionally coded as masculine. Conversely, woman's affinity with repetition and cyclical time is noted by numerous writers; Simone de Beauvoir, for example, claims that "woman clings to routine; time has for her no element of novelty, it is not a creative flow; because she is doomed to repetition, she sees in the future only a duplication of the past."[13] Here, repetition is a sign of woman's enslavement in the ordinary, her association with immanence rather than transcendence. Unable to create or invent, she remains imprisoned within the remorseless routine of cyclical time. Lefebvre's perspective is less censorious: women's association with recurrence is also a sign of their connection to nature, emotion, and sensuality, their lesser degree of estrangement from biological and cosmic rhythms. As I have already noted, Julia Kristeva concurs with this view in seeing repetition as the key to women's experience of extrasubjective time, cosmic time, jouissance.[14]

Why are women so persistently linked to repetition? Several possibilities come to mind. First, women are almost always seen as embodied subjects, their biological nature never far from view. Biorhythmic cycles affect various aspects of male and female behavior, yet menstruation and pregnancy become the preeminent, indeed the only, examples of human subordination to natural time and a certain feminine resistance to the project of civilization. Second, women are primarily responsible for the repetitive tasks of social reproduction: cleaning, preparing meals, caring for children. While much paid work is equally repetitive, only the domestic sphere is deemed to exist outside the dynamic of history and change. For example, in his well-known discussion of industrial time, E. P. Thompson suggests that women's everyday lives conform to a premodern temporal pattern. "The rhythms of women's work in the home are not wholly attuned to the measurement of the clock. The mother of young children has an imperfect sense of time and attends to other human tides. She has not yet altogether moved out of the conventions of 'pre-industrial' society."[15]

Finally, women are identified with repetition via consumption. For Marxist scholars of the everyday, commodification is its paramount feature, evident in ever greater standardization and sameness. As the primary symbols and victims of consumer culture, women take on the repetitive features of the objects that they buy. Femininity is formed through mass production and mass reproduction, disseminated through endless images of female glamour and female domesticity. Women become the primary emblem of an inauthentic everyday life marked by the empty homogeneous time of mass consumption.

The different aspects of women's association with repetitive time are captured in a suggestive passage that is quoted by Lefebvre from a novel by the popular American writer Irwin Shaw. As the hero of Shaw's novel walks down Fifth Avenue looking at women shopping, he idly imagines a museum exhibit devoted to the theme of modern femininity. Like the tableaux at the Museum of Natural History, with their stuffed bears opening honeycombs against a background of caves, this diorama would display modern American women in their natural habitat and engaged in their most typical activities. What would such an exhibition consist of? It would display to the curious viewer "a set of stuffed women, slender, high-heeled, rouged, waved, hot-eyed, buying a cocktail dress in a department store." While these women engaged in democratic acts of mass consumption, "in the background, behind the salesgirls and the racks and shelves, there would be bombs bursting, cities crumbling, scientists measuring the half-life of tritium and cobalt."[16]

This image eloquently crystallizes the gendering of time. In the background, dwarfing the indifferent shoppers, is the technological sublime of science and war. This is cataclysmic time: the catastrophe of nuclear explosion, mass destruction, monumental history. But the female customers remain caught within the repetitive time of everyday life; passionate yet compliant consumers, they continue to buy dresses, oblivious to the possibility of catastrophe. They are governed by a law of repetition that is both social and natural. Creatures of artifice, they embrace the capitalist imperative to "shop till you drop." Yet they also embody the inexorable rhythms of nature. Like the stuffed animals at the museum, their behavior is framed as the inevitable result of natural instinct combined with appropriate environment. Indistinguishable members of the species woman, they are caught within a repetitive cycle of natural desire.

Such visions of the horror of repetition, we need to recognize, are distinctively modern. For most of human history, activities have gained value precisely because they repeat what has gone before. Repetition, understood as ritual, provides a connection to ancestry and tradition; it situates the individual in an imagined community that spans historical time. It is thus not opposed to transcendence, but the means of transcending one's historically limited existence. In the modern era, by contrast, to repeat without questioning or transforming is often regarded as laziness, conservatism, or bad faith. This disdain for repetition fuels existentialism's critique of the unthinking routines of everyday life, its insistence on the importance of creating oneself anew at each moment. It is behind the shock of the new in modern art that is intended to liberate us from our habitual, entrenched perceptions. And it is evident in Freud's view of repetition as a form of pathology, linked to the dark, antisocial urge of the death drive. Repetition is seen as a threat to the modern project of self-determination, subordinating individual will to the demands of an imposed pattern.

Yet the attempt to escape repetition is a Sisyphean project, for, as Lefebvre rightly insists, it pervades the everyday. He further argues that daily life is "situated at the intersection of two modes of repetition: the cyclical, which dominates in nature, and the linear, which dominates in processes known as 'rational.'"[17] Here as elsewhere, Lefebvre conceives of repetition as taking one of two forms: natural bodily rhythms or the regimented cycles of industrial capitalism. Yet many everyday routines cannot be easily fitted into either of these categories. They are neither unmediated expressions of biological drives nor mere reflexes of capitalist domination but a much more complex blend of the social and the psychic. Continuity and routine are crucial to early child development and remain important in adult life. Repetition is one of the ways we organize the world, make sense of our environment, and stave off the threat of chaos. It is a key factor in the gradual formation of identity as a social and intersubjective process. Quite simply, we become who we are through acts of repetition. While recent cultural criticism has stressed the innovative dimensions of the everyday, it has paid much less attention to the need for routine in the organization of daily life.[18]

Furthermore, there is a tendency, clearly visible in the work of Lefebvre, to equate repetition with domination and innovation with agency and resistance. Yet this is to remain trapped within a mind-set that assumes the superior value of the new. In our own era, however, the reverse is just as likely to be true. In the maelstrom of contemporary life, change is often imposed on individuals against their will; conversely, everyday rituals may help to safeguard a sense of personal autonomy and dignity, or to preserve the distinctive qualities of a threatened way of life. In other words, repetition is not simply a sign of human subordination to external forces but also one of the ways individuals engage with and respond to their environment. Repetition can signal resistance as well as enslavement.

Finally, Lefebvre's often illuminating discussion of the quotidian is weakened by his persistent opposition of cyclical and linear time, the everyday and the modern, the feminine and the masculine. Yet the passing of time surely cannot be grasped in such rigidly dualistic terms. Thus acts of innovation and creativity are not opposed to, but rather made possible by, the mundane cycles of the quotidian. Conversely, even the most repetitive of lives bears witness to the irreversible direction of time: the experience of aging, the regret of past actions or inactions, the premonition of death. The temporality of everyday life is internally complex; it combines repetition and linearity, recurrence with forward movement. The everyday cannot be opposed to the realm of history, but is rather the very means by which history is actualized and made real.[19] Thus repetition is not an anachronism in a world of constant flux, but an essential element of the experience of modernity. Rather than being the sign of a uniquely feminine relationship to time, it permeates the lives of men as well as women.

## HOME

While everyday life expresses a specific sense of time, it does not convey a particular sense of space. In fact, everyday life is usually distinguished by an absence of boundaries, and thus a lack of clear spatial differentiation. It includes a variety of spaces (the workplace, the home, the mall) as well as diverse forms of movement through space (walking, driving, flying). Moreover, our everyday experience of space is now powerfully affected by technology; thanks to television, telephones, and computers we can have virtual knowledge of places and cultures quite remote from our own.

In spite of these varied locations, several philosophers of everyday life focus on the home as its privileged symbol. Agnes Heller writes, "Integral to the average everyday life is awareness of a fixed point in space, a firm position from which we 'proceed' (whether every day or over larger periods of time) and to which we return in due course. This firm position is what we call 'home.'"[20] Like everyday life itself, home constitutes a base, a taken-for-granted grounding, which allows us to make forays into other worlds. It is central to the anthropomorphic organization of space in everyday life; we experience space not according to the distanced gaze of the cartographer, but in circles of increasing proximity or distance from the experiencing self. Home lies at the center of these circles. According to Heller, familiarity is an everyday need, and familiarity combines with the promise of protection and warmth to create the positive everyday associations of home.

Home is also important to Lefebvre's discussion of everyday life, but his attitude is more ambivalent. Home becomes an occasion for meditating on his own discomfort with the everyday lives of others. Describing a suburban development on the outskirts of Paris, he is unable to suppress his own sense of irritation. "The owners' superficiality oozes forth in an abundance of ridiculous details, china animals on the roofs, glass globes and well-pruned shrubs along the miniature paths, plaques adorned with mottos, self-important pediments."[21] Home is a symbol of complacency, pretentiousness, and petitbourgeois bad taste. Yet Lefebvre is also critical of his own reaction. He admits that going into one of these suburban houses would probably seem like entering heaven to the migrant workers at Renault. "Why should I say anything against these people who—like me—come home from work every day? They seem to be decent folk who live with their families, who love their children. Can we blame them for not wanting the world in which they live reasonably at home to be transformed?"[22]

This is surely a key citation in understanding the spatial dimensions of theories of everyday life. Home is not just a geographical designation, but a resonant metaphysical symbol. Lefebvre perceives the petitbourgeois individual to be reasonably at home in the world. Being at home in the world is an implicit affront to the existential homelessness and anguish of the modern intellectual. Adorno writes, "Dwelling, in the proper sense, is now impossible. . . . It is part of morality not to be at home in one's home."[23] The vocabulary of modernity is a vocabulary of anti-home. It celebrates mobility, movement, exile, boundary crossing. It speaks enthusiastically about movement out into the world, but is silent about the return home. Its preferred location is the city street, the site of random encounters, unexpected events, multiplicity and difference. David Harvey, for example, sketches an image of the city as the "place of mystery, the site of the unexpected, full of agitations and ferments."[24] This chaotic ferment is in tune with the spirit of the critic, described as a restless analyst, constantly on the move. Home, by contrast, is the space of familiarity, dullness, stasis. The longing for home, the desire to attach oneself to a familiar space, is seen by most theorists of modernity as a regressive desire.

Home is, of course, a highly gendered space. Women have often been seen as the personification of home and even as its literal embodiment. Houses are often imagined as quasi-uterine spaces; conversely, the female body, notes Freud, is the "former home of all human beings."[25] As a result, feminists have often been eager to demystify the ideal of home as haven. One nineteenth-century female novelist, for example, imagined a utopian future in which the word "home" would no longer exist.[26] Modern feminism, from Betty Friedan onward, has repeatedly had recourse to a rhetoric of leaving home. Home is a prison, a trap, a straitjacket. In recent years, this critique of home has intensified: the discourse of contemporary feminism speaks enthusiastically of migrations, boundary crossings, nomadic subjects.

Much of the same language pervades cultural studies. De Certeau dedicates *The Practice of Everyday Life* to "a common hero, a ubiquitous character, walking in countless thousands on the streets." His image of the agile pedestrian, adeptly weaving a distinctive textual path across the grid of city streets, has become a resonant symbol of the contemporary subject. Freedom and agency are traditionally symbolized by movement through public space. Cultural studies, in stressing the resistive dimensions of daily life, has drawn heavily on such images of mobility, as in Lawrence Grossberg's references to nomadic subjects "wandering through the ever-changing places and spaces, vectors and apparatuses of everyday life."[27]

In response, Janet Wolff has suggested that such metaphors are masculine and hence problematic for feminism. She notes the persistent association of maleness with travel and femininity with stasis. But, as she also acknowledges, women have always traveled, and they now do so in vast numbers, as tourists, researchers, aid workers, guest workers, refugees. To describe metaphors of travel as inherently alienating to women seems too simple. Wolff also ignores the geopolitical dimensions of such metaphors. They derive at least partly from greater interest in examining the geographical, ethnic, and cultural differences among women, although, as I argue in chapter 5, images of nomadism in feminist theory are hardly free of problems.[28]

Still, it is true that such metaphors are partial, casting light on particular aspects of experience only to relegate other parts of daily life to the shadows. In spite of the hyperbole in postmodern theory about nomadism, hyperspace, and time-space compression, writes Doreen Massey, "much of life for many people, even in the heart of the first world, still consists of waiting in a bus-shelter with your shopping for a bus that never comes."[29] Similarly, Massey questions the assumption that postmodern global space has done away with the need for home and has left us placeless and disoriented. She notes the continuing importance of place and locality in everyday life, while questioning the belief that a desire for home is inauthentic or reactionary. This assumption, she argues, arises out of a recurring tendency to see space and time as ontological opposites rather than as interconnected dimensions of human experience. Time, typically, is equated with history, movement, and change, whereas space is seen as static, ahistorical, and conservative.[30]

The everyday significance of home clearly needs to be imagined differently. First, home is, in de Certeau's terms, an active practicing of place. Even if home is synonymous with familiarity and routine, that familiarity is actively produced over time, above all through the effort and labor of women. Furthermore, while home may sometimes seem static, both the reality and the ideology of home change dramatically over time. Second, the boundaries between home and non-home are leaky. The home is not a private enclave cut off from the outside world, but is powerfully shaped by broader social currents, attitudes, and desires. Think, for example, of the Martha Stewart phenomenon, where we see a distinctively new vision of the home as *Gesamtkunstwerk*, a highly stylized and labor-intensive blend of folkloric authenticity and postmodern chic.

Finally, home, like any other space, is shaped by conflicts and power struggles. It is often the site of intergenerational conflicts, such that an adolescent sense of identity can be predicated on a burning desire to leave home. Home can be a particularly fraught place for those whose sexual identities and practices do not conform to the expectations of their family of origin. It can be a place of female subordination as well as an arena where women can show competence in the exercise of domestic skills. Home is often a place for displaying commodities and hence saturated by class distinctions; a recent ethnography of working-class women notes their embarrassment at the perceived insufficiency of their home.[31]

Home also acquires particularly poignant meanings for migrants and their descendants. In *Zami*, for example, Audre Lorde shapes the meaning of a life story around changing definitions of home. As a child, Lorde absorbs her mother's nostalgic yearning for her Caribbean homeland, as a young adult she must leave her mother's house in order to help create a "house of difference" in the New York lesbian community, and finally she arrives at a vision of home informed by both her American lesbian identity and her Caribbean heritage.[32]

As this example suggests, the idea of home is complex and temporally fluid. Home should not be confused with a fantasy of origin; any individual life story will contain different and changing visions of home. Home need not be "where you're from"; it can also be "where you're at."[33] My definition is intentionally minimal; it includes any often-visited place that is the object of cathexis, that in its very familiarity becomes a symbolic extension and confirmation of the self. As Roger Silverstone argues, home is "an investment of meaning in space."[34] Such a familiar location fulfills both affective and pragmatic needs. It is a storage place, both literally and symbolically; home often contains many of the objects that have helped to shape a life history, and the meanings and memories with which these objects are encrypted. Home is, in Mary Douglas's phrase, a "memory machine."[35] In this regard, Heller's focus on home as central to the spatial organization of everyday life provides a useful corrective to the current infatuation with mobility and travel.

A number of feminist scholars are developing alternative visions of the symbolism and politics of home. bell hooks, for example, suggests that the history of home has very different meanings for African American women as well as men. "Historically, African American people believed that the construction of a homeplace, however fragile and tenuous (the slave hut, the wooden shack) had a radical political dimension. Despite the brutal reality of racial apartheid, of domination, one's homeplace was the one site where one could freely confront the issue of humanization, where one could resist."[36] The title of an early black feminist anthology, *Home Girls*, underscores this more positive, though by no means uncritical, vision of home as a potential source of warmth and strength.[37]

In a recent essay, Iris Marion Young also makes a thoughtful case for rethinking feminist attitudes to house and home. Questioning the nostalgic longing for home as a place of stable identities predicated on female self-sacrifice, she nevertheless wants to recognize the symbolic richness and cultural complexity of "home-making" (which is not just housework). Home, she argues, is a specific materialization of the body and the self; things and spaces become layered with meaning, value and memory. This materialization does not fix identity but anchors it in a physical space that creates certain continuities between past and present. "Dwelling in the world means we are located among objects, artifacts, rituals, and practices that configure who we are in our particularity."[38] Young explicitly tackles the oppressive aspects of home in a moving account of her own mother's failure to conform to the ideal of the 1950s housewife and its tragic consequences. Yet she also wants to insist that home can be a place of important human values, including safety, individuation, privacy, and preservation, that need to be reclaimed rather than disdained by feminism.

A masculinist cultural tradition, Meaghan Morris suggests, has perceived home as the site of both "frustrating containment (home as dull) and of truth to be rediscovered (home as real)."[39] In both cases, it has been seen as existing outside the flux and change of an authentically modern life. Yet home is not always linked to tradition and opposed to autonomy and self-definition: on the contrary, it has been central to many women's experience of modernity. A feminist theory of everyday life might question the assumption that being modern requires an irrevocable sundering from home, and simultaneously explicate the modern dimensions of everyday experiences of home.[40]

## HABIT

The temporality of everyday life and its spatial anchoring are closely connected. Both repetition and home speak to an essential feature of everyday life: its familiarity. The everyday is synonymous with habit, sameness, routine; it epitomizes both the comfort and boredom of the ordinary. Lefebvre writes, "The modern . . . stands for what is novel, brilliant, paradoxical . . . it is (apparently) daring, and transitory," whereas "the quotidian is what is humble and solid, what is taken for granted . . . undated and (apparently) insignificant."[41]

The idea of habit crystallizes this experience of dailiness. Habit describes not simply an action but an attitude: habits are often carried out in a semiautomatic, distracted, or involuntary manner. Certain forms of behavior are inscribed on the body, part of a deeply ingrained somatic memory. We drive to work, buy groceries, or type a routine letter in a semiconscious, often dreamlike state. Our bodies go through the motions while our minds are elsewhere. Particular habits may be intentionally cultivated or may build up imperceptibly over time. In either case, they often acquire a life of their own, shaping us as much as we shape them.

"Habit," writes Samuel Beckett dourly, "is the ballast that chains the dog to its vomit."[42] Modern literature has exposed these congealed patterns of daily life and questioned the sleepwalking demeanor inspired by the tyranny of habit. Its relationship to the everyday is often paradoxical, seeking to both preserve and negate it. On the one hand, literature is often passionately interested in the ordinary; think of the great realist novels of the nineteenth century, the encyclopedic scope of *Ulysses* as an "inventory of everyday life,"[43] the domestic details of a postmodern novel such as *White Noise*. On the other hand, it also tries to redeem the everyday by rescuing it from its opacity, defamiliarizing it and making us newly attentive to its mysteries. Yet this act of magnifying and refracting taken-for granted minutiae transcends the very dailiness it seeks to depict. Literature's heightened sensitivity to the microscopic detail marks its difference from the casual inattentiveness that defines the everyday experience of everyday life.

A similar critique of habitual perception lies at the heart of contemporary critical theory. From Barthes, Althusser and others we have learned to see the taken-for-granted as the ruse of bourgeois ideology. Judith Butler has shown that sedimented practices are the means by which repressive regimes of gender do their work. Postmodern accounts of the "aestheticization of everyday life," the invasion of our inner selves by the images and slogans of the mass media, only intensify this suspicion of everyday beliefs and attitudes. There is nowhere to run and nowhere to hide: no sanctum of the ordinary that escapes the tentacular grip of late capitalist consumer culture. The commonsense assumptions and routines by which we organize our lives are insidious precisely because they seem natural; we can counter their power only by ongoing critical vigilance. The work of theory is to break the spell of the habitual and the everyday.

Phenomenological studies of everyday life are, by contrast, much less censorious of habit. Indeed, they suggest that everyday life is self-evident and that this is a necessary rather than unfortunate fact. Everyday life simply *is* the routine act of conducting one's day-to-day existence without making it an object of conscious attention. "The reality of everyday life is taken-for-granted as reality. It does not require additional verification over and beyond its simple presence. It is simply *there*, as self-evident and compelling facticity. I *know* that it is real. While I am capable of engaging in doubts about its reality, I am obliged to suspend such doubt as I routinely exist in everyday life."[44]

In other words, everyday life is the sphere of what Schutz calls the natural attitude. This does not mean that the forms of everyday life are inevitable or unchanging. Long before the current interest in gender as performance, ethnographers such as Goffman were describing the performance of self in daily life and noting the socially constructed and conventional nature of our identities. The point is, however, that such performances are for the most part automatic, conducted with a constant but semiconscious vigilance. Unless a specific problem emerges to demand our attention, we rarely pause to reflect on the mundane ritualized practices around which much of our everyday life is organized. As Schutz and Luckmann point out, "our natural attitude of daily life is pervasively determined by a *pragmatic motive*."[45]

Agnes Heller also insists on this point, claiming that it is impossible in principle to adopt a critical, self-reflexive attitude toward all aspects of everyday life: "we would simply not be able to survive in the multiplicity of everyday demands and everyday activities if all of them required inventive thinking. . . . Disengagement is an indispensable precondition for . . . continued activity."[46] Heller's defense of habit is a pragmatic one: in order to survive in the world and get things done, we depend on routine. Certain facets of everyday life can be called into question, but it is simply impossible to doubt everything at once. Heller insists, "it is absolutely imperative that in certain types of activity our praxis and our thinking should become repetitive."[47] Habit is the necessary precondition for impulse and innovation.

Of course, phenomenological studies of everyday life are concerned with description rather than explanation and thus do not address questions of politics and power. An overreliance on habit can be personally constraining and socially detrimental, promoting a complacent acceptance of the way things are. In this sense, habit can serve conservative ends. Yet contemporary theory tends to overpoliticize the routines of everyday life in presenting the "natural attitude" as nothing more than a vehicle of ideology. At its most extreme, this results in a denunciation of any form of fixity in favor of permanent flux. Habit becomes the enemy of an authentic life.

This is, however, to see habit only as a straitjacket and constraint, and to ignore the ways routines may strengthen, comfort, and provide meaning. Furthermore, the distracted performance of routine tasks is surely a quintessential feature of the everyday, occurring across a wide range of histories and cultures. This is not to deny the vast differences between particular experiences of everyday life nor the fact, stressed by Foucault and Elias, that the modern era has led to distinctively new forms of internalized discipline. It is, however, to argue that the ritualized activity known as habit constitutes a fundamental element of being-in-the-world whose social meanings may be complex and varied.

From such a perspective, habit is not something we can ever hope to transcend. Rather, it constitutes an essential part of our embeddedness in everyday life and our existence as social beings. For example, the contemporary city may constitute a chaotic labyrinth of infinite possibilities, yet in our daily travels we often choose to carve out a familiar path, managing space and time by tracing out the same route again and again. Furthermore, habit is not opposed to individuality but intermeshed with it; our identity is formed out of a distinctive blend of behavioral and emotional patterns, repeated over time. To be suddenly deprived of the rhythm of one's personal routines, as often happens to those admitted to hospitals, prisons, retirement homes, or other large institutions, can be a source of profound disorientation and distress. Furthermore, even the most esoteric and elevated of activities contain routinized elements. Lefebvre notes that no cultural practice escapes the everyday; science, war, affairs of state, philosophy all contain a mundane dimension.[48]

Paula Treichler has observed that cultural studies pays little attention to the daily life of academics, as if everyday life were something that only others experience.[49] As a result, everyday life often has the lure of an exotic anthropological object. Cultural critics treat it with reverential respect and endow it with the rich complexity and ambiguity previously attributed to the modern work of art. In some versions of cultural studies, daily life constantly seethes with subversive energies. Yet everyday life is the realm not just of the other but of the self, not just the realm of transgression but also the realm of familiarity, boredom, and habit. To recognize that we all inhabit everyday life is not to deny social differences but simply to acknowledge a common grounding in the mundane.

Conversely, no life is defined completely by the everyday. Here I disagree with the common claim that only the elite are free to transcend the quotidian, that "most persons have *nothing but* that ordinary everyday life."[50] This is to impose a fantasy of sameness and profound limitation onto the lives of ordinary individuals. Surely every life contains epiphanic moments, experiences of trauma, and points of departure from mundane routines: religious ecstasy, sexual passion, drug taking, childbirth, encounters with death, or simply moments of distanced and thoughtful reflection on the meaning and purpose of one's life. Such heightened, intense, and often self-conscious episodes break just as dramatically with everyday routines as do the aforementioned realms of philosophy, high art, or male heroism. It is hard to see how any specific transcendence of everyday life can be deemed more or less genuine than any other. Every life, in other words, interweaves the everyday and the non-everyday, though some lives are clearly more anchored in the mundane than others.

Everyday life, furthermore, does not afford any automatic access to the "realness" of the world. Of course, it is true that daily life does involve certain forms of practical knowledge and skills without which we could not survive. Yet the assertion that everyday life is the realm of the concrete rather than the abstract needs to be qualified.[51] As both Heller and Schutz point out, everyday life is also the sphere of typification, that is, a reliance on type, analogy, and generality. Precisely because we cannot pause to question everything in the daily rush, we often depend on commonsense assumptions and preexisting schema that may not be supported by empirical evidence. According to Schutz, to live in the life-world is to take preexisting knowledge as simply given "until further notice," until a particular encounter or event serves to render it problematic. Heller suggests that everyday thinking is often fetishistic, accepting things and institutions as they are and bracketing them off from their origins.[52]

Of course, we may also question our own beliefs; the everyday includes the ever-present possibility of innovation and change. Furthermore, everyday life should not be conceptualized as a homogeneous and predictable terrain. It embraces a diverse range of activities, attitudes, and forms of behavior; it contains "broken patterns, non-rational and duplicitous actions, irresolvable conflicts and unpredictable events."[53] Nevertheless, we typically conduct our daily lives on the basis of numerous unstated and unexamined assumptions about the way things are, about the continuity, identity, and reliability of objects and individuals. For Schutz and Heller this is a necessary condition of everyday life rather than a moral or political failing. They would agree with Wittgenstein that theoretical critique is a specific language game that cannot provide a guide for the conduct of an entire life. The everyday is not necessarily more real, more authentic, or more immediate than the non-everyday, but it has a certain pragmatic priority simply because, as Blanchot notes, it is "what we are, first of all, and most often."[54]

## MAKING PEACE WITH THE EVERYDAY

In conclusion, I want to draw together the various threads of my argument and to elaborate on its implications. How useful is the idea of everyday life? What exactly does it mean? How should it be applied? While much of this chapter has focused on the contrasting definitions of everyday life in sociology and cultural studies, I now want to make more explicit connections to feminist scholarship.

Feminism has, of course, traditionally conceived itself as a politics of everyday life. In practice, this has meant very different things. On the one hand, feminists have deployed a hermeneutics of suspicion vis-à-vis the everyday, showing how the most mundane, taken-for-granted activities—conversation, housework, body language, styles of dress—serve to reinforce patriarchal norms. The feminist gaze reveals the everyday world as problematic, in Dorothy Smith's phrase;[55] it is here, above all, that gender hierarchy is reproduced, invisibly, pervasively, and over time. This sensitivity to the power dynamics of everyday life has been heightened by the impact of poststructuralist thought, with its suspicion of any form of fixity. As a result, much current feminist scholarship is

THE INVENTION OF EVERYDAY LIFE

involved in a persistent questioning of the commonsensical, taken-for-granted, and mundane.

On the other hand, everyday life has also been hailed as a distinctively female sphere and hence a source of value. The fact that women traditionally cook, clean, change diapers, raise children, and do much of the routine work of family reproduction is perceived by some feminists as a source of strength. Because of this grounding in the mundane, it is argued, women have a more realistic sense of how the world actually operates and are less estranged from their bodies and from the messy, chaotic, embodied realities of life. Thus, from the perspective of feminist standpoint theory, women's connection to daily life is something to be celebrated. Here everyday life is not a ruse of patriarchy but rather a sign of women's grounding in the practical world.

My discussion has shown, I hope, that this ambivalence has a history, that everyday life has long been subject to intense and conflicting emotional investments. Without wishing to deny the new insights generated by feminism, I would suggest that it also continues a tradition of thought that has viewed the everyday as both the most authentic and the most inauthentic of spheres. It is in this context that one can speak of the invention of everyday life. In one sense, the phrase sounds paradoxical, precisely because daily life refers to the most mundane, routine, overlooked aspects of human experience—those seemingly beyond the reach of invention, abstraction, and theory. Yet I have tried to show that everyday life is not simply a neutral label for a preexisting reality, but is freighted down with layers of meanings and associations.

One of these associations is, of course, gender. I have explored some of the ways everyday life has been connected to women, without simply endorsing the view that women represent daily life. The problem with this view, as the work of Lefebvre makes particularly clear, is that it presents a romantic view of both everyday life and women by associating them with the natural, authentic, and primitive. This nostalgia feeds into a long chain of dichotomies—society versus community, modernity versus tradition, public versus private—that do not help us understand the social organization of gender and that deny women's contemporaneity, self-consciousness, and agency. Furthermore, to affirm women's special grounding in everyday life is to take at face value a mythic ideal of heroic male transcendence and to ignore the fact that men are also embodied, embedded subjects who live, for the most part, repetitive, familiar, and ordinary lives.

What I have found helpful in the phenomenological scholarship is that it takes seriously the ordinariness of everyday life without idealizing or demonizing it. In cultural studies, by contrast, everyday life is often made to carry enormous symbolic weight. Either it is rhapsodically affirmed and painted in glowing colors or it is excoriated as the realm of ultimate alienation and dehumanization. Yet if the everyday is an indispensable aspect of all human lives, as I have argued, it becomes harder to endow it with an intrinsic political content. The everyday is robbed of much of its portentous symbolic meaning.

Thus it makes more sense to think of the everyday as a way of experiencing the world than a circumscribed set of activities within the world. Everyday life simply is the process of becoming acclimatized to assumptions, behaviors, and practices, which come to seem self-evident and taken for granted. In other words, everydayness is not an intrinsic quality that magically adheres to particular actions or persons (women, the working class). Rather, it is a lived process of routinization that all individuals experience. Certain tasks that at first appear awkward or strange—driving is an obvious example—gradually become second nature to us over time. Conversely, the everyday lives of others can seem deeply alien to us, precisely because the quotidian is not an objectively given quality but a lived relationship.

Such routinization may be problematic or even dangerous in some contexts, but it is surely a mistake to see habit as such as intrinsically reactionary. The work of Heller and Schutz is valuable in affirming the pragmatic need for repetition, familiarity, and taken-for-grantedness in everyday life, as a necessary precondition for human survival. As Susan Bordo points out in another context, it is an intellectual delusion to think that we can simply abandon our habits, blind spots, and assumptions and embrace an infinitely shifting, self-undermining multiplicity of perspectives. This belief is a delusion because such habits form the very basis of who we are.[56] Influenced by modernist ideals of innovation and irony, contemporary theorists have tended to either excoriate the everyday for its routine, mundane qualities, or celebrate the everyday by pretending that such qualities do not exist. It is time, perhaps, to make peace with the ordinariness of daily life.

## NOTES

This paper was first published in *New Formations* 39 (Autumn 1999–Winter 2000). Thanks to Sara Blair for helpful references and to Allan Megill for stylistic suggestions.

1. Quoted in Peter Osborne, *The Politics of Time: Modernity and Avant-Garde* (London: Verso, 1995), 192.
2. Maurice Blanchot, "Everyday Speech," *Yale French Studies,* no. 73 (1987): 14.
3. See, however, Roger Silverstone, *Television and Everyday Life* (London: Routledge, 1994), which draws extensively on sociology, phenomenology, and anthropology; and Meaghan Morris, "On the Beach," in *Cultural Studies,* ed. Lawrence Grossberg, Cary Nelson, and Paula Treichler (New York:

Routledge, 1992). See also Dorothy Smith, *The Everyday World as Problematic: A Feminist Sociology* (Milton Keynes: Open University Press, 1987), for a brief discussion of Schutz; Kristin Ross, *Fast Cars, Clean Bodies: Decolonization and the Reordering of French Culture* (Cambridge: MIT Press, 1995), for a feminist application of Lefebvre; and Nancy Fraser, "What's Critical about Critical Theory? The Case of Habermas and Gender," in *Unruly Practices: Power, Discourse and Gender in Contemporary Social Theory* (Minneapolis: University of Minnesota Press, 1989), for a feminist critique of Habermas's conception of the life-world. As this book was going to press, I discovered Laurie Langbauer's stimulating *Novels of Everyday Life: The Series in English Fiction, 1850–1930* (Ithaca: Cornell University Press, 1999). Though she comes to slightly different conclusions, Langbauer's survey of different theoretical conceptions of everyday life and their relationship to questions of gender reveals intriguing parallels to my own discussion.

4. Henri Lefebvre, *Everyday Life in the Modern World* (New York: Transaction, 1984), 38. For the history of writing on daily life, see Alvin W. Gouldner, "Sociology and the Everyday Life," in *The Idea of Social Science,* ed. Lewis A. Coser (New York: Harcourt, Brace, Jovanovich, 1975).

5. Thomas Moore, *The Re-Enchantment of Everyday Life* (New York: Harper-Collins, 1996).

6. Alfred Schutz and Thomas Luckmann, *The Structures of the Life-World*, vol. 1 (Evanston, IL: Northwestern University Press, 1983).

7. Alice Walker, "Everyday Use," in *Love and Trouble: Stories of Black Women* (New York: Harcourt, Brace, Jovanovich, 1973).

8. Mike Featherstone, "The Heroic Life and Everyday Life," *Theory, Culture and Society* 9, 1 (1992): 165.

9. Lefebvre, *Everyday Life in the Modern World,* 73.

10. Henri Lefebvre, "The Everyday and Everydayness," *Yale French Studies*, no. 73 (1987): 10.

11. Henri Lefebvre, *Critique de la vie quotidienne*, vol. 2 (Paris: L'Arche, 1961), 54.

12. Johannes Fabian, *Time and the Other: How Anthropology Makes Its Object* (New York: Columbia University Press, 1983), ix.

13. Simone de Beauvoir, *The Second Sex* (London: Picador, 1988), 610.

14. Lefebvre, *Everyday Life in the Modern World,* 17; Julia Kristeva, "Women's Time," in *Feminist Theory: A Critique of Ideology,* ed. Nannerl O. Keohane, Michelle Z. Rosaldo, and Barbara C. Gelpi (Chicago: University of Chicago Press, 1982). See also Frieda Johles Forman, ed., *Taking Our Time: Feminist Perspectives on Temporality* (Oxford: Pergamon, 1989) for similar arguments.

15. E. P. Thompson, "Time, Work-Discipline and Industrial Capitalism," *Past and Present* 38 (1957): 79

16. Henri Lefebvre, *Critique of Everyday Life*, vol. 1 (London: Verso, 1991), 28.

17. Lefebvre, "The Everyday and Everydayness," 10.

18. See, however, Silverstone, *Television and Everyday Life* for a systematic engagement with these issues.
19. Osborne, *The Politics of Time*, 198.
20. Agnes Heller, *Everyday Life* (London: Routledge and Kegan Paul, 1984), 239.
21. Lefebvre, *Critique of Everyday Life*, 43.
22. Lefebvre, *Critique of Everyday Life*, 43.
23. Theodor Adorno, *Minima Moralia: Reflections from Damaged Life* (London: Verso, 1974), 38–39.
24. David Harvey, *Consciousness and the Urban Experience* (Oxford: Basil Blackwell, 1985), 250.
25. Sigmund Freud, "The Uncanny," in *Sigmund Freud, vol. 14, Art and Literature* (Harmondsworth: Penguin, 1985), 368.
26. Dolores Hayden, *The Grand Domestic Revolution: A History of Feminist Designs for American Homes, Neighborhoods and Cities* (Cambridge: MIT Press, 1981), 137.
27. Lawrence Grossberg, "Wandering Audiences, Nomadic Critics," *Cultural Studies* 2, 3 (1988): 384.
28. Janet Wolff, "On the Road Again: Metaphors of Travel in Cultural Criticism," in *Resident Alien: Feminist Cultural Criticism* (New Haven: Yale University Press, 1995).
29. Doreen Massey, "A Place Called Home?" *New Formations* 17 (1992): 8.
30. Doreen Massey, "Politics and Space/Time," *New Left Review* 196 (1992): 65–84.
31. Beverley Skeggs, *Formations of Class and Gender* (London: Sage, 1997).
32. Audre Lorde, *Zami: A New Spelling of My Name* (London: Sheba Feminist Publishers, 1982).
33. See Paul Gilroy, "It Ain't Where You're From, It's Where You're At . . . The Dialectics of Diasporic Identification," *Third Text* 13 (1990–91): 3–16; Ien Ang, "On Not Speaking Chinese: Postmodern Ethnicity and the Politics of Diaspora" *New Formations* 24 (1994): 1–18.
34. Silverstone, *Television and Everyday Life*, 28.
35. Mary Douglas, "The Idea of a Home: A Kind of Space," in *Home: A Place in the World*, ed. Arien Mack (New York: New York University Press, 1993), 268.
36. bell hooks, "Homeplace: A Site of Resistance," in *Yearning: Race, Gender and Cultural Politics* (Boston: South End Press, 1990), 42.
37. Barbara Smith, ed., *Home Girls: A Black Feminist Anthology* (New York: Kitchen Table Women of Color Press, 1983).
38. Iris Marion Young, "House and Home: Feminist Variations on a Theme," in *Intersecting Voices: Dilemmas of Gender, Political Philosophy and Policy* (Princeton: Princeton University Press, 1997), 153.
39. Meaghan Morris, "At Henry Parkes Motel," *Cultural Studies* 2, 1 (1988): 12.
40. "The domestic has become a complex and contradictory reality. . . . Do-it-yourself decoration and house improvement, the increasing personalisation

of media and information technologies, consumption itself in all its various manifestations, the intensification of the home as a leisure centre, as well as a place of paid work, all signify its changing status." Silverstone, *Television and Everyday Life*, 51. For one case study of the gender politics of home, see Lesley Johnson, "'As Housewives We Are Worms': Women, Modernity and the Home Question," *Cultural Studies* 10, 3 (1996): 449–63. Jane Juffer's recent book *At Home with Pornography: Women, Sex and Everyday Life* (New York: New York University Press, 1998), is an important contribution to rethinking the meanings of home, modernity, and space as well as redefining feminist approaches to pornography.

41. Lefebvre, *Everyday Life in the Modern World*, 24.
42. Samuel Beckett, *Proust and Three Dialogues* (London: John Calder, 1965), 19.
43. Lefebvre, *Everyday Life in the Modern World*, 3.
44. Peter Berger and Thomas Luckmann, *The Social Construction of Reality: A Treatise in the Sociology of Knowledge* (Harmondsworth: Penguin, 1967), 37.
45. Schutz and Luckmann, *Structures of the Life-World*, vol. 1, 6.
46. Heller, *Everyday Life*, 129.
47. Heller, *Everyday Life*, 259.
48. Lefebvre, *Critique de la vie quotidienne*, vol. 2, 61.
49. John Fiske, "Cultural Studies and the Culture of Everyday Life: Discussion," in Grossberg, Nelson, and Treichler, *Cultural Studies*, 167.
50. Dorothee Wierling, "The History of Everyday Life and Gender Relations: On Historical and Historiographical Relationships," in *The History of Everyday Life*, ed. Alf Lüdtke (Princeton: Princeton University Press, 1995), 151.
51. Fiske, "Cultural Studies and the Culture of Everyday Life."
52. Schutz and Luckmann, *Structures of the Life-World*, vol. 1, 8; Heller, *Everyday Life*, 52.
53. Silverstone, *Television and Everyday Life*, 7.
54. Blanchot, "Everyday Speech," 12.
55. Smith, *The Everyday World as Problematic*.
56. Susan Bordo, "Feminism, Postmodernism and Gender-Skepticism," in *Feminism/Postmodernism*, ed. Linda Nicholson (New York: Routledge, 1990). For a discussion of parallel issues in queer theory, see Biddy Martin, "Extraordinary Homosexuals and the Fear of Being Ordinary," in *Feminism Meets Queer Theory*, ed. Elizabeth Weed and Naomi Schor (Bloomington: Indiana University Press, 1997).

# 4

# JUDITH KRANTZ, AUTHOR OF
# *THE CULTURAL LOGICS OF*
# *LATE CAPITALISM*

A new form of mass-market fiction has flooded the bookstores and beaches of the Western world. The "money, sex, and power" novel, associated with such authors as Judith Krantz, Jackie Collins, and Barbara Taylor Bradford, is an interesting phenomenon that deserves more sustained attention than it has yet received. One striking feature of the genre is its bold reinterpretation of gender identities and relations. Rather than either repeating the age-old story of feminine romance or reinvigorating traditional masculine plots (the Western, the hard-boiled crime novel) by adding a female protagonist, it offers a new script characterized by gender hybridity and transvestite themes. The money, sex, and power novel thus raises interesting questions about changing images of gender in late capitalist culture.

Another distinctive feature of the genre is its simultaneous allegiance to what are often seen as historically distinct and mutually exclusive notions of the self. The money, sex, and power novel tells a classic modern narrative of individual self-development and social mobility, while also evincing a fascination with postmodern themes of consumption, image, celebrity, and other aspects of the society of the spectacle. This uneven temporality, the sense of being caught between contradictory modes of thought, behavior, and historical understanding, surely speaks to many individuals in our own time, but perhaps above all to women. Gender hybridity and uneven temporality—these two, not unconnected, phenomena are the most noteworthy features of this new genre, suggesting its relevance not just for cultural studies but also for debates in feminist and postmodern theory.

For those not familiar with the genre, I should begin by explaining that the money, sex, and power novel has a distinctive plot. It features a glamorous, ambitious heroine who fights her way to the top of a corporate empire while engaging in conspicuous consumption of men and designer labels. The form became almost synonymous with the best-selling novel in the 1980s, its cultural visibility intensified by the frequent transformation of its authors into glamorous media celebrities paid huge advances by their publishers. The Krantzian heroine, furthermore, soon appeared in other media texts and genres, as similar images of striving corporate femininity began to appear in prime-time television drama, advertising, and women's magazines. A complex mélange of Balzacian *Bildungsroman*, prime-time soap opera, and brand-name commodity aesthetic, the money, sex, and power novel raises interesting questions about the changing images of femininity in popular culture and the ability of current feminist methodologies to address such changes.

Feminist cultural critics have devoted much of their energy to analyzing traditional women's genres such as melodrama, soap operas, and romance fiction. The reasons behind this strategy are self-evident; there has been a long-standing devaluation of all things feminine and a consequent interest among scholars in exploring and reclaiming a tradition of women's popular culture. As a result, however, feminist media studies has frequently worked with a relatively static model of femininity—often conflated, as Liesbet van Zoonen notes, with the figure of the housewife. Gender is seen as a preexisting entity that precedes and justifies particular cultural practices, rather than an identity that is realized through such practices.[1]

Some of the frameworks deployed by feminist critics reflect and contribute to this view. Various forms of psychoanalysis ranging from Freud to Lacan to object relations theory have been used to elaborate models of the female psyche that can account for women's pleasures and investments in popular forms. An-

JUDITH KRANTZ

chored in the eternal verities of the Oedipal script, such models cannot account for historical changes in how gender is portrayed. Nor can they explain how such changes are influenced by economic or political structures. Even when linked to a discussion of female subcultures or interpretative communities, feminist readings of popular forms often assume an impermeable boundary between men's and women's texts. This boundary firmly separates the public world of goal-oriented activity from the private world of emotion and affect. Women's culture comes across as a separate zone of romantic and maternal longings that is strangely uncontaminated by worldly desires and ambitions.

Much contemporary popular culture, however, questions these very gender divisions. Here we can see an instance of the time lag that often characterizes cultural studies, as scholars struggle to keep up with the rapidly mutating texts that are the objects of their analysis. At the very moment when feminist critics were rushing to interpret romance as the quintessential example of women's popular fiction, some rather different women's genres were achieving commercial and cultural prominence. In examining the money, sex, and power novel, then, I hope to address some of the broader cultural implications of these new fictions of femininity. I also want to extend the discussion of postmodernism and literature, which has focused almost exclusively on self-conscious, experimental forms of writing. A popular, formulaic genre may also have something to contribute to our view of the postmodern.

Of course, the recent interest in gender hybridity and transvestism has also made its way into cultural studies. See, for example, the many readings of Madonna's media personae as a subversive parody of gender norms. What is often missing from such discussions, however, is any discussion of how such refashionings of gender link up to the logics and imperatives of late capitalist culture. This is not to invite automatic denunciations of capitalism, but to wonder about the connections and lines of influence between economic structures, popular images and narratives, and commonsense understandings of gender.

What is so interesting about the money, sex, and power novel is its preoccupation—nay, its obsession—with precisely this question. Judith Krantz and Fredric Jameson may not otherwise have much in common, but they share a burning interest in the cultural logic of late capitalism. The title of my essay plays off Jorge Luis Borges's famous short story "Pierre Menard, Author of the *Quixote*." Unlike Borges's hero, however, Krantz repeats Jameson's classic discussion of postmodernism yet also rewrites it differently.[2] For if Jameson posits a relatively coherent cultural logic ("postmodernism") that differs substantially from modernism, Krantz's novels suggest something complicated: the simultaneous existence of differing temporalities, worldviews, and modes of experience. Late capitalism, in other words, has not one logic, but several. Even as

JUDITH KRANTZ

women are placed at the heart of a postmodern era of consumption, pleasure, and spectacle, they are also protagonists of a quintessential modern narrative of self-realization, autonomy, and upward mobility. Looking at the distinctive features of an enormously popular genre may throw more general light on the historical modalities of contemporary culture.

## POSTMODERN KRANTZ: COMMODITIES AND CELEBRITIES

Postmodernism is the ultimate example of a floating signifier, a term whose meaning fluctuates dramatically according to context. As I noted in the introduction, there is little consensus as to whether it constitutes a historical period, an artistic style, or a theoretical perspective, or indeed all three at once. Within one subset of discourses around "postmodernism," nonetheless, we can identify some recurring beliefs and motifs. We live in an era of ubiquitous commodification, it is argued, where every last pocket of culture has been saturated by the texts and images of capitalist-driven media industries. This "society of the spectacle" has engendered a new sense of depthlessness, a fragmentation of identity, and a weakening of historical consciousness. Any meaningful distinctions between popular and high culture have been effaced as the latter is seamlessly incorporated into a capitalist system of profit and marketability. Indeed, the very distinction between text and reality is extinguished. Theodor Adorno and Max Horkheimer's mournful observation that "real life is becoming indistinguishable from the movies" is intensified a thousandfold in an epoch when we live our lives through the images and scripts of an all-pervasive commodity culture.[3]

The money, sex, and power novel provides a highly apposite context for exploring such questions. It is, after all, the only literary genre explicitly devoted to representing—and indeed glorifying—consumption. Individual novels are usually organized around a dual theme of the commodity and the celebrity, that is, the self as commodified sign. This theme permeates the genre at various levels. Most obviously, much of the narrative is devoted to descriptions of shopping. The department stores and specialty boutiques of Paris, Rodeo Drive, or Manhattan provide the fictional backdrop for detailed evocations of women's surrender to the seductive power of the commodity. When the Krantzian heroine is lonely or frustrated, consumption offers the promise of both sensual fulfillment and spiritual transfiguration.

The equation of shopping and sex is a recurring theme. Billy Ikehorn, the fabulously wealthy heroine of *Scruples*, feels a powerful "sexual buzz" as she prowls through the department stores of Beverly Hills, "buying supremely unnecessary clothes to feed, but never fill, the emptiness within."[4] In the novel's sequel, *Scruples Two*, when the same character is suddenly overwhelmed by a passionate eagerness to buy, this urge signals the return of her characteristic energy and exuberant vitality; "she was feeling desire again, desire, that life-giving force; desire, that need that can't be called up by any force of will."[5] The links between eroticism and consumption are clearly spelled out. "Where there was shopping," Billy Ikehorn ruminates at a later point, "sex would somehow follow."[6] The yearning for commodities, however, is not just a precursor or substitute for sexual desire, but an impulse of equal power and intensity. The desire to consume—and here Krantz is in complete agreement with Jean Baudrillard— bears no relationship to the use value of what is bought. Rather, it is triggered by the aura of the commodity; its magic allure holds forth the promise of an imaginary plenitude. Indeed, at the heart of *Scruples* is the elaboration of a "Disneyland concept of retailing," where the distinctions between consumption and entertainment, shopping and pleasure are artfully blurred.[7] The Scruples store is presented as "a shopper's perfect playground, a great caravan of choice, a never-ending source of real and fantasy gratification."[8]

These novels, then, refer to yet also rewrite a long-standing association between femininity and consumption. The female consumer has often been portrayed as both symbol and symptom of the dangerous seductions of modern capitalism. Her excessive desire erodes traditional values of discipline and self-restraint, replacing them with a new feminine ethos of luxury, narcissism, and hedonistic excess.[9] In the postmodern world of the money, sex, and power novel, however, conventional oppositions between work and leisure, production and consumption have lost much of their meaning. Rather, the consumer skills of the Krantzian heroine are the essential preconditions for her entrepreneurial and professional success in the lifestyle, marketing, and image industries. Thus the heroine of *Scruples* runs an exclusive department store, Jazz Kilkullen of *Dazzle* is a celebrity photographer, Maxi in *I'll Take Manhattan* works as a magazine publisher; other major characters in the Krantzian world work in advertising, modeling, interior decorating, and similar fields. This is not simply a case of women's continuing association with traditional feminine industries, as one critic suggests, but rather a sign of the changing status and importance of such industries within the society of the spectacle. Women's affinity with the commodity is no longer devalued but triumphantly affirmed as a source of their economic power. This affinity equips them with newfound authority and professional expertise as media magnates and captains of industry in a culture that is increasingly feminized in its preoccupation with image, surface, and style.

This focus on commodity culture also permeates the genre at the level of form, pandering to the reader's own pleasures in vicarious consumption. Of course, we do not consume actual objects, only their representations. Yet the difference between real and imaginary consumption becomes murky as commodities are freighted with ever more portentous meanings and layers of symbolism. Increasingly, what we are sold are not objects but elaborate fantasies and glamorous lifestyles. Thus the experience of reading a Judith Krantz novel is not unlike that of watching *Lifestyles of the Rich and Famous* while simultaneously flicking through the glossy advertisements in *Vogue*. Much of the money, sex, and power novel is given over to depicting the lifestyles of the fabulously rich. The reader is a window-shopper, vicariously experiencing the pleasures of elegant interiors, chic designer clothes, and opulent styles of entertaining. Spectacle and display are key features of a genre that opens panoramically onto exotic yet curiously similar vistas from Saint Tropez to Los Angeles. The result is a distinctive literary expression of a commodity aesthetic usually found in prime-time American television dramas and Hollywood films; a glamorous and glossy world of abundance, beauty, health, and wealth from which all traces of poverty, abjection, and dissonance have been firmly expunged.[10]

The narrative function of the brand name is all-important in this context. This motif is both exemplified and parodied in a typical passage from Julie Burchill's *Ambition*.

> On Madison Avenue, at the soft-tech, Italo-Japanese, black-beige Armani shop, she bought black label, and at Krizia she bought sportswear that would have a nervous breakdown if one did anything more rigorous than hail a cab in it. She avoided Walter Steiger but did succumb to a pair of pewter, lace and plastic Vittorio Riccis for Zero. She snapped up a brace of six-hundred-dollar sweaters at Sonia Rykiel and half a dozen pairs of cashmere tights at $178 dollars a throw at Fogal. . . . On Fifth Avenue she ignored Gucci as a matter of principle, bought lots of Michael Kors black at Bergdorf's and Donna Karan cashmere and a Rifat Ozbeck tuxedo dress for under four hundred dollars at Saks. On East 57th St she bought a Chanel suit, against her better judgement, for just over two thousand dollars, a three-thousand-dollar handbag at Prada, and after browsing in La Marca for two minutes, understood completely why it was Cher's favorite store, made her excuses and left.[11]

This brand-name fetishism has a specific effect. It does not just describe particular distinctions between commodities, but also impresses such distinctions on the reader, who is thereby alerted to the crucial differences between Gucci and Prada, Armani and Versace. Similarly, Krantz's pronouncements on the cut of a genuine Chanel jacket or the location of the best table at Spago's carry with them an unmistakable accent of authority. As Angela Carter notes, these novels thereby combine entertainment with instruction, serving as handbooks to a certain kind of social mobility. They address, yet simultaneously call into being, a reader attuned to the most subtle forms of stylistic discrimination, a brand-name connoisseur.[12]

This "in-the-know" quality of the money, sex and power genre, the sense of a confident familiarity with the intimate details of a glamorous, wealthy lifestyle, is reinforced by the media visibility of many of its authors. Jackie Collins and Judith Krantz are almost as likely to appear in *People* magazine as the characters they depict. In this way, they acquire the status of participant-observers, authentic inhabitants of the opulent world that they faithfully chronicle for others. The glossy airbrushed photograph and accompanying text on the back cover intensify this authorial aura. In the case of Krantz, for example, the reader learns that all her novels are best-sellers that have been made into major television series, and that her husband is the "movie and television producer Steven Krantz." Such devices help to authenticate Krantz's depictions of jet-set society, while simultaneously cloaking the author with the same glamour and prestige as the characters she depicts.

The cult of celebrity is not limited to the marketing of the author, but informs the money, sex, and power genre at several levels. Most obviously, Krantz's protagonists are often famous personalities. Celebrity, along with the related accoutrements of money, sex, and power, emerges as a desideratum that bestows an incandescent aura on the fictional heroine. One exists only in being seen and worshiped by innumerable others. More interesting, however, are the recurring references to real celebrities in the genre. We discover that Jazz Kilkullen, the heroine of *Dazzle*, has photographed "François Mitterrand, Isabelle Adjani, Princess Anne, Jesse Jackson, Marlon Brando, Muammar Khaddafy, Woody Allen."[13] Valentine, a couture designer and key character in *Scruples*, is commissioned to dress Raquel Welch, Barbra Streisand, and Cher for the Oscar awards. Maxi, the protagonist of *I'll Take Manhattan*, is a neighbor and friend of Donald Trump. Such devices add to the genre's claim to authenticity as an insider guide to the lifestyles of the rich and famous. Part of its appeal, then, would appear to lie in the voyeuristic frisson engendered by a sense of intimate familiarity with the private lives of famous people.

One of the paradoxes of this genre, then, is that celebrity—seemingly the most artificial of social phenomena—becomes one of the ways the genre signals its closeness to reality. As Richard Dyer points out, stardom is a contradictory blend of artifice and authenticity; celebrities are completely fabricated yet uniquely original. Everyone knows that their personae are manufactured by the mass media, yet stars nevertheless radiate a powerful aura of immediacy and authenticity. As latter-day saints, they are worshiped as emblems of a heightened

JUDITH KRANTZ

and more intense reality.[14] In the money, sex, and power novel, this contemporary preoccupation with the famousness of the famous finds its most explicit literary expression.

The function of celebrities, according to James Monaco, "isn't to act, just to be."[15] There is an obvious parallel between being a celebrity and the traditional feminine role; both are consumed as image and object of the gaze. As Joanne Finkelstein has pointed out, the assumptions of nineteenth-century physiognomy continue to exercise a powerful influence on our contemporary perceptions of the self. In a culture dominated by visual technologies, character and identity are yoked ever more tightly to physical appearance. The tautness of a body or the curve of a mouth is an unambiguous sign of moral or personal worth.[16] Such a physiognomic logic explicitly underpins the techniques of visualization and representation in the money, sex, and power novel. The heroine's striking but idiosyncratic physical beauty is an unambiguous marker of her identity; as in the fairy tale, there is a seamless connection between inner and outer selves. The narrator's references to the impudent line of a character's nose or to the sensual unruliness of her hair are unmistakable guides to the essence of her true personality. In the Krantzian universe, identity *is* performance, unambiguously displayed on the surfaces and planes of the body.

The money, sex, and power novel, one might argue, is thus an exemplary illustration of a late capitalist semiotic, reducing agency to appearance, depth to surface, personality to a stylized presentation of self through commodity consumption. The "femininity" of the genre, as exemplified in its focus on and address to women, results from the persisting role of women as consumers as well as a more general feminization of contemporary culture through the sovereignty of appearance, image, and style. The genre's preoccupation with pleasure, luxury, and "fun" further intensifies this association with the feminine. As Zoe Sofia and Maria Angel point out, a feminist psychoanalysis that equates the symbolic order with phallic authority, repression, and the law of the father does not help us make sense of much contemporary culture. Many of the texts that surround us do not preach self-discipline, restraint, and control, but extol the virtues of hedonism, abundance, and instant pleasure. Capitalism is increasingly portrayed as the good mother rather than the repressive father, the munificent breast rather than the phallus.[17] The money, sex, and power novel confirms this vision of the social world as playground and pleasure dome, offering the promise of immediate gratification to the voracious reader/consumer.

### MODERN KRANTZ: THE SELF-MADE WOMAN

Such a reading, however, highlights only one aspect of this genre. As well as celebrating a feminine realm of style, pleasure, and consumption, the money, sex, and power novel also has a classic *Bildungsroman* plot espousing such values as individualism, ambition, and self-realization. In this sense, it both exemplifies and rewrites the quintessential narrative of modernity as a project of ongoing self-development and Faustian struggle. The crucial difference, of course, is that this dynamic hero is now a woman.

Thus the Krantzian heroine issues her challenge to the city from the heights of a New York penthouse rather than a Parisian cemetery ("I'll take Manhattan"), but in other respects her development from ingénue to triumphant metropolitan subject is a striking echo of such classic realist novels as *Père Goriot*. Franco Moretti notes that the nineteenth-century *Bildungsroman* is the literary embodiment of distinctively modern values of exploration, mobility, and restlessness. The novels of Balzac, in particular, reveal a fascination with social mobility as an end in itself, offering panoramic imaginings of individual achievement and self-creation opened up by the social upheavals of modernity. "The desire for success appears for the first time as a wholly 'natural' impulse needing no justification."[18] Like Balzac's Eugène Rastignac, the heroine of the money, sex, and power novel comes to regard the metropolis as both worthy opponent and ultimate prize, offering an exhilarating and unlimited array of personal, sexual, and economic possibilities. The narrative will trace her gradual ascension to full personhood through struggle, ambition, and a process of active self-formation. As in the classic *Bildungsroman*, this scenario relies on an opposition between tradition and modernity, between the constraints of old and repressive conventions and the exhilarating freedoms and pleasures of urban life ("she loved the city, she needed the city, she *belonged* to the city").[19]

Of course, Balzac's fascination with the spectacular energy unleashed by the development of modern capitalism is accompanied by a bleak recognition of its destructive effects on human relations and moral values. Krantz's vision is adulatory rather than critical, upbeat rather than censorious. Her texts embrace the utopian sensibility of fantasy rather than the penetrating, critical gaze of social realism. Her heroines radiate the undiluted energy, self-presence, and intensity of will of the mythic protagonist. Thus the money, sex, and power novel appropriates and rewrites the classic capitalist narrative of the self-made man. It is now the figure of woman who embodies the modern promise of freedom and self-invention afforded the triumphantly mobile public subject.

The narrative trajectory of *I'll Take Manhattan*, for example, traces the development of its heroine, Maxi, from consumer to producer, from playgirl to skilled entrepreneur. Born into wealth and privilege, Krantz's protagonist spends much of her early life in pursuit of pleasure: endless shopping and traveling, a string of husbands, a life of guilt-free hedonism. It is only after her father's publishing empire is threatened that she is spurred into purposeful action, her subsequent transformation as much personal as professional. By the end of the novel, she has learned to run a magazine, to be a successful publisher, to use money to make more money; in other words, to be a successful capitalist. But she has also acquired self-knowledge, maturity, and a greater sense of autonomy. That public success and personal development are equated rather than opposed in the genre underscores its worldly, anti-Romantic perspective. Like the Balzacian hero, the Krantzian protagonist desires what is in the world rather than outside it. She identifies with the prevailing social values of her time, albeit values that have been traditionally denied to women. Her achievement will be to master the rules of social and economic advancement more skillfully than anyone else.

As Margaret Marshment points out, the money, sex, and power novel contains two basic plot variants. Either a young woman is born into relative poverty and rises through determination and hard work to a position of wealth and power, or she inherits money and status, but must prove herself worthy of them.[20] In either case, the narrative is propelled forward by the passionate striving of the protagonist, her yearning for both personal fulfillment and public self-realization. She embodies what are often seen as quintessentially modern, as well as masculine, values: ambition, self-discipline, hard work, even egoism. The protagonist of *Scruples*, for example, possesses the following qualities: "total dedication to a cause, stern self-discipline, the willingness to struggle toward achievement at all costs, the determination to move relentlessly toward an ideal of perfection."[21] Originally harnessed to the goal of disciplining and perfecting her body, these traits will in turn come to motivate her spectacular entrepreneurial success.

Particularly interesting in this regard is the genre's fascination with work as the key to self-realization. With some exceptions, the traditional novel has rarely focused on the workplace; when labor is depicted, it is often equated with either exploitation or dehumanization.[22] In the money, sex, and power novel, by contrast, work is integral to the process of authentic self-formation. Krantz, for example, devotes numerous pages to detailing the professional training and achievements of her heroines (for example, as photographer, pilot, or entrepreneur). These pages are infused with an exhilaration and highly charged affect rarely found in contemporary fictional representations of men at work. This view of the workplace as a site of self-actualization points to a significant ideological shift that is, of course, dependent on class and race privilege. For the wealthy heroine, labor becomes a source of creative self-fulfillment and prestige rather than monotony and exhaustion.

The money, sex, and power novel also draws on a distinctively American tradition of popular stories depicting "the pursuit of happiness through social mo-

JUDITH KRANTZ

bility and financial accumulation."[23] The late nineteenth century saw the publication of numerous books testifying to the success and character of the self-made man, a figure seen as owing nothing to aristocratic privilege or European tradition. What was distinctive about the American version of this narrative was its seamless welding of material success with moral and spiritual qualities; public achievement served as a testimony to personal virtue. As Leo Braudy notes, "success was a spiritual concept. It came entirely from within the self and it built from the ground up, both financially and psychically. The individual's prime recourse was 'character', which itself was not innate so much as self-controlled and self-created."[24] While Braudy suggests that this narrative had lost much of its cultural centrality by World War I, the contemporary visibility of the money, sex, and power novel points to its rebirth and revitalization.

What sanctions the current efflorescence of the genre is, of course, the changed gender of the protagonist. While white men's struggle for power and success can no longer be celebrated with quite the same insouciance as in the past, the fictional representation of ambitious and powerful white heroines has a novel appeal that can also be justified, at least implicitly, as a redressal of past inequality. In this sense, the money, sex, and power genre would not be possible without feminism. At the same time, there is no simple or straightforward link between political ideology and popular fantasy. These novels are "feminist" only in the very limited sense of affirming an individual woman's right to wealth, power, and success. As such, their closest analog in the political sphere would be liberal feminism. Yet Krantz's novels are popular myths, not political documents. Myth, by its very nature, requires an exemplary, heroic, larger-than-life protagonist: this is an aesthetic requirement as much as an ideological one. In the money, sex, and power novel, this exceptionalism is expressed through a late capitalist value system of fame, power, and success. However, a reader's enjoyment of a popular image of powerful femininity does not automatically imply an endorsement of the Krantzian narrative as a blueprint for a desirable social reality.

In other words, we can best assess the cultural significance of the money, sex, and power novel not by reading it as a prescriptive guide to real-life behavior but by comparing it to other popular representations of femininity. In this context, the genre departs from a long-standing tradition of presenting female power as inherently evil, dangerous, and worthy of punishment.[25] The money, sex, and power novel is the only popular form that celebrates and rewards the female desire for power and the power of female desire. In this context, it offers a marked contrast to conventional feminine forms such as romance and soap opera, which explore such themes only in veiled and muted fashion, as well as a contrast to the ubiquitous representations of frustrated and unbalanced "career women" in recent Hollywood cinema.

JUDITH KRANTZ

At the same time, this coupling of a heroic narrative of individual achievement with a female protagonist also brings some significant changes. For example, the emphasis on the heroine's glamour and beauty serves to deflect any potential anxieties about her masculinization. She offers reassurance that women can achieve traditional forms of male economic success without sacrificing familiar forms of female (hetero)sexual power. Furthermore, the theme of conflict and struggle so central to the Balzacian *Bildungsroman* is often downplayed. Thus the heroine typically assumes the mantle of her father's authority as the head of a corporation or dynasty only after his death. A direct Oedipal struggle is thus avoided. The line of inheritance passes from father to daughter; either there are no sons, or potential male claimants to paternal power are carefully disinvested of legitimacy. In Krantz's *I'll Take Manhattan*, for example, one of Maxi's brothers goes blind and the other turns out to be homosexual. These facts are obviously intended to "explain" their renunciation of the family dynasty and provide an alibi for the heroine's own assumption of the role of paternal heir. In these and similar instances, the money, sex, and power novel reveals an ongoing negotiation and an attempted resolution of conflicting models of the female self. Even as it draws on a quintessentially modern plot of social mobility and self-formation, the genre thus reveals important, gendered differences.

## A CONTRADICTORY AMALGAM OF PLOTS

I have sketched out the contours of two coexisting narratives and thematic clusters in the money, sex, and power genre. How, then, should we make sense of this doubleness? A possible solution would be to classify one plot as superficial, a distracting device that conceals a deeper structural logic. For example, a Marxist critic might see the theme of female agency and self-actualization as an anachronistic residue, a simulacrum of bourgeois subjectivity that obscures the real erasure of the individual in late capitalist consumer culture. Alternatively, a feminist critic might choose to focus exclusively on the genre's presentation of an active and assertive female protagonist. She could argue, as some feminists have done, that theories about the dissolution of the self, the omnipresence of simulation, and the end of history are irrelevant to women's lives and are, indeed, contradicted by women's entry into the public realm. Women's experience, in other words, lies outside the temporal schema of the postmodern.

What is most striking about the money, sex, and power novel, however, is the interdependence and importance of both of its plots. It thus serves as a good example of the broader arguments about multileveled experiences of history and time that I make throughout this book. To dismiss history, agency, and self-development as obsolete ideas is to ignore the fact that such ideas continue to matter, and that they are being revitalized by social groups who have yet to participate fully in the heritage of modernity. Hence the trajectory of the Krantzian heroine, while clearly not a reflection of the lives of the vast majority of women, nevertheless points to important changes in female fantasy and representations of women in popular culture. Such ideological changes can in turn have important material consequences. Yet to focus only on positive images of women and affirm the value of female agency does not take us very far. Female identity is not an authentic ground or a solid foundation, but a fluctuating fiction that owes a great deal to the contemporary media and the society of the spectacle.

The money, sex, and power novel, then, alerts us to the coexistence of multiple temporalities and modes of the self. Here Judith Krantz cleverly anticipates a point made by Terry Eagleton:

> The bourgeois humanist subject is not in fact simply part of a clapped-out history we can all agreeably or reluctantly leave behind; if it is an increasingly inappropriate model at certain levels of subjecthood, it remains a potently relevant one at others. Consider, for example, the condition of being a father and a consumer simultaneously. The former role is governed by ideological imperatives of agency, duty, autonomy, authority, responsibility; the latter, while not wholly free of such strictures, puts them into significant question. . . . The subject of late capitalism, in other words, is neither simply the self-regulating synthetic agent posited by classical humanist ideology, nor merely a decentered network of desire, but a contradictory amalgam of the two.[26]

It is precisely this contradictory amalgam of temporalities and identities that shapes the money, sex, and power novel and that speaks in particular to the diverse and changing social roles of women.

This theme comes to the fore in the genre's interest in gender ambiguity. While a casual reading of the money, sex, and power novel might consider it a fictional rendition of the ideology of liberal feminism, the Krantzian heroine is not the ostensibly gender-neutral subject of classic liberalism. Rather, she is gendered in contradictory ways. This motif is repeated obsessively throughout the genre. Maxi, of *I'll Take Manhattan*, combines a "masculine, piratical swagger" with the feminine body of a "great courtesan of the Belle Epoque."[27] Billy Ikehorn's beauty is "almost virile," at the same time as she is a "female of rampant sexual vitality."[28] Jazz, in *Dazzle*, usually identified with "feminine, long-legged grace," at another point "could almost have passed for a young man."[29] Any notion of an innate gender identity is replaced by a sense of multiple and

JUDITH KRANTZ

shifting identifications with femaleness or maleness. In this regard, the narrator's description of Jazz as "a player of games, a mistress of disguises, a creature of many moods"[30] applies to all of Krantz's characters, for whom gender is a self-conscious performance rather than a natural attribute. The theme of transvestism, a recent concern of feminist theory, has defined the money, sex, and power novel since its inception. In this regard, Krantz's novels reveal some suggestive parallels to the theme of "fin de sexe, fin de siècle" that I explore in chapter 6.

Krantz's frequent descriptions of sexual encounters certainly do not conform to conventional gender scripts. In contrast to traditional women's genres, the money, sex, and power novel sanctions both sexual promiscuity and sexual explicitness, borrowing freely from the conventions and vocabulary of pornography. What is particularly striking about the Krantzian oeuvre is its openness to a wide range of fantasy scenarios. Women are alternatively dominating and submissive, sexual objects but also desiring and active subjects of the gaze. At certain points the author caters to a traditional female fantasy of being overwhelmed by a dominant male, exploring the masochistic pleasures of humiliation and submission. More frequent, however, are sexual scripts that depict a powerful woman subjugating and controlling a dependent or subservient male. These scripts draw on an extensive repertoire of sadomasochistic motifs and images. Furthermore, while heterosexual relations are the primary focus, there are occasional and equally detailed descriptions of sexual encounters between lesbians and between gay men. In this regard, Krantz's texts offer the closest approximation of polymorphous perversity yet to be found in mainstream popular fiction.

Unlike some cultural critics, however, Krantz is aware of the interconnections between sexual transgression and the logics of a consumer culture geared to the incitation of desire and the shock of the new. She does not idealize desire as a subversive force that wreaks havoc on the status quo, but firmly locates it in the lifestyles and attitudes of a specific sector of late-twentieth-century American culture. In this regard, while the money, sex, and power novel asserts women's right to guilt-free, hedonistic sex, it does so by robbing it of any ethical or psychological significance. Sex is transformed into a glamorous, commodified, lifestyle activity, a recreational pleasure and display of proficiency techniques on a rough par with regular workouts at the gym. Similarly, Krantz's exploration of the fluid and multivalent meanings of gender does not lose sight of the changing social and economic structures that make this fluidity possible. Her hyperbolic descriptions of the lifestyles of the rich and famous, while containing many fantasy elements, also provide some suggestive insights into the consumer culture that we all inhabit.

I hope, in conclusion, to have shown why I find the money, sex, and power novel to be an intriguing genre, as well as its surprising congruence with many current theoretical concerns. My tongue is at least partly in my cheek; I do not really think that Judith Krantz is a fan of Jean Baudrillard, or that most of her readers turn to her work because they are seeking clarification about postmodernism. My reading is idiosyncratic, not an attempt to sum up the political meanings and effects of this new genre. In fact, I am broadly sympathetic to an axiom of cultural studies: those who want to make pronouncements about the political effects of popular culture need to talk to actual readers, viewers, or fans rather than speculate on the basis of textual evidence.

Still, I do not agree that textual analysis should always defer to ethnography. This is to assume an overly simple distinction between the social sciences, which give us truth about the world, and literature and art, as second-order discourses, which do not. These distinctions are much less clear-cut than they used to be. If we are now more aware of the rhetorical and aesthetic aspects of ethnography and sociology, surely we can also concede that works of fiction may help to throw light on our social theories. Reading Krantz alongside theorists of postmodernism suggests the possibility of a mutual, rather than one-way, illumination.

Interestingly enough, Krantz is often singled out by literary critics as a particularly egregious example of the trashiness of popular culture. For example, Alberto Manguel writes, "A novel by Judith Krantz . . . locks itself into one exclusive airtight reading, and the reader cannot escape without knowingly exceeding the limits of common sense (there are few who read *Princess Daisy* as an allegory of the voyage of the soul)."[31] Indeed, hunting for "voyages of the soul" in Krantz might prove to be something of a stretch. But the parallels between Krantz's explorations of contemporary culture and postmodern theories are not far below the surface and do not require particularly ingenious acts of excavation. Her novels may not be quite as simple and simpleminded as Manguel suggests.

In fact, what is interesting about the money, sex, and power novel is its blurring of categories that some cultural critics want to keep separate. The feminine, rather than existing outside the social and public world, is explicitly situated at the heart of commodity culture. At the same time, a traditionally masculine script of ambition and achievement is re-created through the figure of woman. Modern themes, values, and plots are not separate from the culture of postmodernity; rather, the modern and postmodern continue to inflect and shape each other in complex ways. Thinking about multiple subject positions and coeval temporalities helps us make sense of contemporary women's culture. In this regard, a Judith Krantz novel provides a useful adjunct and corrective to the more sweeping pronouncements of contemporary theorists. It also provides, perhaps, a more enjoyable read on the plane.

## NOTES

This essay was first published in *Women: A Cultural Review* vol. 8, no. 2 (1997). Taylor & Francis Ltd., 11 New Fetter Lane, London EC4P 4EE.

1. Liesbet van Zoonen, *Feminist Media Studies* (London: Sage, 1984), 123.
2. Jorge Luis Borges, "Pierre Menard, Author of the *Quixote*," in *Labyrinths* (New York: New Directions, 1964); Fredric Jameson, *Postmodernism, or The Cultural Logic of Late Capitalism* (London: Verso, 1991).
3. Theodor Adorno and Max Horkheimer, "The Culture Industry: Enlightenment as Mass Deception," in *The Dialectic of Enlightenment* (London: Verso, 1979), 126.
4. Judith Krantz, *Scruples* (New York: Crown, 1978), 171.
5. Judith Krantz, *Scruples Two* (New York: Bantam, 1993), 228.
6. Krantz, *Scruples Two*, 234.
7. Krantz, *Scruples,* 260.
8. Krantz, *Scruples Two*, 87.
9. Rita Felski, *The Gender of Modernity* (Cambridge: Harvard University Press, 1995), chap. 3.
10. See Ien Ang, *Watching Dallas* (London: Methuen, 1985), 55.
11. Julie Burchill, *Ambition* (London: Corgi, 1989), 252–53.
12. Angela Carter, *Nothing Sacred* (London: Virago, 1992), 188.
13. Judith Krantz, *Dazzle* (New York: Bantam, 1992), 3.
14. Richard Dyer, "A Star Is Born and the Construction of Authenticity," in *Stardom: Industry of Desire*, ed. Christine Gledhill (London: Routledge, 1991).
15. Quoted in Joshua Gamson, *Claims to Fame: Celebrity in Contemporary America* (Berkeley: University of California Press, 1994), 10.
16. Joanne Finkelstein, *The Fashioned Self* (Cambridge: Polity Press, 1991).
17. Maria Angel and Zoe Sofia, "Cooking Up: Intestinal Economies and the Aesthetics of Specular Orality," *Cultural Studies* 10, 3 (1996).
18. Franco Moretti, *The Way of the World: The Bildungsroman in European Culture* (London: Verso, 1987), 130.
19. Burchill, *Ambition*, 15.
20. Margaret Marshment, "Substantial Women," in *The Female Gaze: Women as Viewers of Popular Culture*, ed. Lorraine Gamman and Margaret Marshment (London: Women's Press, 1988), 31.
21. Krantz, *Scruples*, 56.
22. Moretti, *The Way of the World*, 165.
23. Leo Braudy, *The Frenzy of Renown: Fame and History* (New York: Oxford University Press, 1986), 512.

24. Braudy, *The Frenzy of Renown*, 512.
25. Marshment, "Substantial Women," 31.
26. Terry Eagleton, "Capitalism, Modernism and Postmodernism," in *Against the Grain: Selected Essays* (London: Verso, 1986), 145.
27. Judith Krantz, *I'll Take Manhattan* (New York: Bantam, 1986), 9.
28. Krantz, *Scruples*, 8.
29. Krantz, *Dazzle*, 5.
30. Krantz, *Dazzle*, 6.
31. Alberto Manguel, *A History of Reading* (New York: Penguin, 1996), 92–93.

# 5

# THE DOXA OF DIFFERENCE

t is tempting, writes Rodolphe Gasché, to see the philosophical history of difference as revealing the progressive emancipation of difference from identity.[1] We are more and more likely to take this view. As Gasché notes, difference reigns supreme in critical thought. By contrast, equality and commonality hardly rate a mention, except as intellectual or political enemies to be vanquished and discarded on the scrapheap of history. Emblazoned on book covers, routinely invoked in intellectual debates, "difference" is an unassailable ideal, a value in itself. Difference has become doxa, a magical word of theory and politics that radiates redemptive meanings.

Feminism has its own version of this story of difference's triumph. The origins of feminism are usually attributed to such figures as Mary Wollstonecraft, who drew on Enlightenment ideals of reason and equality to challenge the subordination of women. Yet such ideals, it soon transpired, were not congenial friends of feminism, but masks for a phallocentric logic that sought to reduce difference to sameness. The universal values of the Enlightenment could recognize the rights and freedoms of others only by assimilating them to male-defined norms. Second-wave feminists sought instead to reclaim the feminine; women's path to freedom lay in affirming their irreducible differences rather than in pursuing equality with men. This woman-centered vision has now lost much of its charge, thanks to the impact of poststructuralism as well as the stringent criticisms of its blindness to material and cultural differences among women. As a result, the story goes, we now find ourselves in a postmodern condition, where female difference has fragmented into multiple differences and any appeal to universal ideals or norms is politically questionable and theoretically naive.

This story has been told often and in different tones of voice. For some it is a narrative of progress, as feminism gradually sheds its attachment to old-fashioned forms of essentialism and universalism and achieves a more sophisticated stage of consciousness. For others it is a narrative of the fall, as feminism is lured from its goal of representing and struggling for all women by internecine squabbles and the prestige of French avant-garde thought. Many feminist scholars are familiar with this story; we may encounter it in scholarly articles, reproduce it in our classes, echo it in our own academic writing. Indeed, it contains a grain of truth, at least as a description of the recent trajectory of mainstream feminist theory in the humanities.

I want, however, to qualify the view of feminism's ascent to the dizzying heights of difference. This unilinear plot does not leave room for thinking about the coexistence and interdependence of different frameworks. Like all grand narratives, moreover, it confuses the internal logic of particular intellectual debates with the condition of the world as a whole. The political interests and needs of women do not always move neatly in step with the various phases of academic feminist theory.

Of course, no doxa is endorsed by everyone, and there have been various challenges to difference within contemporary feminism. Already in 1986, in an article ably summarized by its title, "The Instability of the Analytical Categories of Feminist Theory," Sandra Harding warned against grounding feminism in a single political-philosophical idea, arguing that Enlightenment ideas, gynocentric politics, and postmodern critiques of identity are all woven into the complex fabric of contemporary feminism. "We should learn how," writes Harding, "to regard the instabilities themselves as valuable resources."[2] Chela Sandoval has also criticized taxonomies of feminism as a series of developmental stages, arguing for a "tactical subjectivity" that can deploy different forms of politics according to context.[3] In addition, as I show in more detail below, some postcolonial theorists are challenging the current vogue of difference in Western feminism.

Not much attention has been paid, however, to thinking through the *philosophical* inconsistencies as well as political problems of trying to ground feminism in difference. Indeed, for the most part, the conceptual primacy of difference remains uncontested. Feminist scholars may question particular images of difference for objectifying or exoticizing others. However, the force of this critique usually relies on the belief that there are real, genuine differences that are obscured by this false representation. One of the aims of this chapter is to rethink alterity as the supreme goal of feminist theory and politics. I do not seek to do away with difference but simply to question the belief that it is the ultimate explanation of how things really are. Instead, I offer a description of equality and difference that is pragmatic rather than ontological, that asks what work these concepts can do rather than whether they are true. But my point is not simply that equality and difference are distinct but equally valid choices within feminism, as Ann Snitow has argued.[4] Rather, I want to show that they are philosophically and politically interdependent. The pursuit of difference thus returns us inexorably to seemingly obsolete issues of equality and commonality.[5]

## SEXUAL DIFFERENCE: THE SUPREME DIFFERENCE?

As Michèle Barrett points out, difference has several, not always compatible meanings in feminist theory.[6] Most commonly, it refers to the difference between women and men, whether this difference is attributed to biological, psychological, or social causes. Second, it points to the differences *between* women as shaped by class, race, sexual preference, age, and so on. This second definition is often used to challenge the claims made in the name of the first: the experiential diversity of real women does not allow us to hazard a general definition of female difference. Third, feminist critics have drawn on Derrida's notion of *différance*, of meaning as both differing and deferred, to talk about the unstable and ambiguous nature of language as linked to the feminine. Finally, psychoanalytical feminists, particularly those indebted to Lacan, refer to sexual difference as an inescapable but unstable division that shapes our psyches and our entry into language.

In this chapter I look at two influential currents in feminist theory: psychoanalytic theories of sexual difference in feminist philosophy and analyses of the cultural and material differences between women in postcolonial studies. These two fields exemplify some of the most sophisticated recent feminist scholarship. They recognize the problems of trying to define women's difference in universal terms. They want, though in dissimilar ways, to radicalize and complicate the notion of difference. Looking at these two areas of inquiry thus provides a good starting point from which to explore the ramifications of alterity, heterogeneity, difference, and the like in feminist thought.

Sexual difference theory first came to the fore in the United States in the late 1970s through the writings of the so-called French feminists (Hélène Cixous, Luce Irigaray, Julia Kristeva). This work helped to inspire a sea change in feminist thought by drawing attention to the primary and far-reaching role of language in shaping our notions of masculine and feminine. It was also criticized in some quarters for essentialist, idealist, and Eurocentric tendencies.[7] At the present time, we are witnessing the emergence of what we might call a "second generation" of sexual difference theorists writing in Europe, Australia, and the United States, including such well-known scholars as Rosi Braidotti and Drucilla Cornell.

For the most part, these writers are more conscious than their predecessors of the pitfalls involved in theorizing the category of woman. As a result, while they want to retain sexual difference as a foundational concept, they also seek to empty it of any substantive or normative content. The goal is to affirm the feminine and women's difference without making any general claims about the nature of female bodies or female psyches. I want to begin by weighing the theoretical as well as political implications of recent theories of sexual difference. My concern here is specifically with feminist philosophy; the related but distinct issue of poststructuralism's influence on feminist aesthetic theory is explored in chapter 8. As much of the prestige of this writing derives from its affiliations with "high theory," we need to consider whether its deployment of poststructuralist ideas is in fact theoretically cogent.

Rosi Braidotti, for example, voices the guiding questions of feminist philosophy as follows: "Can we formulate otherness, difference without devaluing it? Can we think of the other not as other-than, but as a positively other entity?"[8] Braidotti, like her colleagues, prefers the term "sexual difference" to "gender." Gender is tied to a sociological view of male and female as externally imposed "roles" that could eventually disappear in some imagined androgynous future. Sexual difference feminists, by contrast, focus on the semiotic and the psychic, stressing the structural centrality of sexual division to the formation of human psyches and human cultures. They agree with Lacan that the definition and content of what it means to be male or female differ across cultures, but that the primary division between male and female is universal and inescapable, if also unstable.

Of course, the two sides of this division do not carry equal weight. Rather, the symbolic order is predicated on the sovereignty of the phallus and the absence of

THE DOXA OF DIFFERENCE

the feminine except as a phantasm of male desire. Braidotti, for example, agrees with Irigaray that women's real difference, their radical otherness, is unrepresentable within existing cultural systems. "Woman as the other remains in excess of or outside the phallogocentric framework."[9] The goal of feminism is thus not to deny difference—which would merely endorse the logic of phallocentrism as male-defined sameness—but to recover the feminine within sexual difference, to generate an autonomous female imaginary beyond existing stereotypes of woman. For Braidotti, difference simply is the grounding concept of feminist theory. She writes, "the problem is also how to free 'woman' from the subjugated position of 'annexed other', so as to make her expressive of a different difference, of *pure difference*, of an entirely new plane of becoming, out of which differences can multiply and differ from each other" (my emphasis).[10]

The recent work of Drucilla Cornell explores these questions of sexual difference in great detail. Cornell, like Braidotti, acknowledges her debt to Lacan and Derrida, whom she regards as potential allies of feminism in their critique of phallocentrism. This affiliation renders Cornell suspicious of any reference to female essences or universals. She devotes considerable time and effort to refuting the arguments of the feminist legal theorists Robin West and Catharine MacKinnon, whose vision of a unitary female destiny she explicitly rejects. Yet Cornell, like Braidotti, is wary of a slippage between women and the feminine in the writings of Derrida and other writers. When woman is reduced to a metaphor, then the feminine becomes a position in language available to either sex. If the feminine is a figure of speech, however, it is one with which women have a particularly urgent affiliation.

Feminism thus finds itself caught between the quagmire of essentialism, the risky attempt to discover features common to all women, and the abyss of a linguistic idealism, where women vanish into the thin air of textuality. How can we avoid either essentializing women or dematerializing them? The solution proposed by Braidotti and Cornell can best be described as a formal theory of sexual difference; it affirms the importance and value of the feminine while refusing to give it any substantive content. This refusal is a deliberate attempt to circumvent a will to truth that is seen as phallocentric. Feminism will refuse to define what it means to be a woman. Rather, the feminine simply is that which resists definition, which cannot be limited, which embodies multiplicity and otherness. It is not to be equated with the false femininity of current gender stereotypes but is a utopian gesturing toward an alternative imaginary beyond the constraints of patriarchal thought. "Feminism," writes Cornell, "demands nothing less than the unleashing of the feminine imaginary—an imaginary made possible, paradoxically, by the lack of grounding of the feminine in any of the identifications we know and imagine as Woman."[11]

The value of such a position, according to Cornell, is that it allows feminism to affirm the feminine without the need for essentialist or naturalist descriptions of woman.[12] A psycholinguistic model of sexual difference, in its emphasis on structural relations rather than essences, can accommodate the complex differences of race, class, sexuality, and culture among women. Thus, by refusing to give any specific content to the feminine, the feminist philosopher hopes to avoid the charge of ethnocentrism. Such a framework can include all rather than only some women. Feminine difference exists outside the binary structures of patriarchal thought, including, paradoxically, the very distinction between masculine and feminine. It is not part of the already thought, but a principle of opposition to it. The feminine simply *is* the sign of heterogeneity, the ultimate sign of difference.

I remain troubled, however, by some contradictions in this nonprogrammatic feminist program. For example, the appeal to an autonomous vision of the feminine seems incompatible with the poststructuralist ideas on which theorists of sexual difference rely. Within such a framework, there can be no possible rupture between an existing male symbolic and a future female imaginary. This is because we can recognize irreducible otherness only in relation to norms and traditions that allow us to perceive this singularity *as* other.[13] Difference *always* involves comparison. Thus Braidotti's wish to conceptualize difference not as "other than" but as "positively other" collides with the most basic premise of poststructuralist thought. This is the belief that the sign has no inherent, positive meaning but exists only through its differential relationship to other signs. The feminine cannot exist outside the masculine because the terms are thoroughly implicated and interdependent.

Another way of phrasing the objection is to ask, how can we ever know for sure whether a particular idea, metaphor, or form of discourse is phallocentric or feminine? What criteria would allow us to decide? (Female authorship alone, clearly, does not suffice.) And how could this expression of feminine difference remain feminine, given the iterability of the sign, its ability to be quoted, repeated, and retrospectively assigned very different meanings in an infinite array of contexts? In other words, it is hard to see how a utopian vision of feminine otherness can be reconciled with a model of language that defines meaning as fundamentally relational, unstable, and impure.

Thus sexual difference theory, at least in its philosophical manifestation, often tends toward absolute distinctions. Either women aspire to a radically other world beyond what already exists or we remain imprisoned forever in the iron cage of phallocentric culture. This dichotomy follows from its reliance on Lacanian premises (although orthodox Lacanians do not believe that we can ever escape the iron cage). Yet this Lacanian view of history and culture as

THE DOXA OF DIFFERENCE

essentially phallocentric is too global for the kind of work feminist scholarship needs to do. It collapses important distinctions and reduces crucial differences to ever present sameness.[14] Were all the women in history—the artists, the revolutionaries, the mothers, the teachers—really nothing more than passive vehicles of phallocentrism?

If not, then feminism needs a more supple framework to grapple with women's specific and complicated relations to particular forms of power. And if this is indeed the case, as Cornell sometimes implies in her account of culture as an exclusively male creation, why should contemporary feminists be able to free ourselves from the relentless grip of phallocentric thought when all previous women in history have failed? If, as Braidotti claims, women's difference has been "unrepresentable" during the long history of phallologocentrism, why should things be suddenly different now? What epistemological break renders contemporary accounts of the feminine so much more authentic than those produced by all the women of past millennia?

There seems to be an important connection between the sweepingly negative view of past history in feminist sexual difference theory and its vision of a radically other future. Cornell's championing of feminine difference is passionately and avowedly utopian, yet there are reasons utopianism has lost much of its luster in recent years. The founding premise of utopian thought is a modern ideal of self-invention, the birth of the absolutely new that will follow the moment of rupture from the alienated and inauthentic past. A similar vision motivates Braidotti, who claims at one moment that we inhabit the postmodern (usually equated with the questioning of the new), yet in the next moment equates the feminist project with radical rupture and the absolute value of the new. "Where can this new theoretical and political creativity be founded? What does 'the new' come from? What paradigms can assist us in the elaboration of new schemes?"[15]

A utopian mentality, suggests Nancy Fraser, can lead to a devaluation of existing political struggles and a preference for the gesture of grand refusal.[16] An opposition between (feminine) revolution and (male-defined) reformism often appears in the work of sexual difference theorists, yet the framing of politics in such starkly antithetical terms has lost much of its force in recent times.[17] This feminist ideal of self-creation *ex nihilo* is another instance of an argument strangely at odds with the poststructuralist ideas on which it draws, most obviously the deconstructive critique of origins. Politics, surely, relies on a much more messy amalgam of identifications, partial self-recognitions, and critical refusals, as social groups negotiate their ambivalent relations to the representations that define them. Women both are and are not "women." A vision of the feminine as pure otherness cannot speak to this mélange of tradition and innovation, recuperation and re-creation, borrowing from the past and imagining the future, that shapes feminist practice.

Furthermore, seizing hold of difference as the defining feature of the feminine often leads to the reverse claim: that the feminine is the exemplary sign of alterity. Cornell, for example, claims that "the 'feminine' is not celebrated just because it is the feminine, but because it stands in for the heterogeneity that undermines the logic of identity purportedly established by phallologocentrism."[18] In other words, even as sexual difference theorists try to evacuate the feminine of any specific content, they continue to assume the primacy and priority of the male/female divide. The feminine becomes the fundamental mark of difference, standing in for all the other possible forms of diversity. Thus Braidotti refers to the difference between men and women as the prototype of all differences, describing feminism as *the* discourse of modernity.[19] She stresses the importance of paying attention to racial and cultural differences among women, but only in relation to the foundational reality of sexual difference. "Meditation on the 'differences' among women" becomes a means to "enact and implement sexual difference"; conversely, sexual difference offers "positive foundational grounds for the redefinition of female subjectivity in all of its complexity."[20]

Yet it is hard to see how feminists can make such claims without reinstating feminism as a "master discourse," a framework that subsumes all others even as it claims to recognize their independent existence. As has often been pointed out, only some women can afford to see sexual difference as primary, usually because their own race, class or sexuality is unmarked and hence invisible.[21] Some sexual difference theorists recognize the force of such objections and have made an effort to bring discussions of race into their work. Cornell, for example, offers a reading of *Beloved* as a rewriting of *Medea,* arguing that the novel dramatizes the very difference of African American motherhood.[22] Yet it is a moot point whether Lacanian theory can help us understand fully the multicausal politics of race. In continuing to identify power with the phallus and subversion with the feminine, Lacanian feminism upholds the fiction that power is an exclusively masculine phenomenon and does not help us think about how women actively support class and race divisions. In assimilating all forms of difference to an idealized vision of the feminine, it does not face up to the many tensions and conflicts between particular axes of difference.

Furthermore, while theorists of sexual difference insist on the fissures and contradictions within femininity, their focus on language means that they often overestimate the reach of phallic power. Masculinity is hardly unified; men of specific classes, races, and sexualities have very different relations to the male ideal. While the transcendental signifier—God, the king, the priest, the judge, the guru, the teacher—is coded masculine, this does not mean that all males are suffused with transcendental authority. For example, while women of color have challenged the sexism within their own communities, they are less likely to see masculinity as the enemy or to assume an automatic connection between men and cultural power. Similarly, some lesbians, particularly since the AIDS crisis and the advent of queer theory, see their affiliation with gay men as equal to or more important than their kinship with heterosexual feminists. Women may have perfectly cogent reasons for choosing to identify with men. Because theorists of sexual difference assume the primary importance of the male-female distinction, which is only subsequently filled in by the details of class, race, sexuality, and so on, they cannot account for women choosing to ally with men as well as, or instead of, with other women except in terms of false consciousness or its equivalent.

## DIFFERENCE AS DISSENSION: POSTCOLONIAL FEMINISM

Sexual difference feminism, I suggest, results in an impasse. Either scholars give feminine difference a specific definition and risk charges of essentialism, or they celebrate the feminine as a general principle of difference, thereby robbing it of any meaningful content and creating what Laura Donaldson dubs "the woman without qualities."[23] At this point I would like to turn to a discussion of feminist perspectives in postcolonial theory to see what alternative positions emerge. What other ways are there of talking about difference?

I am aware that "postcolonial feminism" is a contested term that is not unequivocally endorsed by all the writers I discuss.[24] I understand postcolonial as a description of countries recently liberated from colonial rule, and postcolonial theory as concerned with the economic, social, and cultural conditions of such countries, often viewed in a broader global context. Even within these specific parameters, however, scholars have objected to the term for erasing important differences between specific nations (for example, India and Australia), for glossing over racial differences and inequalities within these nations (Australia may be postcolonial to white settlers, but not to indigenous peoples), and for implying a clear-cut transition to a postcolonial condition that ignores continuing Western influence in the cultural and economic, if not the political, realm.[25] Furthermore, the current visibility of postcolonial studies has given rise to suspicions about the ease with which displays of alterity can be marketed in Western institutions.[26] Clearly, postcolonial does not function as a neutral label, but carves out an intellectual field that includes certain objects and excludes others.

Like any contested term, then, it can serve only as a starting point, rather than an endpoint, for inquiry. My main concern, however, is less with the ultimate accuracy of "postcolonial" as a description of current realities than with considering how the field of postcolonial feminism helps to clarify the value and limits of difference. In one important sense, difference is magnified. Racial, ethnic, and cultural diversity cut across female difference and fragment its coherence as a category. Criticizing the clichés of the third world woman propagated by Western feminism, postcolonial feminists insist on attending to the specific and heterogeneous lives of the majority of the world's women.

For example, Chandra Mohanty's influential article "Under Western Eyes" examines how feminist theories of women's oppression combine with a Euro-American conception of the third world to produce the composite image of the "Third World Woman." This woman is depicted as sexually repressed, tradition-bound, and uneducated, in contrast to the educated, modern, autonomous, first world feminist. The third world woman thus becomes the ultimate proof of the universal nature of patriarchy and female bondage. She is depicted as same, part of a putative global sisterhood, yet mysteriously other, an exotic and enigmatic figure.[27]

Mohanty assails this still prevalent stereotype, arguing for careful and context-specific analyses of how women are constituted as a group within particular locations. Attention to the interweaving of gender with ethnicity, class, religion, and other factors will inevitably weaken the force of Western feminist stories of male power and female powerlessness. In this sense, postcolonial feminist theory calls into question Western feminist notions of difference by arguing that they obscure many other important differences. Feminism needs to pay more attention to difference, not less.

Yet the place of difference in postcolonial feminism is more complicated than this suggests. In "Under Western Eyes" Mohanty's emphasis on the specific and the local seems to indicate skepticism about the value of large-scale social theory. In another context, however, Mohanty insists on a broad view and the need for cross-national and cross-cultural analyses that can clarify the socioeconomic and ideological systems within which women of the third world are enmeshed.[28] Here she wants to retain the category of the "Third World Woman," not as a natural identity, but as a way of enabling coalitions among diverse groups of women through the creation of "imagined communities." Thus an emphasis on the particular is qualified by a turn to systematic analysis of global disparities. In a similar vein, Gayatri Spivak warns of the limits of microanalyses that remain oblivious to "the broader narratives of imperialism," while Rey Chow chafes at the current fetish of cultural, local, and ethnic difference, suggesting that difference cannot be understood outside broader structures of communication and domination.[29]

This suspicion of a Western feminist politics of difference is voiced with particular force and clarity in a recent article by Ien Ang. "As a woman of Chinese descent," Ang writes, "I suddenly find myself in a position in which I can turn my 'difference' into intellectual and political capital, where 'white' feminists invite me to raise my 'voice,' *qua* a non-white woman, and make myself heard."[30] The politics of assimilation, as Ang notes, has given way to that of multiculturalism. Yet this seemingly benevolent attention to multiple voices is much less laudatory than it seems. Rather, white feminism appropriates difference in an unthinking, often imperialist fashion. "Difference is 'dealt with' by absorbing it into an already existing feminist community without challenging the naturalised legitimacy and status of that community *as* a community."[31]

Ang thus questions the happy celebration of differences among women by drawing attention to the real, often profound gulf that separates them. This is, in her phrase, "the tension between difference as benign diversity and difference as conflict, disruption, dissension."[32] While visions of common female experience have become untenable in feminism, the turn toward a politics of diversity is no solution if it does not face up to the inequalities among women in access to power, knowledge, and material resources. For Ang, such inequalities arise from the structure of white, Western hegemony, which she defines as "the systemic consequence of a global historical development over the last 500 years— the expansion of European capitalist modernity throughout the world, resulting in the subsumption of all 'other' peoples to its economic, political and ideological logic and mode of operation."[33]

These and similar arguments in postcolonial feminism underscore the connections between difference, hierarchy, and inequality. Difference, for the most part, is still linked to the experience of suffering, exploitation, and pain. Against Braidotti's attempt to recast difference as "positively other," they insist on the continuing relevance of difference as "other than." Acts of comparison are crucial in making visible the pervasive inequalities of money, power and access to material resources.

To make such comparisons, furthermore, is to believe in the possibility of systematic analysis and normative critique. It is to assume that we do not just have a postmodern plurality of viewpoints, but that some perspectives are better than others in making sense of structural patterns of inequality. If epistemological norms cannot easily be abandoned, neither can ethical ones. Thus the diagnosis of inequality assumes a norm of equality that is found to be lacking. In this sense, equality is not simply a phallocentric or imperialist concept but, rather, an indispensable term for analyzing the pathologies of patriarchy and imperialism.

In this respect, the field of postcolonial feminism reveals an ongoing tension between the particular and the general, between the "thick description" of cultural practices that remains faithful to how particular individuals see themselves, and the "big picture" of transnational structures of inequality that requires a more distanced perspective. Moreover, much of this work refuses to separate gender from other social determinants, including the distinct if overlapping axes of race and class, and frequently looks at questions of difference in material and institutional as well as linguistic and cultural terms.[34] Both of these ideas strike me as indispensable to any adequate feminist account of difference.

At the same time, the postcolonial analysis of inequality is often combined with a deconstructive critique of identity. Here again, the power of difference is qualified. Postcolonial theorists are likely to note that nativist visions of racial or cultural difference do not make much sense in an era of pervasive migration, media globalization, and transnational information flow. The insurgent voices of the colonized are shaped by the experience of colonization; the colonizer's culture is irrevocably altered by contact with the native. As a result, a view of distinct, singular, and homogeneous groupings gives way to a model of *métissage*, of borrowing and lending across porous cultural boundaries.

These ideas of hybridity, creolization, and *métissage* have inspired some controversy with postcolonial studies but strike me as the most viable alternative to the doxa of difference. For example, Robert Young claims that hybridity is compromised by its links to nineteenth-century racist genetics and the assumptions of compulsory heterosexuality. Yet, as Young recognizes, the power of hybridity as an idea lies in embracing the logic of both/and. "Hybridity thus makes difference into sameness, and sameness into difference, but in a way that makes the same no longer the same, the different no longer simply different," thereby engendering "difference and sameness in an apparently impossible simultaneity."[35]

This reformulation strikes me as crucially important. Metaphors of hybridity and the like not only recognize differences *within* the individual subject, fracturing and complicating holistic notions of identity, but also look at connections *between* subjects by recognizing affiliations and repetitions. For example, Susan Stanford Friedman has recently made a detailed and compelling case for hybridity and syncretism as a way of working through certain dilemmas and deadends in feminist theory.[36] Difference is no longer the master trope. Rather than encouraging an ever greater atomization of identity, we can explore the many strands of affiliation as well as differentiation among individuals, groups, and cultures. Affiliation, I would stress, does not prevent disagreement but rather makes it possible. It is only in the context of shared premises, beliefs, and vocabularies that dissent becomes possible.

For this reason, while I am in sympathy with most of Ang's argument, I am not persuaded by her recourse to incommensurability to describe the relations between women of different races. This claim arises out of Ang's discussion of conflicting interpretations of Madonna as an example of the gulf that separates white women from women of color. Ang claims that most white feminists view Madonna in a positive light, whereas black writers such as bell hooks are critical of the racial ideologies that shape such media images of idealized whiteness. Ang comments, "What we see exemplified here is a fundamental incommensurability between two competing feminist knowledges, dramatically exposing an irreparable chasm between a white and a black feminist truth. No harmonious compromise or negotiated consensus is possible here."[37]

Ang's own example, however, surely does not warrant such a strong conclusion. Both black and white feminist readings of Madonna draw on overlapping political vocabularies and conceptual frameworks that allow them to use terms such as *identity* or *oppression*. Furthermore, they both partake of the historically specific "language game" of cultural studies in interpreting a media phenomenon such as Madonna in a broader cultural framework. At the same time, differing political locations may result in a disagreement about the subversive impact of this particular cultural icon.[38] What we see here is a complex entanglement of shared assumptions and differing assumptions, not a clash of incommensurable discursive universes.

Furthermore, it is precisely this entanglement that makes criticism possible, that allows hooks to point out the contradictions between feminism's claim to represent all women and its actual race blindness. It also means that white feminists can in principle learn from this criticism and analyze Madonna in terms of racial as well as sexual politics.[39] Incommensurability, by contrast, does not allow for disagreement, critique, or persuasion because there are no common terms that would allow one argument to latch onto and address another. Incommensurability means untranslatability. Furthermore, the recourse to incommensurability *works both ways*. If the knowledges of white women and women of color are incommensurable, this does not simply justify the latter's refusal to have their concerns subsumed within white Western feminism. It also means that such concerns are by definition inaccessible to white women, who are thereby relieved of any need to engage with them. Thus, an actual incommensurability between the positions of women of different races would deny the very point of Ang's argument, making it incomprehensible to those very readers to whom it is addressed.

I read Ang's argument as a strategic move in a specific debate, a provocation intended to startle white Western feminists out of arrogant assumptions about who constitutes the subject of feminism. However, while I agree that "idealized unity" is no longer an option for feminism, the turn toward incommensurability strikes me as counterproductive, both conceptually tenuous and politically defeatist. Conceptually tenuous because the notion of incommensurable or untranslatable worlds does not address the actual overlappings of vocabularies, frameworks, and assumptions. Politically defeatist because it seems to rule out, in advance, any possibility of one discourse acting on and influencing another. Yet how else, one wonders, is politics possible?

Of course Ang is right to point out that the vast material and cultural divisions between women cannot be overcome by mere fiat or good intention. Yet her statement that "We might do better to start from point zero and realise that there are moments at which no common ground exists whatsoever, and when any communicative event would be nothing more than a speaking past one another" seems to offer only the alternative of silence and separatism.[40] It is hard to see how such an *a priori* belief in the impossibility of communication can be squared with Ang's own careful critique of Western feminism. After all, why bother with such a critique if your audience is incapable of understanding you?

At the same time, Ang is obviously right to insist that cultural interchange does not take place on an equal footing, that borrowing and citation are framed by asymmetrical grids of power. In this context, explorations of hybridity have been criticized for effacing material conflicts between the colonizer and the colonized and denying the agency of the oppressed.[41] This criticism may have some force when directed at those writers who discuss hybridity in purely linguistic terms, but it does not strike me as generally true. To recognize the leakages and interconnections between cultures does not require us to deny inequality. Nor should hybridity be seen as synonymous with celebrating cultural fragmentation and geographical displacement. Such experiences of dislocation may be appealing to the jet-setting Western intellectual but may be viewed very differently by those who are torn from their homes as refugees or guest workers.

For example, Rosi Braidotti develops at length her vision of the nomadic subject as a realization of postmodern and feminist themes. Yet, as she also recognizes, images of the nomad in contemporary theory can be harshly insensitive to the very different economic and social conditions under which people travel. The point, in my mind, is not to idealize nomadism and hybridity as a new source of political value (the more hybrid you are, the better). It is simply to admit that cultural impurity is the backdrop of *all* contemporary struggles—including struggles for self-determination and cultural autonomy—in a global context of voluntary and involuntary cultural interchange.

In other words, hybridity means coming to terms with the fact that the oppressed cannot free themselves of all taints of the oppressor's culture and that a pursuit of absolute difference is thus untenable. For example, as I showed in chapter 2, recent postcolonial theory is interested in the translation of influences and ideas into local contexts. Rather than simply dismissing certain ideas—modernity, universality, progress, and the like—as vehicles of an imperialist agenda, it looks at how these ideas are actually used. The complex intermingling of indigenous traditions and external influences means that discourses once linked to the colonizer may acquire very different meanings when adopted by the colonized to challenge their own condition. Such a pragmatic concern with the use of particular ideas strikes me as a more viable—and more hopeful—basis for politics than a striving for radical otherness.

## RETHINKING DIFFERENCE

I want, finally, to explore in more detail the contradictory and impure status of difference as a philosophical category and to show its necessary dependence on the norms and ideals it tries to negate. First, as Joan Scott points out, the common opposition in feminist thought between equality and difference is in fact a false antithesis.[42] The opposite of equality is not difference but rather inequality, a principle to which presumably no feminist would subscribe. Similarly, the opposite of difference is not equality but identity. Thus a difference-based feminism refuses a logic of identity that would subsume women within male-defined norms. It does not, however, reject equality but argues for an expanded understanding of equality that can also respect difference. Cornell helpfully refers us to Amartya Sen's notion of equivalence as a way of conceptualizing this vision of "equal differences": "'Equivalence' means of equal value, but not of equal value *because of likeness*."[43]

In other words, affirming difference involves a tacit appeal to equality, if it is not to result in a mere endorsement of current inequality. "Equivalence" means paying attention to the irreducible particularity of certain forms of experience but also making a general argument about why these forms of experience deserve to be treated fairly and with respect. Hence it does not make sense to oppose Enlightenment ideals of equality to incommensurability and difference. Rather, the very critique of such ideals as lacking presumes, even if only implicitly, a more adequate vision of equality that is genuinely open to diversity.

Similarly, to defend the value of difference and specificity is to call up some universal maxim, such as the rule that "all differences should be treated with respect." It is soon clear, however, that this minimal norm does not get us very far. What differences are we talking about? Those of gender, race, class, sexuality, education, age, intelligence, opinion, politics, lifestyle? Are all these differences equal? Can they all be given equal amounts of respect? For example, can the Ku Klux Klan's desire to express its political differences from mainstream values be reconciled with the desires of specific racial groups to have their own cultural differences respected? The appeal to difference, it soon becomes clear, does not lead us out of the labyrinth of norms, values, and truth claims, but takes us into its very heart.

There are two distinct issues that come to the fore in recent defenses of difference. First, there is a claim for the *significance* of a difference, and second, there is a claim for its *value*. In this sense, as Charles Taylor points out, affirming difference does not involve a total departure from shared norms. Rather, it means making a case for the value of a particular difference by appealing to a shared horizon of meaning. There are infinite examples of differences among the people in the world. Identifying certain kinds of difference (gender, class, race, sexual preference) as more important than others (shoe size, ability to sing in tune) means appealing to intersubjective norms. "Defining myself means finding what is significant in my difference from others."[44] Of course, we cannot predict in advance which differences will matter; the social movements of the last twenty years have been precisely about expanding the criteria for "significant difference." In the future, no doubt, these criteria will shift again. But asserting a difference always involves showing why this specific difference matters in the broader scheme of things. It means putting difference in a framework.

The second issue refers to the *value* of particular forms of difference. Certain axes of differentiation may be important without anyone wanting to preserve them. One example might be the difference of severe poverty or starvation. Alternatively, someone who is sympathetic to diversity may nevertheless balk at celebrating the "difference" of the racist or misogynist. Contemporary affirmations of difference often assume, in an oddly naive way, that all differences are necessarily benevolent and hence deserving of recognition. Yet this is clearly not the case. Difference cannot be a value in itself, not only because some differences are inconsequential and uninteresting, as Taylor notes, but also because specific forms of differences may be harmful to the freedom of others. To argue for openness to diversity thus does not do away with but rather exacerbates the problem of formulating values and norms that can mediate between the claims of competing forms of difference. Such "contingent foundations" are inescapable, yet subject to ongoing revision; their status is rhetorical rather than ontological.[45]

In a similar vein, Steven Connor points out that appeals to difference and incommensurability within poststructuralist theory always refer back to norms, values, and universalizable assumptions.[46] The recourse to absolute alterity is incoherent. Equality and difference, identity and otherness, universality and particularity always bleed into each other. Much poststructuralist thought relies on a surface/depth opposition; the discourse of equality is seen as an illusory veil concealing the hidden "truth" of difference. Yet difference is not a foundation but a relation; it is not an inherent property of things or people but a distinction engendered by a particular framework. It is possible to take any two randomly chosen objects in the world and find criteria that will reveal them to be

THE DOXA OF DIFFERENCE

either similar or different. In other words, there is no reality-in-itself that can *prove* difference or similarity once and for all. To affirm a commonality with others or to assert a difference from others is to engage in a rhetorical and political act. It is only in these contingent terms that the value of such statements can be assessed.

One possible objection to my argument is that it continues to rely on oppositions between universality and particularity, sameness and difference instead of going beyond binary categories and dualistic thought. While contemporary scholars often use this reproach to disarm their opponents, its logic is dubious. Specifically, it relies on a misreading of deconstruction, which recognizes by contrast that dualism cannot be overcome, but at best displaced.[47] It also relies on a certain reading (or as Gasché would say, misreading) of Hegel, in which dialectical opposition always leads to difference being subsumed and canceled out by identity.

Yet feminist attempts to overcome philosophical dualism, as exemplified in sexual difference theory, have been spectacularly unsuccessful. In some instances they lead to dualism being replaced by monism; difference alone becomes the new foundational category of feminist thought. It is hard to see how making sense of the world through one concept instead of two constitutes progress. Alternatively, dualism is rejected only to be reproduced at a more abstract level. Hence the male-female distinction is decried as an instance of bad, binary, phallocentric thinking, but this very argument in turn sets up a new binary opposition between phallocentric and feminine thought.

In my view, feminists should stop worrying so much about trying to overcome dualistic thinking (for a discussion of the problem of trying to "overcome" anything, see chapter 6). Instead, we can think of dualism as an oscillation and productive conflict between distinct terms that is not resolved through a harmonious synthesis. I have tried to approach the equality/difference distinction in this light. Furthermore, I have questioned the assumption that feminism should be tied to either one of these terms, pointing out that particular groups of women may ally themselves variously, and indeed simultaneously, to both of them.

Thus a *deconstructive* reading of the equality/difference distinction links up with a *pragmatic* assessment of the political stakes of appealing to either term in specific times and places. For example, the reasons for the current feminist focus on difference might include the unprecedented move of women into traditionally male institutional structures, with a consequent collision of vocabularies, experiences, and forms of life; the impact of poststructuralism on intellectual work in the humanities; and the sustained critique of mainstream feminism for its lack of attention to race, class, and sexuality.

At the same time, the status of difference as a guiding concept is contested even, or rather especially, by those women who are defined as "different" from mainstream white feminism. Many women are unlikely to dismiss equality as passé, given the continuing and vast disparities in the global distribution of power and resources. As Chow notes, the recent feminist interest in female otherness derives from the specific material and ideological conditions of Western feminism and cannot be carelessly generalized.[48] The political meanings of appeals to difference differ, just as the meanings accruing to the struggle for equality are not always equal.

In this context, I want to conclude by noting that categories often invoked disparagingly by feminist theorists—equality, reason, history, modernity—are not stable, uniform entities. The meanings and political uses of such ideas vary dramatically. It is here that much of feminist poststructuralist philosophy, with its sweeping vision of the *longue durée* of Western history as a history of phallocentrism, reveals its limitations. Rather than postmodern, it often strikes me as profoundly antimodern. In chapter 2, I surveyed the new approaches to modernity, which explicitly refute the view that women, or any other disenfranchised group, can embody absolute difference or otherness. Rather, in addressing the position of women in both the past and the present, feminists might do better to think in terms of "difference within sameness" and "sameness within difference." The *interference* with the purity of such categories can be enormously productive in challenging conventional frameworks and definitions. By contrast, the resort to eternal incommensurability and otherness simply assigns women to the ghetto of difference and hence leaves the realm of sameness untouched.

## NOTES

This chapter was originally published in *Signs* and was aided by a University of Virginia summer grant. I would like to thank my *Signs* readers and Farzaneh Milani for their help in drafting the original version. I have revised and briefly expanded my original arguments. *Signs* also published responses from Rosi Braidotti, Drucilla Cornell, and Ien Ang, who expressed varying levels of disagreement with my interpretation of their work, as well as publishing my response to their responses. In particular, Drucilla Cornell drew my attention to her book *The Imaginary Domain: Abortion, Pornography and Sexual Harassment* (New York: Routledge, 1995), which makes an important and powerful contribution to feminist theories of equality. See *Signs: Journal of Women in Culture and Society* 23, 1 (1997)

1. Rodolphe Gasché, *Inventions of Difference: On Jacques Derrida* (Cambridge: Harvard University Press, 1994), 82.
2. Sandra Harding, "The Instability of the Analytical Categories of Feminist Theory," *Signs: Journal of Women in Culture and Society* 11, 4 (1986): 664.

3. Chela Sandoval, "U.S. Third World Feminism: The Theory and Method of Oppositional Consciousness in the Postmodern World," *Genders* 10 (1991): 1–24.

4. Ann Barr Snitow, "A Gender Diary," in *Conflicts in Feminism*, ed. Marianne Hirsch and Evelyn Fox Keller (New York: Routledge, 1990).

5. My original essay acknowledged some helpful feminist discussions of difference, including Christine Sypnowich, "Some Disquiet about Difference," *Praxis International* 13, 2 (1993): 99–112; Françoise Collin, "Plurality, Difference, Identity," *Women: A Cultural Review* 5, 1 (1994): 13–24; Iris Marion Young, "Together in Difference: Transforming the Logic of Group Political Conflict," in *The Rights of Minority Cultures*, ed. Will Kymlicka (Oxford: Oxford University Press, 1995). An important new contribution to this debate is Susan Stanford Friedman, *Mappings: Feminism and the Cultural Geographies of Encounter* (Princeton: Princeton University Press, 1998). Friedman presents a dazzling and eminently persuasive case for going "beyond" difference.

6. Michèle Barrett, "The Concept of 'Difference,'" *Feminist Review* 26 (1987): 29–41.

7. See, among others, Ann Rosalind Jones, "Towards an Understanding of *l'écriture féminine*," *Feminist Studies* 7, 2 (1981): 264–87; Gayatri Chakravorty Spivak, "French Feminisms in an International Frame," in *In Other Worlds* (New York: Methuen, 1987).

8. Rosi Braidotti, *Patterns of Dissonance: A Study of Women in Contemporary Philosophy* (Cambridge: Polity Press, 1991), 177.

9. Rosi Braidotti, *Nomadic Subjects: Embodiment and Sexual Difference in Contemporary Feminist Theory* (New York: Columbia University Press, 1994), 160.

10. Braidotti, *Nomadic Subjects*, 115.

11. Drucilla Cornell, "What Is Ethical Feminism?" in Seyla Benhabib, Judith Butler, Drucilla Cornell, and Nancy Fraser, *Feminist Contentions: A Philosophical Exchange* (New York: Routledge, 1995), 147.

12. Drucilla Cornell, *Transformations* (New York: Routledge, 1993), 57.

13. Gasché, *Inventions of Difference*, 2.

14. In one of her contributions to *Feminist Contentions*, entitled "Pragmatism, Feminism and the Linguistic Turn," Nancy Fraser notes that such a position "misleadingly posits unity and coherence among what are actually a diverse plurality of discursive regimes, subject positions, signifying practices, public spheres and significations—including divergent and conflicting significations of femininity, which are surely not all reducible to 'lack'" (165).

15. Braidotti, *Nomadic Subjects*, 3.

16. Fraser, "Pragmatism, Feminism and the Linguistic Turn," 165.

17. John McGowan, *Postmodernism and Its Critics* (Ithaca: Cornell University Press, 1991), 154.

18. Drucilla Cornell, *Beyond Accommodation: Ethical Feminism, Deconstruction and the Law* (New York: Routledge, 1991), 34.

19. See Braidotti, *Patterns of Dissonance*, 210, 10. See also Luce Irigaray's claim in *An Ethics of Sexual Difference* (Ithaca: Cornell University Press, 1993) that "sexual difference is one of the major philosophical issues, if not the issue, of our age. According to Heidegger, each age has one issue to think through, and one only. Sexual difference is probably the issue in our time which could be our 'salvation' if we thought it through" (5).

20. Braidotti, *Nomadic Subjects*, 80, 149.

21. See, e.g., Elizabeth V. Spelman, *Inessential Woman: Problems of Exclusion in Feminist Thought* (Boston: Beacon Press, 1988); bell hooks, *Feminist Theory: From Margin to Center* (Boston: South End Press, 1984).

22. Cornell, *Beyond Accommodation*, 195.

23. Laura Donaldson, *Decolonizing Feminisms: Race, Gender and Empire Building* (Chapel Hill: University of North Carolina Press, 1992), 126.

24. Perhaps the most detailed case for the disjuncture between postcolonial theory and a race-conscious feminism is made by Carole Boyce Davies in *Black Women, Writing and Identity: Migrations of the Subject* (New York: Routledge, 1994), chap. 4. In my view, however, Davies overstates her case; there is a much more substantial feminist presence in postcolonial studies than she acknowledges. Furthermore, her own argument relies heavily on postcolonial theory.

25. Ruth Frankenberg and Lata Mani, "Crosscurrents, Crosstalk: Race, 'Postcoloniality' and the Politics of Location," *Cultural Studies* 7, 2 (1993): 292–310; Anne McClintock, "The Angel of Progress: Pitfalls of the Term 'Postcolonialism,'" in *Colonial Discourse and Post-Colonial Theory*, ed. Patrick Williams and Laura Chrisman (New York: Columbia University Press, 1994).

26. Gayatri Chakravorty Spivak, "Can the Subaltern Speak?" *Marxism and the Interpretation of Culture*, ed. Cary Nelson and Lawrence Grossberg (Urbana: University of Illinois Press, 1988); Rey Chow, *Writing Diaspora: Tactics of Intervention in Contemporary Cultural Studies* (Bloomington: Indiana University Press, 1993).

27. Chandra Talpade Mohanty, "Under Western Eyes: Feminist Scholarship and Colonial Discourse," *boundary 2* 13, 1 (1984): 333–57.

28. Chandra Talpade Mohanty, "Cartographies of Struggle: Third-World Women and the Politics of Feminism," in *Third-World Women and the Politics of Feminism*, ed. Chandra Talpade Mohanty, Ann Russo, and Lourdes Torres (Bloomington: Indiana University Press, 1991), 2.

29. Spivak, "Can the Subaltern Speak?" 291; Chow, *Writing Diaspora*, 47; see also Trinh Minh-ha, *Woman, Native, Other: Writing Postcoloniality and Feminism* (Bloomington: Indiana University Press, 1989).

30. Ien Ang, "I'm a Feminist But . . . 'Other Women' and Postnational Femi-

nism," in *Transitions: New Australian Feminisms* (New York: St. Martin's, 1995), 57.

31. Ang, "I'm a Feminist But," 60.
32. Ang, "I'm a Feminist But," 68.
33. Ang, "I'm a Feminist But," 65.
34. Mohanty, "Cartographies of Struggle."
35. Robert Young, *Colonial Desire: Hybridity in Theory, Culture, and Race* (London: Routledge, 1995), 26.
36. Friedman, *Mappings.*
37. Ang, "I'm a Feminist But," 64.
38. I am not convinced that race is the only or most salient issue in feminist disagreements about Madonna. Generational and disciplinary differences are also crucial. While cultural studies has encouraged numerous celebrations of Madonna, many feminist scholars in other disciplines, as well as women still affiliated to the social movement ideals of 1970s feminism, criticize Madonna for buying into, rather than subverting, patriarchal notions of feminine beauty.
39. Susan Bordo, *Unbearable Weight: Feminism, Western Culture and the Body* (Berkeley: University of California Press, 1993).
40. Ang, "I'm a Feminist But," 60.
41. Benita Parry, "Problems in Current Theories of Colonial Discourse," *Oxford Literary Review* 9, 1 (1987): 27–58.
42. Joan Scott, "Deconstructing Equality-versus-Difference: Or the Uses of Poststructuralist Theory for Feminism," *Feminist Studies* 14, 1 (1988): 33–50.
43. Cornell, *Transformations*, 141.
44. Charles Taylor, *The Ethics of Authenticity* (Cambridge: Harvard University Press, 1991), 35–36.
45. The term "contingent foundations" comes from Judith Butler, "Contingent Foundations," in Benhabib et al., *Feminist Contentions.*
46. Steven Connor, *Theory and Cultural Value* (Oxford: Basil Blackwell, 1992).
47. One might express this recognition by noting that any claim to overcome binary oppositions inevitably sets up a new opposition between binary and nonbinary thought.
48. Chow, *Writing Diaspora*, 66.

# 6

# FIN DE SIÈCLE, FIN DE SEXE

## TRANSSEXUALITY AND THE DEATH OF HISTORY

W hen exactly did history die, and how? Was its demise sudden and catastrophic, as the unspeakable horrors of Auschwitz and Hiroshima shat-
tered, once and for all, any lingering belief in Western myths of progress? Or did
it go more slowly, gradually dissolving into glossy media images and nostalgic simulations of an ever more enigmatic past? At what point in time did the idea of history become history, did it become possible to say, "that was then, this is now"?
And how does this perception of a temporal gulf between "then" and "now," between the era of past history and *posthistoire*, tally with the claim that we no longer
possess a historical consciousness? Finally, what is the connection between discourses of the end of history and the end of sex? How does our sense of historical
time relate to changing perceptions of gender and sexual difference?

I begin some tentative responses to these questions by pointing to the many references to transsexuality and transgenderism in much postmodern thought. Why has the transsexual become such a popular figure in postmodern theory? In *The Transparency of Evil,* Jean Baudrillard writes, "the sexual body has now been assigned an artificial fate. This fate is transsexuality—transsexual not in any anatomical sense but rather in the more general sense of transvestism, of playing with the commutability of the signs of sex . . . we are all transsexuals."[1] Here Baudrillard's metaphor seeks to capture the dissolution of once stable polarities of male and female. Sexual nature becomes sexual artifice, inner self turns into performance, depth is replaced by surface. Sex is simply the deployment of the signs of sex through the skillful manipulation of clothing, bodies, and gestures. According to Baudrillard, such celebrities as Madonna, Michael Jackson, and La Cicciolina underscore our contemporary fascination with the exaggeration, parody, and inversion of conventional signs of sexual difference.

Poststructuralist theory echoes and intensifies these practices of gender bending and blending. In many cases, it provocatively challenges the reality and stability of the male/female divide. On the one hand, theorists like Derrida, Deleuze, and Baudrillard profess their desire to "become woman" by aligning themselves with a feminine principle of undecidability and masquerade. On the other hand, feminists increasingly appeal to metaphors of transvestism to stress the mutable and plastic qualities of the sexed body. The most influential feminist theorists of recent times, Donna Haraway and Judith Butler, have both tried to break out of the prison house of gender by thinking of gender as a performance rather than an identity. Gender is something you do rather than something you are, and this doing is uncertain, unstable, and contingent.

"Fin de siècle, fin de sexe," the epigram coined by the French artist Jean Lorrain to express the affinities between gender confusion and historical exhaustion in the late nineteenth century, seems even more apt for our own time.[2] As our millennium winds to its end, writers are looking back to the last fin de siècle and plundering its repertoire of references to decadence, apocalypse, and sexual crisis. Yet these references are also acquiring new meanings, as images of sex and gender connect up to postmodern stories about history and time. As the male/female divide becomes ever more fragile and unstable, it is claimed, so we are also witnessing a waning of temporality, teleology, and grand narrative. The end of sex, in this view, echoes and affirms the end of history. Phallocentrism and linear time are the evil twins of modernity, closely intertwined in a symbiotic relationship. Their joint demise is a foregone conclusion, as binary logic and historical totalities give way to an altogether more ambiguous and indeterminate condition. Indeed, the idea that history has come to an end is perhaps the most ubiquitous commonplace of postmodern thought.

My aim in this chapter is not to prove or disprove such claims. The end of history is clearly not a thesis that is amenable to empirical adjudication. Rather, I want to think about who is making these claims and why. What does it mean to talk about the death of history? To what extent does such a claim reaffirm the order of time that it appears to negate? How do changing conceptions of history and time link up to the struggles of contemporary social movements? And to what extent should feminism affirm or question the thesis of the end of history and the end of sex?

First, I look briefly at the work of Jean Baudrillard and Donna Haraway, two figures who have crafted highly influential diagnoses of the postmodern condition. I suggest that their writings are imbued with large-scale visions of historical time that echo their diverging views of the transgendered subject as a figure of either apocalypse or redemption. I then turn to the work of the Italian philosopher Gianni Vattimo, who delivers some important insights on history in postmodern thought. Yet I also suggest that Vattimo's work does not pay much attention to the political stakes in struggles over the meaning of history and temporality. Finally, I look at discourses of the end of history and the end of sex from the standpoint of feminist theory.

## (TRANS)GENDERED HISTORIES: BAUDRILLARD AND HARAWAY

Baudrillard's rant against the pathology of Western culture depicts a world that is overflowing with meaning and hence empty of it, a zone of promiscuous information and communication that is obscene in its total transparency. Media saturation, the spread of computers and cybernetic culture, the inescapable injunction to consume, all conspire to create a hallucinatory limbo of the hyperreal. No point exists outside this all-embracing network of simulation. Notions of history, reality, and linear time live on only as fossilized remains endlessly replayed on the screens of our video terminals. Since the debacle of 1968, politics can be nothing more than self-delusion. Any form of liberation—sexual, political, aesthetic—merely engenders an escalation of networks of simulation that subsume, neutralize, or dissolve all meaning. One of Baudrillard's most intriguing insights is that power works not through silencing and prohibition but rather through the proliferation and excess of communication. In his work, the model of the cultural code gradually gives way to that of the virus, evoking the endless, invasive multiplication of contagious signifiers.

In Baudrillard's later work, questions of gender and sexuality are at the heart of this nightmarish vision of an epidemic of signification. *The Transparency of Evil* mourns the reduction of sexuality to "the undifferentiated circulation of the signs of sex."[3] The erotic falls prey to the logic of simulation through its ubiquitous presence as image and spectacle on our screens, magazines, and billboards. "After the demise of desire," Baudrillard writes, "a pell-mell diffusion of erotic simulacra in every guise, of transsexual kitsch in all its glory."[4] In Baudrillard's relentlessly heterosexual and -sexist universe, the waning of desire is due to the disappearance of sexual difference. We have become "indifferent and undifferentiated beings, androgynous and hermaphroditic,"[5] creatures without gender and hence without sex. Biotechnology heralds a brave new world of cloning, parthenogenesis, serial reproduction by celibate machines replicating like protozoa. Feminists in turn accelerate this confusion of gender categories by reducing the inexorable destiny of being male or female to a pedestrian matter of preference and rights. The figure of the transsexual in Baudrillard thus points to a general process of implosion and de-differentiation that renders all terms commutable and equally indeterminate. The end of sex echoes and affirms the end of history, understood as the failure of both agency (the eclipse of the subject by the sovereignty of the object) and knowledge (the impossibility of imputing any meaning or direction to temporal processes).

Yet, even as he insists that narrative has become impossible, Baudrillard's writings offer a powerful and nostalgic narrative of the fall. Harking back to an imagined era when signs conveyed a richness and fullness of meaning, he recounts a doleful parable of cultural decline from the standpoint of the latecomer, the one who comes after. At one point, Baudrillard writes, "we are merely epigones. . . . The highest level of intensity lies behind us. The lowest level of passion and intellectual illumination lies ahead of us."[6] Such a melancholic vision of cultural decadence is of course a recurring theme in modernity, the faithful shadow of history as progress.

For Baudrillard, a meaningful future is no longer possible. He claims that linear and progressive time no longer exist in an imploding universe where history turns back on itself in a self-consuming spiral of infinite regression. In the mythic no-time of TV that we all inhabit, history is flattened out into a smorgasbord of endlessly recycled images and perpetual presents. Yet this very diagnosis explicitly posits a history that once *was* and is no more. Indeed, Baudrillard's account of the four stages of the sign, which moves from being "the reflection of a basic reality" to "pure simulacrum" is a deeply elegiac narrative.[7] Thus Baudrillard voices a profoundly historical sense of the current impossibility of history. Even as he insists that linear time has been replaced by reversibility and repetition, Baudrillard appeals to a temporal schema structured around the triadic relation of a disappearing present, an absent future, and an authentically self-present, if no longer knowable past.

We can highlight this point by considering Donna Haraway's very different emplotment of historical time. Like Baudrillard, Haraway argues that social experiences and relations have been radically transformed by cybernetic systems, biotechnological innovation, and the spread of media networks. She too argues that old oppositions of masculine and feminine, along with their corollary distinctions of private versus public, mind versus body, culture versus nature, no longer hold in the new world system that she terms "the informatics of domination." In this context she introduces her resonant symbol of the cyborg, a hybrid blend of male and female, organism and machine. The cyborg stands for the messy intermingling of previously distinct categories that characterizes the postmodern. We are all cyborgs now, she states; "the cyborg is our ontology, it gives us our politics."[8]

Haraway's transgendered cyborg, however, bears little kinship to Baudrillard's transsexual subject. An ironic and polyvalent symbol of both domination and resistance, it gestures resolutely toward the future rather than gazing back at the past. The force of Haraway's essay lies in her adamant critique of feminism's hostility toward science and technology and its nostalgic attachment to an idea of organic female identity. Rather, she insists, feminists need to explore the new possibilities, pleasures, and politics made possible by transgressed boundaries and fragmented selves. Postmodern science is their potential ally. The cyborg serves as a feminist icon for the postmodern era, an unruly child of technological systems that it simultaneously exploits and contests.

How, then, do cyborgs embody or subvert existing patterns of historical time? Haraway explicitly rejects the redemptive frame of Western progress as well as the countermyth of a lost paradise. The cyborg, she declares, is outside salvation history and has no origin story; it rejects the seductive pull of vanguard politics and a teleological vision of agency. Yet even as it weaves its way among multiple perspectives, Haraway's manifesto (a quintessentially modern genre that she both parodies and reproduces) expresses a deeply historical awareness of the irreversible and linear nature of time. Drawing on Fredric Jameson's tripartite scheme of capitalist development, Haraway insists on the distinctiveness of our own epoch and the impossibility of returning to an earlier moment. "We cannot go back ideologically or materially," she writes; "it's not just that 'god' is dead, so is the 'goddess.'"[9]

The "Manifesto for Cyborgs" is a text permeated by a strong sense of its own temporality. It points to the irrevocable transformation of our material and conceptual universe, thanks to the impact of cybernetics and biotechnology. Recent scientific and social change has definitively severed us from our recent past. Without denying the grinding exploitation, oppression, and poverty that permeate our own time, Haraway wants nonetheless to affirm political agency and the redemptive potential of the future. Coding the transgendered subject of the postmodern as liberating icon rather than nightmarish catastrophe, she sees new and exciting possibilities in hybrid gender identities and complex fusions of previously distinct realities. In its expectant and hopeful gesturing toward a "not yet" that may liberate women from the naturalized oppressions and dichotomies of the past, Haraway carves a resolutely utopian, forward-looking vision out of social conditions often identified with the dwindling of political possibilities.

The texts of Baudrillard and Haraway, then, offer two very different political and philosophical responses to the de-differentiation of sexual difference. Transsexuality, Sandy Stone observes, is currently a hotly contested subject. Stone discusses some of these struggles over meaning as they play themselves out among doctors, feminists, and transsexuals themselves. However, Stone's statement also has more general resonance when one thinks about the widespread fascination with transsexuality in the rhetoric of fin de millennium.[10] Interpreted as historical symptom or philosophical symbol, this figure inspires a chorus of claims and counterclaims about its redemptive or catastrophic meanings.

Nowhere is this more apparent than in two anthologies on gender and the postmodern body edited by Arthur and Marilouise Kroker, *Body Invaders* and *The Last Sex*.[11] Here upbeat celebrations of transsexuality couched in the vocabulary of postmodern feminism and queer theory are juxtaposed alongside gloomy scenarios of docile bodies under the sway of biotechnology and consumer culture. While *Body Invaders* offers a more pessimistic reading of a postmodern body subject to the omnipresent tyranny of simulation, *The Last Sex* gestures euphorically toward a future transgender liberation and the emergence of a third sex. Thus the editors look to a "new sexual horizon" that is "post-male and post-female"; their goal, they write, is to achieve the indeterminate state of "female, yet male, organisms occupying an ironic, ambivalent and paradoxical state of sexual identity."[12] Ends of centuries are important moments for the appearance of highly charged myths of death and rebirth, senescence and renewal. In our own era such hopes and anxieties are writ large across proliferating representations of transsexual and transgendered bodies.

## PARADOXES OF HISTORY AND POSTMODERNITY: GIANNI VATTIMO

What interests me here is not just the weighty yet conflicting meanings assigned to transsexuality in recent theories of the postmodern. It is also the stubborn reappearance of history in its very disavowal. Even as they question conventional forms of historical thinking and big philosophical stories, the texts I have been discussing reveal a strong sense of being located in time. They see themselves in relation to pasts and futures that are richly endowed with redemptive and dystopian meanings.

This paradox is explored in some detail by the Italian philosopher Gianni Vattimo, an important commentator on *posthistoire*. Vattimo argues that the defining feature of the modern is a particular consciousness of time. To be modern is to be oriented to the future, as an untapped potential of authenticity and freedom. The new becomes the supreme value to which all other values refer. Hence we justify and explain our ideas by presenting them as new, radical, even revolutionary. Conversely, to be old-fashioned, outmoded, antiquated, out of date, regressive, or behind the times is to be doomed to insignificance. This time consciousness leads us to think of the history of thought as a progressive enlightenment that allows us to transcend the errors of the past. Vattimo summarizes this perception in the idea of *Überwindung*, overcoming and transcending past history. He agrees with Lyotard and others that postmodernism brings a dissolution of this story of progress and overcoming. What has come to an end, Vattimo insists, is not simply a certain set of ideas about history, but history itself, insofar as history cannot be separated from its expression as a metaphysical narrative.

Yet Vattimo also attends to the obvious paradoxes of using a historical term to discuss the end of history. "If we say that we are at a later point than modernity, and if we treat this fact as in some way decisively important, then this presupposes an acceptance of . . . the point of view of modernity itself, namely the idea of history with its two corollary notions of progress and overcoming."[13] This paradox defines many contemporary accounts of postmodernism. To assume the superiority of the postmodern is to make the quintessentially modern gesture of valuing the present for superseding the errors of the past. To reject the errors of modernity is to repeat the motif of historical overcoming that defines modernity itself. Much postmodern thought thus turns out to be deeply enmeshed within the very historical and temporal dynamic that it wants to disavow. As many writers have noted, the claim that metanarratives have come to an end is itself a grand narrative of the first order.

According to Vattimo, then, we cannot get beyond the heritage of modernity. To make such a claim is to remain ensnared in the very logic of overcoming that defines a modern time consciousness. We cannot "transcend" metaphysics. Instead, we can at best hope to recover from it slowly and painfully, as if from a sickness. As an alternative to *Überwindung*, Vattimo turns to the Heideggerian notion of *Verwindung*. "This term," he writes, "suggests a number of different meanings: to recover from an illness, to resign oneself to something, or to accept (another's judgement)."[14] *Verwindung* thus involves a self-conscious sense of being implicated in history and metaphysics. We cannot create ourselves *ex nihilo* or cleanse ourselves of the contaminating influence of the past in order to emerge reborn and redeemed. There are no absolute breaks or completely new beginnings. The use of the term *Verwindung* recognizes the dangers of metaphysics, but also that claiming to go beyond metaphysics is the most metaphysical of statements. We cannot simply escape or transcend our heritage in this way, though we can seek to be cured of it by twisting metaphysics in a different direction in order to drain it of its strength.[15] Here we can see Vattimo's use of "weak thought," a style of philosophizing that seeks to undermine the heroic consciousness of modernity as an Oedipal triumph against the errors of tradition.

Vattimo is not as well-known in the English-speaking world as some other postmodern theorists, yet he offers an astute analysis of the historical and temporal paradoxes of the postmodern. After one reads Vattimo, it becomes obvious how often discussions of the postmodern continue to draw on modern ideas about history and time. Just as modernity sees itself as transcending tradition, so defenders of the postmodern often see themselves as transcending modernity, defined as the new tradition. In doing so, of course, they simply repeat the modern obsession with the new and the now. Postmodern simply becomes a synonym for neo–avant-garde. If the postmodern is to have any distinctive meaning at all, it must surely rely, as Vattimo points out, on a different relationship to history and tradition.

Although Vattimo's diagnosis of the historical paradoxes of postmodernism is often illuminating, his own account of history is in certain respects highly unilinear. He insists that the postmodern is not a new stage in history, but rather the dissolution of the category of the new. Yet he also claims that the disenchantment with history arises from "general traits of our common experience" in contemporary Western societies.[16] These traits include the routinization of progress (the new becomes the norm) and the growing awareness of the rhetorical and narrative dimensions of historical thought. Vattimo contrasts this contemporary sense of disenchantment with an earlier time when everyone believed in universal history and the absolute value of the new.

Here he lays himself open, as he recognizes, to the charge of an "oversimplifying sociology" often leveled at philosophers.[17] First, this philosophical reading of the time-consciousness of modernity is excessively schematic. As I suggested in chapter 2, modernity's relationship to the new is more complex than Vattimo's summary indicates. Certainly, newness does become a value in itself, but modernity also includes a turn to tradition and a powerful distrust of the new, most obviously in Romanticism. Linear time is intertwined with circular time, revolution with tradition, change with repetition. Furthermore, the history of modernity also contains the voices of disenfranchised others—laborers, slaves, suffragettes—who are often at odds with the dominant perspectives on history and time. As I have already observed, postmodern stories often present an oversimplified view of the modern past as an oppressive sea of sameness.

Second, Vattimo's account does not pay much attention to the different uses and abuses of history in our own time. Not all groups experience their relationship to time and history in the same way. For example, the current explosion of women's texts exploring issues of memory, time, tradition, and change seems at odds with the bland assertion that "we" live in a posthistorical era. As a philosopher, Vattimo tends to see history only in terms of the self-critique of Western metaphysics. In this way of thinking, to expose the metaphysical nature of history is to offer a decisive rebuttal of its claims. Yet history, unperturbed, continues to flourish in many forms: academic history, public history, oral history, historical fiction. History is not just a philosophical problem but a pressing social and pragmatic concern. For many individuals and groups, it remains crucial to their sense of themselves as human and social subjects. Indeed, from a sociological perspective, one might speak not of the death of grand narratives but the proliferation of them, as ever more groups identify themselves as historical actors in the public domain.

Second-wave feminism, for example, has inspired several different visions of historical time. One of its most familiar stories recounts the growing freedom of women as they liberate themselves from the manacles of tradition in order to realize themselves as autonomous individuals in the public world. Another influential story rewrites the myth of the fall, claiming that we can find an authentic experience of femininity only in a prelapsarian condition (nature, the organic, the pre-Oedipal) that precedes the alienating subject-object split of modernity. Both of these stories have come to seem increasingly dubious, and poststructuralist feminists are eager to point out their flaws. Yet these critiques in turn spawn their own evolutionary stories and binary oppositions. We often hear how the naive beliefs of early feminist thought have given way to the more enlightened, sophisticated, and self-conscious perspectives of the present. Indeed, M. J. Devaney points out that poststructuralist and postmodernist thought often relies on a very conventional view of progress in claiming to refute the errors of a monolithic entity variously defined as modernity/Enlightenment thinking/the Western metaphysical tradition.[18]

Instead of trying to "transcend" narrative, teleology, and the like, feminists would do better to admit that they, along with everyone else, are enmeshed in story and history. Yet the political and cultural meanings of feminist stories are not always obvious. They do not, after all, cover the same ground as the grand narratives of liberalism or Marxism. The politics of big historical stories cannot be read off from their form. Rather, we need to think about how they circulate, how they are used, and what kind of work they do. Myths of origin or visions of utopia may inspire an exhilarating sense of solidarity and create or cement affiliations among members of disadvantaged groups. Powerful stories can help to engender social change. These same narratives can also deny or gloss over

**145**

differences within a group by assuming that everyone shares the same story. They can encourage feelings of self-righteousness, an us-versus-them mentality, and an aggrieved sense of martyrdom, *ressentiment*, and victimhood. Which of these scenarios will turn out to be true is not something that can be decided in advance. The political meanings of stories are contingent, not absolute.

In his recent work, Vattimo both acknowledges and minimizes the force of oppositional voices in the postmodern era. He points to the new visibility of social movements and minorities and argues that their presence has pluralized, and hence dissolved, the category of history. For Vattimo, like Baudrillard, the proliferation of histories signals the death of history, because history, as the claim to offer an objective account of what really happened, can exist only in the singular. All we have left after the demise of this univocal history are multiple "images of the past projected from different points of view."[19]

This argument is frequently made in reckonings with the current state of history. Yet it relies on an overly simple dichotomy between the universal and the particular. Once the belief in a single true history has died, the argument goes, what remains is a bunch of local narratives, a bouquet of historical perspectives. Plurality becomes a value in itself, indeed, the ultimate value to which all other values refer. In at least some instances, however, this account is misleading. Recent historians of slavery, for example, do not claim only to approach history from a "black" point of view. Their aim is not just to offer one interpretation among many and to celebrate pluralism for its own sake. Rather, they hope to intervene in, contest, and transform other accounts, rather than simply exist alongside them. They do this by claiming to offer a more plausible account of what actually happened. They want to correct, rewrite, and extend rather than negate history.

The discourses of contemporary social movements often seem in this respect to blur the clarity of the distinction between *grands* and *petits récits*. The writings of women, people of color, gays and lesbians, and other disenfranchised groups arise from a strong sense of being left out of the conventional stories and myths of Western culture. As such, they question rather than affirm the notion of a universal subject of history. At the same time, they also aspire to change our understanding of the past and present in a manner that transcends the local. Rather than luxuriating in their specific identities, scholars from these groups make claims about the world that they hold to be generally true (not true just for them). They believe that paying careful attention to the diverse groups who helped to fashion the modern world makes for better history, not the end of history.

Of course, there is no metaphysical guarantee that writing from the standpoint of an oppressed group will produce truth (I discuss the problems of standpoint theory in chapter 9). But the desire to do justice to the past is often particularly urgent for those seeking to excavate the history of underrepresented groups. In other words, the problem of history is closely tied to passionate debates and struggles over what is to count as legitimate historical knowledge. What version of history will be disseminated throughout our culture, which stories will be passed down in our books, museums, and schools? From the perspective of those involved in such debates, Vattimo's meditations on *posthistoire* may say more about the philosopher's crisis of faith in a particular metaphysical tradition than the status of history as such.

In this context, Agnes Heller observes that the end of history is a performative statement rather than an empirical observation, a ritualistic act of murder or death wish often carried out by philosophers. Before committing such a murderous act, she suggests, the philosopher should consider whether he really wishes history dead, "or whether his death wish is but the manifestation of his despair and sorrow because the thing in which he invested affections turned out to be different from what he had expected and hoped for."[20]

## AN END TO THE END OF HISTORY?

Thinking about differing investments in history brings me back to my starting point: the figure of transsexuality or transgenderism as a symbol for contrasting visions of history and time. I do not want to suggest that the works of Baudrillard and Haraway should serve as capsule summaries of male and female perspectives on the postmodern. Both of these writers are far too idiosyncratic to stand in for their sex. Moreover, there are diverse and often conflicting representations of history on both sides of the gender divide.

At the same time, it is clear that our cultural affiliations and identifications do shape the way we think about history and time. For example, the obsessive relationship to a lost history in the works of Marxist and post-Marxist theorists such as Baudrillard, Jameson, Lyotard, and Vattimo inspires a sense of melancholia and loss that is by no means as universal as these writers often assume. Thus even a cursory glance at recent feminist writing reveals an array of rather different temporalities. Even as they call into question existing Oedipal stories, many of these texts insist that history is a vital concern rather than a defunct concept. Furthermore, as my discussion of Haraway indicates, the questioning of sexual difference does not always lead to a waning of the historical imagination. Rather, such questioning may engender powerful new historical stories and inspire imaginative visions of alternative worlds and possible feminist futures.

Such a claim, of course, undermines the postmodern trope of transgenderism and the claim that "we" are all transsexuals. It suggests that gender may help to shape the stories we tell about beginnings and ends, pasts and futures. Like the end of history, the end of sex is metaphorically rather than literally true. Even as a metaphor, however, it captures only one aspect of the contemporary cultural imagination. Baudrillard points to our obvious fascination with postmodern symbols of gender ambiguity such as Michael Jackson and Madonna. But what about the enormous popularity of the "Men Are from Mars, Women Are from Venus" empire of books, videos, infomercials, and seminars? Or the widespread appeal of a popular feminism that seeks to affirm and celebrate female identity? On the one hand, traditional gender divisions are becoming less and less stable, thanks to the technological, economic, and social changes so adeptly summarized by Haraway. On the other hand, many of these gender divisions are redrawn as the question of women's difference comes to the fore as never before. The erosion of gender and the affirmation of gender are indissolubly linked.

Themes of transgender, postgender, transvestism, and the like have an ambiguous relationship to feminism. I have questioned the view that symbols of gender crisis automatically imply a loss of history and agency. In both the last fin de siècle and our own, this seems much more true of the feminized male than of the masculinized woman. Her ambiguous gender is often charged with historical purpose and an exhilarating vision of new possibilities rather than with a sense of belatedness and exhaustion. Thus the remarkable influence and impact of Haraway's essay surely derive in part from the powerful resonance of its key image. The cyborg has become a new feminist icon, a bold and visionary ideal of a postgendered subject that breaks with a long history of representing woman as the archetype of both nature and nurture.

Inevitably, however, some feminists are less than sanguine about the postgendered subject. Susan Bordo, for example, is skeptical about the value of the cyborg as a feminist icon. She suggests that it will help relegate female experience and embodiment to the shadows before they have been adequately explored. The postmodern and poststructuralist fascination with shifting identities is helping to erase women's specific concerns. From another angle, the feminist fascination with images of transvestism is questioned by Eve Sedgwick and Michael Moon. This usage, they claim, is often careless as well as oblivious to the history of transvestite cultures and practices, including their complex relationship to the history of homosexuality.[21]

In the original version of this argument, besides drafting some rather tortuous prose, I did not pay much attention to the field of transgender scholarship. My main concern was to puzzle through some of the parallels and differences between images of gender blurring in male postmodernist and feminist theory. My use of "transsexual" and "transgender" echoed the often casual metaphorical usage of these terms by postmodern theorists. In the last few years, however, we have witnessed an efflorescence of writing on transgender and transsexual issues ("transgender" is sometimes used as an umbrella term for any form of gender dysphoria and gender-crossing, including transsexuality, while at other times it refers specifically to those who cross gender without surgical intervention). Ranging from the personal to the theoretical, this new writing maps out a complicated constellation of alliances and disagreements between various scholars, writers, and activists.

This constellation also includes queer theorists. For example, some lesbians who are attracted to the idea of female masculinity have found the concept of "trans" relevant to their exploration of perverse bodies, identities, and desires. In a controversial essay published in 1994, Judith Halberstam explored "a postmodern lesbian desire" that was linked to "the spectacle of the female body becoming male."[22] Halberstam argued that the boundaries between gay, lesbian, and straight have become increasingly incoherent, given the mind-spinning array of gender affiliations and sexual practices. Insisting that we explore the strangeness of all gendered bodies, Halberstam echoes Baudrillard. "Within a more general fragmentation of the concept of sexual identity, the specificity of the transsexual disappears. In a way, I claim, we are all transsexuals."[23]

This elevation of transsexual to a universal metaphor has a provocative force. It seeks to challenge our conventional distinctions between male and female, normal and deviant, real and fake. It insists that all gender is engineered rather than given, prosthetic rather than natural. Yet it also blurs key distinctions. Whether or not we are all transsexuals at an abstract metaphorical level, we certainly don't all *feel* transsexual. Some people have a very strong sense of belonging, body and soul, to a particular gender; others have an intense conviction that particular bodies, sexual practices, and forms of behavior go naturally together and feel deeply threatened by any challenge to this belief.

The claim that we are all transsexuals has inspired particular ire, not surprisingly, among transsexuals, who resent being raised to the status of a universal metaphor. Such usage erases differences that matter: differences between those who occasionally play with gender ambiguity and others for whom the experience of crossing gender is a far more urgent and life-defining experience. Kathleen Chapman and Michael du Plessis address this question in looking at attitudes to transsexuality in feminist and queer theory.[24] There are well-known instances of conflict between feminists and transsexuals; feminists who accuse transsexuals of misogyny and reproducing stereotypes of women, transsexuals who accuse feminists of wanting the final say on gender and policing who counts as a woman, most notoriously at the Michigan Womyns' Music Festival.

Chapman and du Plessis suggest that the seemingly more progressive treatment of transsexuality in queer theory is little better. Either transsexuals are patronized as naive literalists who still believe in a "real" gender identity, or they are simply subsumed within the broader transgender rubric. In the latter case, we find the emergence of the transsexual as simulacrum. "Transsexuals 'r' us," notes Jay Prosser sarcastically, "full of postmodern liberatory promise, their very constructedness encapsulating the essential inessentiality, what we take for granted as the unnaturalness of the body."[25] For Prosser, as for Chapman and du Plessis, this celebration of the transsexual is accompanied by a disturbing elision of the experiences of transsexual subjects.

In her more recent book on female masculinity, Halberstam retracts her claim that "we are all transsexuals," but still wants to explore the often blurry and confused boundaries between queers and transsexuals. In this context, she questions a sentence in my original argument that ran: "Not all social subjects, after all, have equal freedom to play with and subvert the signs of gender, even as many do not perceive such play as a necessary condition of their freedom." My discussion, she suggests, counterposes the political earnestness of the transsexual to the mere gender play of queers, drag queens, and the like, who are thereby cast in the role of "dilettantes and recreationalists in the game of gender."[26]

When I first drafted this sentence, I was thinking of Jean Baudrillard rather than queer theory, but I agree that such an opposition is too simple. Play can be deadly serious; pleasure is not opposed to politics. Let me propose an alternative taxonomy: those for whom "trans" is only a scholarly metaphor, those for whom it also connects to everyday modes of self-presentation and "troubling" gender, and those who actually change sex or undergo gender reassignment. These categories are still crude, and there are many individuals who see themselves as existing in the interstices of such categories. Yet it is important to recognize key differences within the field of transgender, broadly defined. There are plenty of border wars as well as border crossings. Jay Prosser, for example, offers a sustained criticism of attempts to subsume the transsexual within the rubric of queer. Rather, he argues, taking the phenomenon of transsexuality seriously requires a major rethinking of the truisms about gender performance and gender fluidity in contemporary theory.

What all this suggests is that people have radically differing views of gender as well as differing degrees of investment in gender. The current state of transsexual and transgender studies graphically displays this conflict rather than going "beyond" gender in any simple sense (Vattimo's cautioning against the hubris of *Überholung* is relevant here). Much the same can be said about history, which flickers persistently on our horizon in a tantalizing dance of presence and absence. Clearly, we do not think of time in the same way as those Victorians who spoke of the purposeful unfolding of the laws of history. Yet in conceding the demise of evolutionism we do not negate, but rather affirm, our own historical awareness. We recognize that we live in a time when certain assumptions, vocabularies, and ways of thought are no longer possible. The waning of nineteenth-century models of history does not mean that we have lost all sense of being located in time or the desire to give meaning to our lives by locating them within larger temporal frames. The difference is, perhaps, that we have become more aware of the speculative nature of our stories and their inevitable plurality.

To put it another way, history has more than one referent. Some scholars of the postmodern, such as Baudrillard and Fredric Jameson, concede the proliferation of histories in our own era only to negate them. It is only because we no longer have access to a true history, the argument runs, that we are surrounded by impoverished simulacra of the historical. Our sense of temporality is created by phony, nostalgia-laden media images of the past. Yet how can these writers distinguish so confidently between true and false forms of representation? And how authentic was the historical sense of the past? Surely feminists and other scholars of disenfranchised groups have made it clear that what counts as history and tradition has often been highly selective. History may have appeared more natural in the past, more grounded in a sense of community and tradition, but it was not therefore more real.

Once we stop thinking about history as a movement from presence to absence, we can begin to ask more interesting kinds of questions. How do current views of historical time echo, transform, or contest those of earlier moments? What do these views tell us about conflicting visions of history and time? How are these visions linked to particular political and cultural agendas? Can we remain alert to the differences and disjunctures in contemporary experiences of time while also keeping in mind the commonalities that link us? When we look at things in this light, it seems that the myth of the end of history merely repeats rather than subverts the idea of a universal history.

## NOTES

This essay was first published in *New Literary History*, 27, 2 (1996). It has been substantially revised.

1. Jean Baudrillard, *The Transparency of Evil* (New York: Verso, 1993), 20–21.
2. Cited in Will L. McLendon, "Rachilde: Fin-de-Siècle Perspectives on Perversity," in *Modernity and Revolution in Late Nineteenth-Century France*, ed. Barbara T. Cooper and Mary Donaldson-Evans (Newark: Delaware University Press, 1992).
3. Baudrillard, *The Transparency of Evil*, 12.
4. Baudrillard, *The Transparency of Evil*, 22.

5. Baudrillard, *The Transparency of Evil*, 25.
6. Jean Baudrillard, *Cool Memories* (London: Verso, 1990), 149.
7. Jean Baudrillard, "Simulacra and Simulations," in *Jean Baudrillard: Selected Writings*, ed. Mark Poster (Stanford: Stanford University Press, 1988), 170.
8. Donna Haraway, "A Manifesto for Cyborgs: Science, Technology and Socialist Feminism in the 1980s," in *Feminism/Postmodernism*, ed. Linda Nicholson (London: Routledge, 1990), 191.
9. Haraway, "A Manifesto for Cyborgs," 204.
10. Sandy Stone, "The Empire Strikes Back: A Posttranssexual Manifesto," in *Body Guards: The Cultural Politics of Gender Ambiguity*, ed. Julia Epstein and Kristina Straub (New York: Routledge, 1991), 294. I am grateful to Andrew Parker for providing me with a copy of this text.
11. Arthur Kroker and Marilouise Kroker, eds., *Body Invaders: Panic Sex in America* (New York: St. Martin's, 1987), and *The Last Sex* (New York: St. Martin's, 1993).
12. Arthur Kroker and Marilouise Kroker, "Scenes from the Last Sex: Feminism and Outlaw Bodies," in *The Last Sex*, 18–19.
13. Gianni Vattimo, *The End of Modernity: Nihilism and Hermeneutics in Postmodern Culture* (Baltimore: Johns Hopkins University Press, 1988), 4.
14. Vattimo, *The End of Modernity*, 39.
15. John R. Snyder, "Translator's Introduction," in *The End of Modernity*, xxvi.
16. Vattimo, *The End of Modernity*, 7.
17. Vattimo, *The End of Modernity*, 6.
18. M. J. Devaney, *"Since at Least Plato" . . . and Other Postmodernist Myths* (London: Macmillan, 1997).
19. Gianni Vattimo, *The Transparent Society* (Baltimore: Johns Hopkins University Press, 1992), 3.
20. Agnes Heller, *A Philosophy of History in Fragments* (Oxford: Basil Blackwell, 1993), 72.
21. Susan Bordo, "Feminism, Postmodernism and Gender-Skepticism," in Nicholson, *Feminism/Postmodernism*, 144–145; Eve Kosofsky Sedgwick and Michael Moon, "Divinity: A Dossier, a Performance Piece, a Little Understood Emotion," in Eve Kosofsky Sedgwick, *Tendencies* (Durham: Duke University Press, 1993), 219–24.
22. Judith Halberstam, "F2M: The Making of Female Masculinity," in *The Lesbian Postmodern*, ed. Laura Doan (New York: Columbia University Press, 1994), 219.
23. Halberstam, "F2M," 212.
24. Kathleen Chapman and Michael du Plessis, "'Don't Call Me *Girl*': Lesbian Theory, Feminist Theory and Transsexual Identities," in *Cross-Purposes: Lesbians, Feminists and the Limits of Alliance*, ed. Dana Heller (Bloomington: Indiana University Press, 1997).

25. Jay Prosser, *Second Skins: The Body Narratives of Transsexuality* (New York: Columbia University Press, 1998), 14.
26. Judith Halberstam, *Female Masculinity* (Durham: Duke University Press, 1998), 167.

# 7

# IMAGES OF THE INTELLECTUAL
## FROM PHILOSOPHY TO CULTURAL STUDIES

**A** recurring theme in both postmodern and poststructuralist thought is the anachronism and exhaustion of philosophy. Whether individual thinkers such as Plato, Descartes, or Kant are placed on trial, or the Western metaphysical tradition *tout court*, the final verdict is often damning. What was once the ultimate repository of human wisdom is now a monument to the hubris of past generations. At best philosophy is subject to gentle mockery for its grandiose aspirations toward eternal truths. At worst, it is roundly condemned for its role in enforcing a Western, phallocentric tyranny of reason.

Of course, the end of philosophy is a long-standing theme; it almost seems as if the condition of philosophy is to be in permanent crisis.[1] But what is distinctively new is the broad reach of this idea. No longer just a subject of debate among philosophers, the demise of philosophy has become a leitmotif of contemporary thought. Even as philosophical concepts permeate more and more disciplines with the spread of "theory," philosophy as a field is under attack. It is now common for cultural critics, sociologists, literary scholars, and even journalists to refer in passing to the end of philosophy as a taken-for-granted event, an integral part of our postmodern cultural condition.

Why, I wonder, has *philosophy* become a scapegoat for so many people? Contemporary philosophers seem to be a relatively innocuous bunch of people. Their departments are usually small, at least in the English-speaking world,[2] and among the first to disappear as academic budgets are slashed and universities bow to corporate criteria of efficiency and vocational relevance. Philosophy's contribution to the grand scheme of things, either intellectually or politically, would appear to be minor. In one sense, of course, this confirms the claims of its critics that it lingers on as "an antiquarian fossil" rather than as a living discipline, an obsolete body of knowledge on a rough par with classical philology.[3] But why expend so much effort castigating a relatively marginal discipline? And why philosophy in particular? The reason is, of course, that philosophy remains haunted by the ghost of its own past as "one of the most prominent pillars of the modern order,"[4] an aura that endows it with a lingering authority and prestige.

In fact, both its critics and defenders may take the preeminence of philosophy too much at face value. Have philosophers really defined the course of Western history and culture? We can clarify philosophy's influence on the world only by looking at the lines of connection between philosophical ideas and such social fields as the judiciary, government, commerce, bureaucracies, education, and everyday life. Much of the time, one suspects, such ideas have furnished convenient but dispensable rationales for actions that are actually inspired by more mundane motives.

Those decrying the Western metaphysical tradition are, however, usually not very interested in such mundane acts of sociological investigation. What is at stake is less the actual historical impact of philosophy than its ethos, its idealized self-image and conception of its own role. Such an ethos, according to Avner Cohen, comprises

> the implicit set of presuppositions, sentiments, self-images, hopes and anxieties that together form the collective *raison d'être* about the ultimate significance of the enterprise in the act of its practitioners. The ethos relates closely to what the members conceive as the deep cause behind the enterprise—what makes it meaningful to its practitioners. It provides its members with a coherent sense of identity and mission.[5]

IMAGES OF THE INTELLECTUAL

What is particularly interesting about the ethos of philosophy is that it reaches beyond the specific practice of philosophers to raise questions about the status, function, and authority of knowledge as such. In inveighing so passionately against philosophy, contemporary scholars are often disassociating themselves from a particular image of the intellectual.

Zygmunt Bauman suggests perceptively that postmodernism tells us less about changes in the world than about the changing position of intellectuals in that world. Because of the rapid expansion of higher education and the information industries, an ever larger sector of the population is engaged in creating or processing knowledge. At the same time, these knowledge workers depend on bureaucratic structures that are felt to compromise the traditional authority and autonomy of scholars. As a result, there is a sense of growing uncertainty about the meaning and value of intellectual work. A flood of recent publications point to an intense and intensive self-scrutiny on the part of scholars and academics.[6] Do intellectuals still form a distinct group or class? Do they have special social or political responsibilities, and if so, on what grounds? Or are the traditional models of the intellectual—as either ivory-tower guardian of culture or visionary political leader—obsolete? And if so, what is to replace them?

It is probably not a coincidence that the era of the end of philosophy is also hailed as the age of cultural studies. Originally a relatively marginal area of inquiry, cultural studies has become a highly visible academic field, particularly in the United States. At first glance, the ethos of cultural studies appears to be the exact opposite of philosophy. Whereas philosophy has traditionally aspired to discover perennial and transcendent truths, cultural studies emphasizes the social embeddedness of human activity and the importance of group identities formed around such categories as class, gender, race, sexuality, age, and ethnicity. In this regard, while cultural studies is usually compared to neighboring disciplines such as literary criticism, sociology, and anthropology, the juxtaposition of philosophy and cultural studies can be illuminating. This comparison throws into sharp relief differing perspectives on what it means to be an intellectual.

One obvious way to compare these two fields is to contrast the universal and the particular. Abandoning grand metaphysical systems leads to a sober acceptance of the partial and limited nature of any attempt to grasp the world in thought. Yet this interpretation may be too simple. Philosophy, however abstract and general its claims, has its own specific logic as an academic discipline. Conversely, the seemingly modest aims of cultural studies often conceal a more ambitious agenda. Cultural studies is by no means free of intellectual hubris. By drawing out some unsuspected parallels, as well as obvious differences, between these two fields, I hope to throw some light on contemporary images of the intellectual.

## THE ETHOS OF PHILOSOPHY

The word "intellectual" was coined in the nineteenth century. To apply the term to the history of Western philosophy is thus to risk the charge of anachronism. Yet there is a sense in which "philosopher" and "intellectual" often function as synonyms. The very etymology of the word "philosophy"—love of wisdom—conjures up the vision of a passionate quest for pure knowledge untrammeled by petty constraints or practical considerations. In the work of Plato and Aristotle, for example, philosophy is an enterprise unlike any other, delving behind the shadowy world of appearances to uncover eternal and immutable truths. Whereas other fields of inquiry are defined by a specific and limited subject matter, metaphysics, according to Aristotle, is the "science of all other sciences," concerned with being as such.[7] From its origins, then, Western philosophy is defined as a mode of thought that can embrace and transcend other more limited forms of knowledge.

This view of philosophy as a pure search for truth was revived and intensified in the Enlightenment. In the seventeenth and eighteenth centuries philosophy came to embrace the entire sphere of knowledge. Only the realms of revealed truth, on the one hand, and rhetoric and belles lettres, on the other, were excluded from philosophy's domain—and even these were held, in their foundations, to be subject to philosophical rationalization. In short, philosophy, in its Enlightenment sense, was not so much the master discipline as *the* discipline; there was no other.[8] Ernst Cassirer describes this view as follows:

> Philosophy . . . is no special field of knowledge situated beside or above the principles of natural science, of law and government, etc., but rather the all-comprehensive medium in which such principles are formulated, developed, and founded. Philosophy is no longer to be separated from science, history, jurisprudence and politics; it is rather to be the atmosphere in which they can exist and be effective. Philosophy is no longer the isolated substance of the intellect; it presents the totality of the intellect in its true function.[9]

At the same time, philosophy's encyclopedic grasp was increasingly skewed in a specific direction, toward the superiority of scientific modes of thought. The *philosophes* of eighteenth-century France, for example, saw philosophy as grounding the rational planning of a more just society. Once the deficits in human society could be explained as failures of reason, the intellectual could boldly assume the role of leader and legislator, speaking with authority on a range of moral and political issues. Subsequently, philosophy played a key role in the creation of the modern university. In the writings of Kant, Humboldt, Fichte, and other German intellectuals of the late eighteenth and early nineteenth centuries, the faculty of philosophy acquired new prestige. As a unified body of knowledge, it would encourage the free play of reason necessary for the education and self-formation of the citizen-subject.[10]

These two aspects of the social mission of philosophy—political emancipation through reason, and the cultivation of the human spirit through reflection and education—are singled out by Jean-François Lyotard in his influential *Postmodern Condition*. According to Lyotard, these modern narratives of Enlightenment have gradually eroded and now inspire incredulity rather than belief. Furthermore, the information revolution is dramatically transforming forms of knowledge in the postmodern era. Science, the most influential field of contemporary thought, has drifted free from any foundational story of human progress. The logic of postmodern science is no longer driven by the quest for Truth but consists of an unstable and often chaotic array of practices. Knowledge is now visualized in terms of information flow and input/output ratios rather than underwriting the growth and self-development of individual or collective subjects.

This crisis of legitimation threatens the Humboldtian model of the university, with its image of the intellectual as pursuing knowledge for its own sake. "The transmission of knowledge," Lyotard notes, "is no longer designed to train an elite capable of guiding the nation towards its emancipation, but to supply the system with players capable of acceptably fulfilling their roles at the pragmatic posts required by their institutions."[11] Lyotard, like Foucault, does not mourn this loss of the intellectual's authority. The big philosophical stories that have often justified scholarly work are not only obsolete, but politically dangerous, totalizing and hence potentially totalitarian. In this regard, the so-called oppositional intellectual is an anachronistic figure, clinging to an outdated vision of politics as enlightenment and the belief in a universal subject-victim. Philosophy, insofar as it continues to exist (and insofar as Lyotard continues to define himself as a philosopher), must abandon its desire to discover a key to all the mythologies. Rather, the role of philosophy must be to challenge all forms of authority, to subvert moral prescriptions and claims to truth. The authentic philosopher, like the artist, questions and experiments; he does not speak to a public, but throws a message into the void.[12]

Richard Rorty, by contrast, sees things rather differently. He argues that philosophy's current malaise is caused not by its aspiration toward wholeness but rather by its increasing narrowness and solipsism. Rorty agrees with Lyotard that the era of philosophy, defined as a search for metaphysical foundations, is over. The traditional philosophical questions are not just anachronistic, but uninteresting. There is no longer any point in trying to pin down the meaning of the good or the true beyond the day-to-day realities of the culture we inhabit. For Rorty, however, the end of foundational philosophy does not mean that we have to give up telling large historical stories and aiming for synoptic overviews.

Here Rorty distinguishes between Philosophy (capitalized) as a nostalgia for eternal and immutable truths, and the more modest ambitions of philosophy, understood as "an attempt to see how things, in the broadest possible sense of the term, hang together, in the broadest possible sense of the term."[13] For Rorty, seeing how things hang together remains an important, indeed indispensable, goal of thought. However, novelists, essayists, and cultural critics are often better at this kind of synoptic vision than professional teachers of philosophy. Thus Rorty's ideal philosopher is an all-purpose intellectual, scornful of disciplinary boundaries and willing to comment on any topic that catches his interest. "He passes rapidly from Hemingway to Proust to Hitler to Marx to Foucault to Mary Douglas to the present situation in Southeast Asia to Gandhi to Sophocles. . . . His specialty is seeing similarities and differences between great big pictures."[14] In other words, Rorty wants to retain one aspect of the philosophical tradition—its interest in "the big picture"—without believing that such pictures bring us closer to a universal truth.

Rorty's complaint about contemporary philosophy is not that it tells too many big stories, but that it tells too few of them. He sees Kant as a key figure in the professionalization of philosophy, its transformation into a discipline or *Fach*. In addition, the proliferation of disciplines and subdisciplines since the early nineteenth century has robbed philosophy of much of its traditional content. For example, the natural and social sciences carved out autonomous fields of inquiry no longer beholden to philosophical concerns. As a result, philosophy was gradually forced to relinquish its encyclopedic aims and ambitions and to become one more specialty among others. However, unlike other disciplines such as sociology, history, and psychology, it had no particular object or field that was distinctively its own.[15]

In the work of postwar Anglo-American philosophers we can see the end results of this narrowing of intellectual scope. These philosophers came to see their discipline as comprising an array of specialized methodologies and vocabularies dealing with technical problems in logic, the philosophy of language, and related fields. The pervasive metaphor was that of *purification*. Philosophy detached itself from a history of woolly, speculative thought in order to achieve a new clarity and scientific rigor. According to Rorty, however, the result of this purification was to turn philosophy into a self-enclosed enclave and academic backwater.[16] Whereas past philosophers such as John Dewey imbued philosophy with an urgent sense of moral and social engagement, contemporary philosophers turn their back on the social world and are in turn ignored by it. Thus the problems facing philosophy, Rorty contends, stem from an increasingly narrow and specialized focus and a refusal to ask questions about things that matter to most people.

This contrast between Lyotard's and Rorty's positions is a striking one. Obviously, it is partly a result of their different biographies. "Philosophy," for Lyotard, means the specter of Hegelian-Marxist thought that continues to haunt many Parisian intellectuals. Rorty, by contrast, seems to be talking about his colleagues at Princeton. Yet they also disagree about important theoretical issues. For example, do large historical stories automatically presume metaphysical foundations? What are the benefits and dangers of appeals to a collective "we"?[17]

I want to suggest that Lyotard's and Rorty's disagreement about whether philosophy is too broad or too narrow points to a recurring tension in contemporary views of philosophy. On the one hand, philosophy is often reproached for its universal ambition, for offering abstract speculations about the nature of reason or the essence of truth that ignore the actual diversity of cultures, histories, and identities. Here philosophy's flaw is that it tries to be too general and all-encompassing. On the other hand, philosophy is also criticized for being narrow and inward-looking, focusing on specialized and technical concerns, and having nothing to say on contemporary social issues. Here its flaw is that it is too particular.

This double-edged critique speaks to different ways of defining the philosopher, both of which have become problematic. Michael T. Ghiselin writes in an elegiac tone, "Where once the term 'philosopher' had some connection with wisdom, now it means nothing more than somebody who occupies a position in a philosophy department."[18] The old idea of philosophers as uniquely wise individuals qualified to pronounce on every social and moral issue no longer gets much support. Yet those who define philosophy more modestly as simply a job description, indicating a professional interest in certain technical or theoretical questions, also attract criticism. Such a self-limitation is seen as a failure of social and political responsibility. Yet what authorizes the public discourse of the philosopher once philosophy no longer has an elevated status? Why should a particular academic training give one a general mandate to voice opinions on social, moral, and political issues?

This double bind, I want to argue, affects intellectuals more generally as they try to puzzle out their role in society. They are caught between two competing visions of their status and function, neither of which is adequate. The old idea of the universal intellectual relies on a cultural authority that can no longer be taken for granted. Yet the model that has replaced it, the expert laboring in a specialized field, lacks any sense of social engagement and responsibility. Is it possible to connect the intellectual to the world without indulging in intellectual hubris and the "arrogant affirmations and imaginings of other peoples' struggles"?[19] And to what extent does expert knowledge in a specific field either authorize or undermine an intellectual's ability to speak on extraprofessional issues?

## THE ETHOS OF CULTURAL STUDIES

Cultural studies, I want to suggest, tries to resolve this dilemma. It offers an alternative vision of intellectual work, one that renounces the hubris of the universal intellectual but without shrinking to the narrowly defined competence of the expert. Rather, the broader social purview of the cultural critic stems from belonging to a disenfranchised group, or in some way representing the interests of such a group. Intellectual work is valued not as the innate wisdom of an academic elite but because it springs from the writer's affiliation with a broader, supra-academic community. In the early days of cultural studies at Birmingham, this affiliation was primarily based on class and the analysis of working-class subcultures. More recently, new social movements have had a dramatic impact on the research program of cultural studies, as scholars have turned toward issues of race, gender, and sexuality.

The politically affiliated intellectual is not of course a new idea. Gramsci's vision of the organic intellectual, first formulated in the 1930s, has inspired a number of people in cultural studies. There is a long history of Marxist reflection on possible alliances between the progressive wing of the intelligentsia and the working class. What is distinctively new about cultural studies, however, is that it places the organic intellectual squarely within the academy. The progressive intellectual is the founder of a new field of study. Political beliefs and alliances are no longer a contingent and covert influence on academic work, but explicitly define a research program. Cultural studies is the first overtly politicized "discipline" to emerge in the modern era. In this regard, it is similar to such interdisciplinary enterprises as women's studies and black studies (I discuss some of these parallels briefly below).

Cultural studies, however, differs conspicuously from traditional Marxism in its suspicion of grand narratives and its refusal to subordinate the everyday experiences of disenfranchised groups to a subordinate moment within an unfolding narrative of human emancipation. In the work of E. P. Thompson, Raymond Williams, and others we can see a refusal to reduce culture to ideology. Rather, there is an intense commitment to rendering and valuing the complexities of working-class culture irrespective of whether it is helping to create a revolutionary proletariat. In much European critical theory, the working class can be redeemed only if it comes to grasp its role in the negation of capitalism and the unfolding of a Marxist dialectic. British cultural studies, by contrast, sought to grant working-class life dignity and value in its own right.[20]

It is here that cultural studies also differs from the political "wings" of neighboring disciplines. After all, Marxist sociology or feminist literary criticism also claims that knowledge is inherently political. However, cultural studies differs not just in taking popular culture as its object, but in suggesting that members of that culture may know as much or more about it than academics. The contrast becomes clear if we think of prominent twentieth-century oppositional intellectuals such as Adorno, Sartre, and Chomsky, whose approach to popular culture relies heavily on ideology critique. They thus draw on a Jacobin ideal of the vanguard intellectual, in spite of their actual, often critical relationship to the heritage of the Enlightenment. Cultural studies, by contrast, redefined the role of ordinary people as dialogic partners rather than objects of study in critical discourse.[21]

The importance of cultural studies thus lies in its questioning of the role of the intellectual and its openness to the potential wisdom of popular knowledge. It sees the practices of everyday life as symbolically rich, often resistive sites of cultural activity. Such descriptions provide a valuable corrective to the bleak pessimism of the mandarin intellectual excoriating the banality of mass culture. Through techniques of ethnography and audience research, as well as through new visions of mass-mediated culture as actively produced by its consumers, cultural studies sought to give greater authority and dignity to the diverse cultures of the nonintellectual majority. The concerns of cultural studies, the editors of a recent anthology conclude, "are not exclusively or even primarily intellectual. Cultural studies proclaims a concern to understand life as it is lived."[22]

The most obvious way cultural studies signals its departure from the universal intellectual is through its rejection of abstract theory and its emphasis on the particular. This narrowing of focus takes place at several levels. First, cultural studies replaces a generic Man with specific identities defined in terms of gender, race, class, sexuality, and so on. This affects not just the object of analysis but also the rhetorical stance of the critic, who is often expected to specify their own social identity. Second, we often see in cultural studies a focus on specific, historically and spatially situated practices rather than claims about culture as a whole. Hence the popularity of such topics as women reading romance novels, the behavior of teenagers at the mall, or the symbolic logic of beach culture. "Local" is a key term in this new mode of analysis. Third, cultural studies often thinks of the insights it produces as useful for a particular moment, rather than holding true for all time. Another important adjective in the rhetoric of cultural studies is "provisional."

These various aspects of particularity are all invoked in the introduction to the well-known anthology *Cultural Studies*. The value of cultural studies work is seen to lie in "conjunctural analysis—analysis, that is, which is embedded, descriptive, and historically and contextually specific."[23] This approach is explicitly distinguished from the "decontextualized scene of philosophical speculation." While acknowledging the influence of contemporary theory on cultural studies, the editors simultaneously distance themselves from "'pure' and implacably ahistorical theory." Contingency is identified as an important category at the level of both content and method. The work of cultural studies is defined—with appealing modesty—as pragmatic and limited; "its interventions are not guaranteed; they are not meant to stand forever."[24]

At the same time, the interest in the particular that defines cultural studies has nothing to do with the particular goals and methods of the disciplines. On the contrary, academic specialization is viewed in a very negative light. A second feature of the rhetoric of cultural studies is its claim to be not only "interdisciplinary" and "transdisciplinary" but also "counterdisciplinary" and "antidisciplinary." Here cultural studies draws on and intensifies a familiar critique of scholarly disciplines. They are artificial constructs that break up the totality of knowledge into isolated, self-enclosed fragments. This kind of compartmentalizing is not only intellectually limiting but also politically dangerous. Disciplines discipline their practitioners, enforce particular norms and protocols, police what does or does not count as legitimate knowledge.

Cultural studies, by contrast, has no "distinct methodology, no unique statistical, ethnomethodological or textual analysis to call its own."[25] It is a field that is not a field, that resists definition and freely crosses boundaries between disciplines. Here cultural critics underscore their distance from the second model of the intellectual that I have discussed, that of the technocrat or expert. Cultural studies draws omnivorously on a range of different methods and traditions while rejecting the straitjacket of academic specialization.

Here, however, we can see a clear parallel between philosophy and cultural studies: both aspire to transcend the disciplines, albeit in different ways. Contemporary philosophy often strives for authority through the language of *purification*, filtering out of other disciplines the essential concepts and logical problems that will form its own subject matter. Cultural studies, by contrast, relies on *accretion*, stockpiling ideas and methods from other disciplines while seeking to avoid the constraints of disciplinarity. As Bill Readings notes, a distinctive feature of cultural studies is its refusal to limit its terms of reference.

IMAGES OF THE INTELLECTUAL

Everything by definition can be understood as culture and therefore subject to analysis by the cultural critic.[26]

This refusal of limits is often presented as a transgressive gesture. Cultural critics speak of making bold raids on other fields, daring to dismantle academic distinctions and defying the guardians of disciplinary purity. Yet we can also put another spin on this self-appointed exceptionalism. Does it not also point to the covert return of a desire to totalize, expressed in an ambition to transcend the blinkered vision that dogs all those unfortunate souls who labor in specific fields? This desire becomes explicit at certain points, as in Cary Nelson and Dilip Parameshwar Gaonkar's heady invocation of a new generation of scholars moving freely across the cultural field, "taking up any and all issues and objects in an interpretive politics with no limits."[27]

Cultural studies, then, means "no limits." This ambitious vision is bolstered, as I've noted, by the unique position of cultural studies: its ability to take all other fields of study as its object. Anything that belongs to the domain of culture—and hence anything—is grist to the cultural critic's mill. While researchers in other fields investigate a particular subject, cultural studies can investigate the investigators, analyzing the conventions of academic knowledge and their links to structures of power. Not surprisingly, taking other disciplines as objects of study sometimes generates negative reactions from scholars in those other disciplines. The brouhaha engendered by Alan Sokal's duping of *Social Text* is one example of such a territorial dispute—in this case, the question of who is qualified to talk about the study of science.[28]

A final feature of cultural studies is its critique not just of the disciplines but of academic institutions. Cultural critics often express their anxiety about a perceived rift between intellectuals and the social world and their desire to heal that rift. This desire is fueled by two impulses. The first is a discomfort with intellectual and cultural hierarchies. Analyzing popular culture often stems from a desire to overcome—or at least to minimize—the divisions between elite and mass culture. The second impulse is a mistrust of institutions and bureaucratic structures that originated in the New Left and was taken up in the new social movements of the 1970s. In cultural studies, the specialized culture of experts and professionals is often seen as alienating and impoverished. Cultural critics speak of "abandoning a narrow circumscribed professionalism in preference for a broad, politically reflective cultivation of the cosmopolitan self."[29] While the university organizes knowledge into tidy, isolated compartments, cultural studies "would speak to the world about the nation and the planet from the vantage point of educated citizenship."[30] The intellectual is no longer imprisoned within the walls of the ivory tower, but engages directly in contemporary social issues. The research program of cultural studies is explicitly linked to a broader mission: the formation of a critical public sphere in which academics form part of a broader community.

There is a clear connection between these two critiques of disciplines and institutions. The discipline that is not really a discipline—that resists any limiting of its intellectual reach and ambitions—will in turn heal the divisions between the university and the rest of society. The fuzziness and shapelessness of cultural studies become the source of its strength. Because everything can be defined as culture, cultural studies offers a way of uniting a fragmented social domain. As several critics have noted, assigning a redemptive social mission to a field of knowledge is not a new idea. At specific moments in the past, both philosophy and English have been hailed as special vehicles of self-knowledge and means to cultural unity.[31] The proliferation of disciplines and subdisciplines inevitably leads to attempts to transcend the fragments and achieve a holistic, all-encompassing vision.

The belief that cultural studies will overcome academic specialization by appealing to a broad public is, however, far from self-evident. Most cultural studies work is published in professional journals and books, garnished with footnotes and references to previous work in the field; its audience for the most part is academics and academics in training. Of course, some cultural criticism does find a broader audience (so, of course, do some books on the canon, such as Harold Bloom's). But what exactly is the political value of this kind of intervention, given the populism of much cultural studies? If ordinary individuals are already as savvy as intellectuals, then, as Janice Radway plaintively asks, "why do they need us?"[32] What is the point of academic intervention in the public sphere once the authority of intellectuals has been called into question? If "the people" are both the object and the addressee of cultural studies, then cultural studies becomes pure tautology. The cultural critic acts as a conduit for popular knowledge, describing the people to itself in a supremely redundant act of intellectual ventriloquism.

Alternatively, if recognizing the value of popular knowledge is part of a discourse about culture primarily created by and for intellectuals, then the demotic claims of cultural studies need to be modified. Like the male identification with the feminine or the Western yearning for the primitive, the fascination of intellectuals with popular culture is a double-edged enterprise. It can point to a genuine desire to disinvest oneself of privilege but also help mask that privilege. As I showed in my discussion of cultural studies and class in chapter 1, academic fantasies about the people do not necessarily coincide with how these people see themselves. For example, one scholar cites her problems in convincing her students of the importance of studying popular culture. Originating from lower-class backgrounds, these students were attending university precisely to gain some

IMAGES OF THE INTELLECTUAL

distance from that culture and to acquire the intellectual and cultural capital that is so easily dismissed by those who already possess it.[33]

## SPECIFIC INTELLECTUALS, SOCIAL MOVEMENTS, AND BIG PICTURES

These contradictions in cultural studies have not gone unnoticed either inside or outside the field. For example, Fredric Jameson sees the populism of cultural studies as a threadbare ideology espoused by intellectuals. This ideology, he claims, "represents a desperate attempt on their part to repress their condition and to deny and negate its facts of life."[34] How, then, should intellectuals make sense of their condition? Deferring to the wisdom of popular knowledge may be a fraudulent and ultimately self-serving gesture. But the solution surely does not lie in reviving the heroic myth of the universal intellectual who will guide and enlighten the befuddled masses.

It is here that Foucault's notion of the specific intellectual offers a more promising alternative. We can best grasp its significance by comparing it to the three other visions of the intellectual sketched out in this chapter. It marks a clear break with the traditional figure of the *universal intellectual* as an authoritative prophet/legislator leading society toward enlightenment. It also differs from the *organic intellectual* as a conduit or spokesperson for the views of an oppressed social group. In spite of important differences between these two models, exemplified in the contrasting ethos of traditional philosophy and cultural studies, both validate the role of intellectuals in similar ways. They think of the intellectual as able to represent the needs and desires of a broader collective (humanity, women, the working class). To make this claim means either ignoring, or claiming to have overcome, the specialized, professionalized, and discipline-driven structures of modern knowledge.

The idea of the specific intellectual, by contrast, does not. Rather, it recognizes the real and irrevocable nature of modern specialization. We can certainly make connections between disciplines, but we cannot go back to a time when biology and sociology, or ethics and aesthetics, were viewed as one. Furthermore, the discourse of intellectuals does not simply voice the views of the oppressed for all to hear. Rather, it is a local intervention within a particular regime of truth. The work of a feminist scholar, for example, may modify the rules of the game within a particular field (how one reads poetry, what counts as an object of study in sociology). These changes are specific, not global; they partake of the intellectual milieu, conventions, and beliefs that they also question.

In this sense, as Foucault notes, the specific intellectual overlaps with the third model that I have discussed, that of the *technocrat* or *expert*.[35] Both terms recognize that intellectuals exist within institutions that shape what they say and how they say it. Professionalism and politics are usually seen as distinct by both conservatives, who endorse the separation, and leftists, who condemn it. However, the idea of the specific intellectual seeks to account for the politics of professionalism. The discourse of intellectuals may have political effects first of all within, but also beyond, its specific field of operation.[36]

> The work of an intellectual is not to shape others' political will; it is, through the analyses that he carries out in his own field, to question over and over again what is postulated as self-evident, to disturb people's mental habits, the way they do and think things, to dissipate what is familiar and accepted, to re-examine rules and institutions, and on the basis of this reproblematization (in which he carries out his specific task as an intellectual) to participate in the formation of a political will (in which he has his role as citizen to play).[37]

The obvious advantage of this model is that it allows intellectuals to accept and think about the specific work they do *as intellectuals* rather than viewing this work as either an anemic supplement to real political action or the superior wisdom of a vanguard elite. In recent years several writers have drawn on Foucault's ideas in order to redraft the project of cultural studies. Bruce Robbins, for example, questions the Left's standard view of professionalism as political self-betrayal. He suggests that the nostalgia for a pure oppositional intelligentsia should give way to an unembarrassed engagement with academic institutions as the supporting context for much critical work. Tony Bennett argues that cultural critics should redefine themselves as cultural technicians, tinkering with practical arrangements in an institutional framework rather than engaging in a heroic struggle against oppression. And John Frow underscores the bad faith of cultural studies scholars who claim to be one with the people, suggesting that their politics should be "openly and without embarrassment presented as their politics, not as someone else's."[38]

These writers are surely correct to insist that cultural studies, which has been scrupulous about particular identities but much less interested in particular institutions, face up to the realities of its own professional context. At the same time, with the notable exception of Robbins, most of the writers on this subject have nothing to say about how being an intellectual is shaped by gender or race. Yet one of the most significant changes in the knowledge class in recent years is its changing constitution. Social groups that have only recently moved into the academy and who remain in a minority are often skeptical that theories of the institution can explain fully their identities and practices. Similarly, they are likely to see themselves as having affiliations that go beyond institutional walls.

Meaghan Morris, for example, notes that "feminism is an unregulated social site from which the actions of feminist professionals are always relentlessly questioned." Feminist scholars are often seen as beholden to a broader public. Hortense Spillers also notes the precarious position of African American intellectuals, suggesting that the "very ability to *differentiate* oneself as *an intellectual worker* . . . has barely been achieved by African Americans across the life world."[39]

In this regard, Anna Yeatman has provided an astute analysis of the contradictory position of what she calls "subaltern intellectuals," who are accountable to the academy for the quality of their intellectual work, but who are also seen as accountable to broader subaltern constituencies. "The subaltern intellectual is one who is positioned as having actually to accord status to that familiar question—why can't you put your ideas in language which ordinary people can understand?"[40] Here, of course, debates about the purpose of cultural studies link up to reflections on the role of women's studies or African American studies.

Some scholars in these fields question the received wisdom that their intellectual work must relate to or serve the needs of a broader community. Robyn Wiegman, for example, argues that the "knowledge formation" known as women's studies needs to uncouple itself from both single and collective female subjects. She rejects the common claim that academic feminism has sold out or become co-opted by its very success. Such apocalyptic narratives of feminism's demise, she points out, rely on unexamined notions about generational continuity and a dubious belief that feminism must remain constant and identical across time and space. Yet the future of academic feminism may turn out to be something very different from its past, or from the forms of feminism that flourish in other, nonacademic contexts.[41]

Hortense Spillers also endorses the view that scholarly work has its own particular logic and that theory is a form of practice. Black intellectuals, she notes, are constantly burdened with responsibility for the plight of black people as a whole. Yet the eternal question, "What will you do to save your people?" is, she suggests, misplaced. This question assumes a nostalgic ideal of a single and unified black community that is in reality long dispersed. Nor can appeals to an organic tradition of music, performance, and preaching provide a plausible model for black intellectual work that will magically knit this work into an all-encompassing cultural whole. The role of black intellectuals, she concludes acerbically, is not the salvation business. They cannot redeem the race, but at best, intervene in the specific contexts they inhabit, as intellectuals engaged in writing, teaching, and rigorous scholarship.[42]

I find such arguments plausible. I do not think we can assume any automatic affinity or connection between subaltern intellectuals and others of the same gender and/or race. But I would also suggest that the movement of women and people of color into the academy complicates some of the standard claims about the position and motivation of intellectuals. For example, Alvin Gouldner's idea of "shopping for an agent" frequently comes up in discussions of the intelligentsia.[43] No longer able to justify their existence according to Enlightenment ideals, the argument runs, twentieth-century intellectuals have sought to resolve this legitimation crisis by attaching themselves to various "authentic" historical subjects: the working class, students, blacks, and so forth.

Whatever the merit of such an explanation, it does not account for those individuals who are both intellectuals *and* members of historically disenfranchised groups. Women and people of color, for example, were never hailed as leaders of the Enlightenment. We cannot argue that they are trying to reassert their cultural centrality by a strategic attachment to an external agent. On the contrary, they themselves *are* that agent, however problematically. Their political affiliations do not derive from an anxiety about the role of intellectuals. On the contrary, such affiliations accompany, and often precede, their entry into the knowledge class.

In other words, there are problems with the claim that the politicizing of the academy is simply due to an intellectual class compensating for its insecurity through an inflated sense of its social mission. The nexus of relations between intellectuals and politics is also shaped by the impact of new social movements on academic life. This is not, I repeat, to assume some essential identity among women or people of color that transcends the very real divisions of class, education, and political ideology. For example, racial identification, as Ien Ang points out, is a rhetorical and political act, an assertion of commonality rather than simply a reflection of ontological sameness.[44] Yet such acts of identification may have important effects. They often inspire, for example, a strong commitment among minority intellectuals to rethinking the ensemble of social relations from new perspectives.

Here I agree with Rorty's view that an interest in big pictures, in seeing how "things . . . hang together," is stubborn, persistent, and important. There will always be individuals interested in making such connections as well as social groups for whom comparison and generalization are politically urgent tasks. These are not "modern" ways of thought, to be jettisoned as we enter a "postmodern" world. It is not the desire for big pictures that is anachronistic, but rather the belief that such pictures are grounded in objective reason, or the laws of history, or some other such metaphysical system. Because it can no longer hope to deliver such cast-iron guarantees, philosophy has for the most part vacated the realm of grand theory. For example, both analytical philosophy and poststructuralist philosophy, in spite of their obvious differences, are deeply suspicious of grand generalizations and big pictures.

Other disciplines have, however, taken up the slack. Less obligated to deliver foundational justifications, they can cater to the interests of those interested in big questions, synoptic overviews, and speculative connections. As Rorty points out, at one time, the study of literature filled this role, providing an intellectual home for those interested in exploring links between art, the history of ideas, and society.[45] Cultural studies is the latest field to encourage the study of diverse, sometimes eccentric topics within a broad, interdisciplinary framework. In recent years, moreover, the term has become an increasingly elastic one. No longer closely or exclusively linked to the Birmingham tradition, cultural studies has come to denote a "broad mix of cultural criticism involving history and anthropology, literature and fine arts, communications and media studies."[46]

Of course expansion always leads to dilution. Some scholars are worried that the new popularity of cultural studies will lead to a watering-down of its original political and media-oriented focus. Furthermore, this visibility makes any claims for its marginal, extra-institutional status much less plausible—though it is a moot point whether such claims were ever accurate in the first place.[47] Nevertheless, cultural studies is currently a place where one can find utopian energies, speculative thought experiments, and political commitments. Here Rorty is way off the mark in excoriating cultural studies as a dry, analytical, anti-Romantic branch of the social sciences that will drive idealistic students away from the university. On the contrary, on present evidence, it attracts numerous enthusiasts and "those interested in better futures," even if it no longer looks for inspiration and redemption to great works of literature.[48]

I do not want to suggest that cultural studies has simply taken over philosophy's traditional role as a provider of "big pictures." Cultural studies owes much to theory, and many cultural critics are familiar with the work of Derrida and Foucault and their questioning of traditional philosophy. Poststructuralism as well as the politics of new social movements shapes the agenda of cultural studies: its emphasis on the specific, its suspicion of the universal intellectual, and its stress on the partial and limited nature of its own findings. At the same time, I've suggested that there are certain clear continuities between cultural studies and philosophy. These include an aspiration to an encyclopedic knowledge beyond disciplinarity that is linked to a powerful sense of social mission.

As has become clear, I have reservations about some claims made in the name of cultural studies. These are well summarized by Lawrence Grossberg: "claims which would make cultural studies into the new organization (and hence salvation) for the humanities; claims which would build its counterdisciplinary impulses into a new totalizing discipline; and claims which demand that cultural studies become the latest incarnation of the academic dream of an intellectual revolutionary agency."[49] Here the idea of the specific intellectual provides a useful reality check. While cultural studies has a complicated relationship to the traditional disciplines, it clearly does not exist outside the constraints of disciplines and institutions. Indeed, it is heavily dependent on them.

In other words, the ethos of cultural studies, like the ethos of philosophy, does not bear any simple relationship to its actual effects. Cultural studies cannot overcome the professionalization of knowledge, abolish social hierarchies, and magically resolve the anxieties of intellectuals about their role and function. But it can provide a space for serious rather than patronizing analyses of popular culture, for thinking about the limits as well as the value of intellectual work, and for eclectic, politically informed scholarship, including both empirical studies and broader, more speculative discussions. It is this messy but fruitful amalgam of concerns, I suspect, that has made it appealing to intellectuals affiliated with new social movements and is the source of its current appeal as an intellectual "home."

## NOTES

This essay was first published in *Continuum* 12, 2 (1998). Reprinted by permission of Taylor & Francis Ltd. Thanks to Niall Lucy for inviting me to think about the relationship between philosophy and cultural studies, to Tom O'Regan for bibliographical information, and to Allan Megill for his careful reading of the manuscript.

1. Avner Cohen, "The 'End-of-Philosophy': An Anatomy of a Cross-Purpose Debate," in *The Institution of Philosophy*, ed. Avner Cohen and Marcelo Dascal (La Salle, IL: Open Court Press, 1989).
2. The position of philosophy in such European countries as France, Germany, and Italy remains more prestigious, though here too its status is being challenged by the social sciences. For a discussion of the French context, see Pierre Bourdieu, *Homo Academicus* (Stanford: Stanford University Press, 1988).
3. Harry Redner, *The Ends of Philosophy* (London: Croom Helm, 1986), 84.
4. Cohen, "The End-of-Philosophy," 112.
5. Cohen, "The End-of-Philosophy," 117.
6. See, inter alia, Zygmunt Bauman, *Legislators and Interpreters: On Modernity, Post-Modernity and Intellectuals* (Cambridge: Polity Press, 1997); Russell Jacoby, *The Last Intellectuals: American Culture in the Age of Academe* (New York: Farrar, Straus and Giroux, 1987); Edward Said, *Representations of the Intellectual* (New York: Vintage, 1994); Bill Readings, *The University in Ruins* (Cambridge: Harvard University Press, 1996); Bruce Robbins, *Secular Vocations: Intellectuals, Professionalism, Culture* (London: Verso, 1993) and his edited collection, *Intellectuals: Aesthetics, Politics, Academics* (Minneapolis:

University of Minnesota Press, 1990); Ron Eyerman, *Between Culture and Politics: Intellectuals in Modern Society* (Cambridge: Polity Press, 1994); Carl Boggs, *Intellectuals and the Crisis of Modernity* (Albany: State University of New York Press, 1993); Paul Bové, *Intellectuals in Power: A Genealogy of Critical Humanism* (New York: Columbia University Press, 1986); Ian Maclean et al., *The Political Responsibility of Intellectuals* (Cambridge: Cambridge University Press, 1990); Jeremy Jennings and Anthony Kemp-Welch, eds., *Intellectuals in Politics: From the Dreyfus Affair to Salman Rushdie,* (London: Routledge, 1997).

7. Redner, *The Ends of Philosophy*, 48.
8. I owe this formulation to Allan Megill.
9. Ernst Cassirer, *The Philosophy of the Enlightenment* (Princeton: Princeton University Press, 1968), vii.
10. In reality, the development of the German university system was much more closely tied to the interests of state bureaucracies than such ideals suggest. See Charles McClelland, *State, Society and University in Germany, 1700–1914* (Cambridge: Cambridge University Press, 1980).
11. Jean-François Lyotard, *The Postmodern Condition: A Report on Knowledge* (Minneapolis: University of Minnesota Press, 1984), 48.
12. See Jean-François Lyotard, "Tomb of the Intellectual," and "A Podium without a Podium: Television According to J.-F. Lyotard," in *Political Writing*, ed. Bill Readings (Minneapolis: University of Minnesota Press, 1993).
13. Richard Rorty, "Introduction: Pragmatism and Philosophy," in *Consequences of Pragmatism* (Minneapolis: University of Minnesota Press, 1982), xiv.
14. Rorty, "Introduction," xl.
15. Redner, *The Ends of Philosophy*, 20.
16. Richard Rorty, "Professionalized Philosophy and Transcendental Culture," in *Consequences of Pragmatism*.
17. Richard Rorty, "Cosmopolitanism without Emancipation: A Reply to Jean-François Lyotard," in *Objectivism, Relativism and Truth: Philosophical Papers*, vol. 1 (Cambridge: Cambridge University Press, 1991).
18. Michael T. Ghiselin, *Intellectual Compromise* (New York: Paragon Press, 1989), 189.
19. Paul Bové, cited in Robbins, *Secular Vocations*, 108.
20. Readings, *The University in Ruins*, 92–96.
21. Of course, some of the work published under the cultural studies rubric continues this tradition of ideology critique. However, what is distinctively new about the project of cultural studies is its break with rather than continuation of that tradition.
22. Valda Blundell, John Shepherd, and Ian Taylor, "Editor's Introduction," in *Relocating Cultural Studies*, ed. Valda Blundell, John Shepherd, and Ian Taylor (London: Routledge, 1993).
23. Lawrence Grossberg, Cary Nelson, and Paula Treichler, "Cultural Studies:

An Introduction," in *Cultural Studies*, ed. Lawrence Grossberg, Cary Nelson, and Paula Treichler (New York: Routledge, 1992), 2.

24. Grossberg, Nelson, and Treichler, "Cultural Studies," 6.

25. Grossberg, Nelson, and Treichler, "Cultural Studies," 2.

26. Reading, *The University in Ruins*, 98.

27. Cary Nelson and Dilip Parameshwar Gaonkar, "Cultural Studies and the Politics of Disciplinarity: An Introduction," in *Disciplinarity and Dissent in Cultural Studies*, ed. Cary Nelson and Dilip Parameshwar Gaonkar (New York: Routledge, 1996), 18.

28. On the relationship between science and cultural studies, Andrew Ross writes, "some cynical commentators might say that it is all part of the colonizing will of cultural studies to penetrate every corner of the field of knowledge in an expansionist movement that masquerades as postdisciplinarity." He concludes, however, that "whatever truth there might be to this ambition, it would still pale beside the reductionist aspirations of science's Holy Grail of a unified theory of the natural world." See "Cultural Studies and the Challenge of Science," in Nelson and Gaonkar, *Disciplinarity and Dissent*, 178.

29. Nelson and Gaonkar, "Cultural Studies," 2.

30. Nelson and Gaonkar, "Cultural Studies," 18.

31. See Ian Hunter, *Culture and Government: The Emergence of Literary Education* (London: Macmillan, 1988); and Readings, *The University in Ruins*.

32. Rosalind Brunt, "Discussion," in Grossberg, Nelson, and Treichler, *Cultural Studies*, 78.

33. Brunt, "Discussion."

34. Fredric Jameson, "On Cultural Studies," *Social Text* 11, 1 (1993): 17–52.

35. Michel Foucault, "Truth and Power," in *Power/Knowledge: Selected Interviews and Other Writings, 1972–1977*, ed. Colin Gordon (New York: Pantheon, 1980), 128.

36. While the notion of the specific intellectual has sometimes been interpreted as encouraging an exclusive focus on the local, Foucault's comments do not justify such a reading. On the contrary, he warns explicitly of the "dangers of remaining at the level of conjunctural struggles" and notes that the "local, specific, struggle" of the intellectual "can have effects and implications which are not simply professional and sectoral" ("Truth and Power," 130–32). The point, as I understand it, is that such effects cannot be presumed in advance, or be assumed to derive from the intellectual's authority as a representative of a social group. For a more critical reading of Foucault's position on intellectuals, see Gayatri Chakravorty Spivak, "Can the Subaltern Speak?" in *Marxism and the Interpretation of Culture*, ed. Cary Nelson and Lawrence Grossberg (Urbana: University of Illinois Press, 1988); and R. Radhakrishnan, "Towards an Effective Intellectual: Foucault or Gramsci?" in Robbins, *Intellectuals: Aesthetics, Politics, Culture*.

37. Michel Foucault, "The Concern for Truth," in *Michel Foucault: Politics, Philosophy, Culture*, ed. Lawrence D. Kritzman (New York: Routledge, 1988), 265.

38. Robbins, *Intellectuals: Aesthetics, Politics, Culture*; Tony Bennett, "Useful Culture," *Cultural Studies* 6, 3 (1992): 406; John Frow, *Cultural Studies and Cultural Value* (Oxford: Oxford University Press, 1995), 169.

39. Meaghan Morris, "A Gadfly Bites Back," *Meanjin* 51, 3 (1992): 546; Hortense Spillers, "*The Crisis of the Negro Intellectual*: A Post-Date," *boundary 2* 21, 3 (1994): 86. For a sociological survey of how African American intellectuals view the connections between their professional and racial identity, see William M. Banks and Joseph Jewell, "Intellectuals and the Persisting Significance of Race," *Journal of Negro Education*, 64, 1 (1995): 75–86.

40. Anna Yeatman, "Postmodern Epistemological Politics and Social Science," in *Postmodern Revisionings of the Political* (New York: Routledge, 1994), 34.

41. Robyn Wiegman, "Feminism and the Afterlife of Identity Politics," *New Literary History*, forthcoming.

42. Spillers, "*The Crisis of the Negro Intellectual*." For a different view, see bell hooks, "Black Intellectuals," in *Killing Rage* (New York: Henry Holt, 1995).

43. Alvin Gouldner, *Against Fragmentation: The Origins of Marxism and the Sociology of Intellectuals* (Oxford: Oxford University Press, 1985), 22–27.

44. Ien Ang, "The Uses of Incommensurability," *Signs: Journal of Women in Culture and Society* 23, 1 (1997): 61.

45. Rorty, "Professionalized Philosophy."

46. Tom O'Regan, "(Mis)taking Policy: Notes on the Cultural Policy Debate," *Cultural Studies* 6, 3 (1992): 409–23.

47. Tony Bennett, "Out in the Open: Reflections on the History and Practice of Cultural Studies," *Cultural Studies* 10, 1 (1996): 133–53.

48. Richard Rorty, "The Inspirational Value of Great Works of Literature," *Raritan* 16, 1 (1996): 8–17. I discuss Rorty's misreading of cultural studies in "Why Those Who Dismiss Cultural Studies Don't Know What They Are Talking About," *Chronicle of Higher Education*, July 23, 1999.

49. Lawrence Grossberg, "Towards a Genealogy of the State of Cultural Studies: The Discipline of Communication and the Reception of Cultural Studies in the United States," in Nelson and Gaonkar, *Disciplinarity and Dissent*, 132.

# 8

# WHY FEMINISM DOESN'T NEED AN AESTHETIC (AND WHY IT CAN'T IGNORE AESTHETICS)

**M**y dissatisfaction with feminist aesthetics does not stem from a belief that there are no connections between art and gender politics. Rather, I do not think that feminist aesthetics helps us understand these connections adequately. One reason for this view is my acquaintance with the long history of attempts to define a Marxist aesthetic and the recent critiques of that history.[1] By contrast, feminist aesthetics has received less systematic attention. This may be because feminism has been most influential in English departments, which are not particularly interested in delving into philosophical debates about aesthetics. Nevertheless, feminist critics in literature, art, film, and related fields often do make general claims about what does or does not constitute good art from a feminist point of view. In this sense, they are embroiled in the project of feminist aesthetics.

In this chapter, I develop further my view that we need to go "beyond feminist aesthetics."[2] I will look at some relevant critical debates in literature but also and to a greater extent in the fine arts. More controversially, perhaps, I suggest that although feminist criticism does not need its own aesthetic, it cannot afford to ignore aesthetics. In fact, it cannot help but be implicated in the aesthetic field. This is, in my view, one of the most helpful insights to come out of postmodern discussions of art as an institution.

## FEMINIST *AESTHETICS* OR *FEMINIST* AESTHETICS?

Because there is now a great deal of work on the male-dominated history of art, I will limit myself to a brief summary of its main conclusions.[3] Feminist critics have discussed in great detail the material obstacles that have limited women's ability to become artists. These include a limited access to education and formal training, lack of social and economic independence for all but the wealthiest of women, and the role of male-dominated cliques and professional elites in the fostering of talent, influence, and reputation. Nevertheless, women's exclusion from art has never been absolute. Women artists have always existed, note Roszika Parker and Griselda Pollock, though they have often been written out of art history.[4] Rather than accepting a tragic narrative of female absence and invisibility, we need to look carefully at the specific circumstances that enable or constrain female creativity. Certain cultures, historical periods, and aesthetic media have been more welcoming to female artists than others.

Perhaps more insidious, because less overt, are the metaphors and myths of creativity that define woman and artist as mutually exclusive terms. Such myths reach an apogee in the Romantic celebration of genius. Here, creativity becomes a quintessentially male act, even as the artist is paradoxically seen to possess feminine qualities of emotional openness and sensitivity. As Christine Battersby notes, "the great artist is a *feminine male*."[5] From Romanticism through to modernism and postmodernism, the artist comes to embody an ideal of subversive masculinity. Women, by contrast, are deemed capable of reproduction and imitation, but not of the bold, insurrectionary vision that defines great acts of creation.

The reception of art often cemented women's place at the margins of the aesthetic. Gender prejudices have permeated the reviews of men and women's art and in turn influenced the process of canon formation. For example, women's art was frequently read in its own time as an expression of the limits of their sex. The transcendent and universal qualities of great art remained almost by definition beyond their reach. Those women who were successful and influential during their own lifetime (George Sand is one obvious example) often disappear from the later annals of literary and art history. Here one encounters, or at least did until recently, a male-centered lineage framed in terms of heroic, cross-generational Oedipal struggles. One striking and often cited example is Ian Watt's *Rise of the Novel.* Middle-class women were important and prolific writers of novels in eighteenth-century England, yet Watt's book attributes the origins of the novel to the work of three men.[6]

Feminist critics have responded to this neglect and trivialization of women's art in various ways. Typically, they have demanded a rethinking of aesthetic criteria from the ground up. Taking women's art seriously changes the way we think about styles, genres, and periods. The marginal position of female artists is not just a material question of lack of money, education, and resources. It is also expressed and reinforced in the very language, vocabulary, and norms of aesthetic evaluation. The history of art, furthermore, is a history of men looking at women, of female bodies being objectified, exoticized, and entombed in works of art. Some scholars have concluded from this critique of the male tradition that feminism needs to fashion its own autonomous aesthetic vision. This feminist aesthetic will ground itself in the distinctive features of female creativity and the subversive undercurrents of a matrilineal tradition.

A feminist aesthetic can take different forms, depending on whether the stress lies on "feminist" or "aesthetics." For example, in her book *Gender and Genius: Towards a Feminist Aesthetic,* Christine Battersby makes a case for a canon of great female artists. While she does not spell out the criteria for such a canon, we would obviously need to rethink the values and standards by which works of art are ranked. For example, women's literature and art that dwell on domestic detail, female friendship, or children have not been treated with the same deference and awe as images of the solitary male struggling against nature or society. Such themes have been deemed minor, not universal. Feminist critics can expose and help to debunk such egregious expressions of male interest and bias. They can make a case for the richness and importance of art by women and describe the distinctive female traditions and genres within which this art acquires much of its meaning. Battersby thus ends her book with a plea for the distinctiveness of female genius that can help us clarify the specific qualities of women's art.

Such defenses of a female "great tradition" are often used to increase the numbers of women in survey courses or art galleries. They have a practical value in this context. Postmodernism notwithstanding, canons show few signs of disappearing. Routine discriminations between major and minor works are part of the day-to-day business of teaching literature and art or running an art gallery. As people feel ever more pressed for time, swamped by information and unsure about the rules of taste, we are also seeing a proliferation of media-generated lists aimed at the uninitiated or insecure: the fifty best novels of the century; the hundred greatest books of all time. It is important to ensure that women are represented on such lists and hence to make a persuasive case for their work on artistic rather than merely political grounds. We need to show why women's art matters to those who care about aesthetics, rather than simply to those who share our politics.

At the same time, proposing a woman-centered canon of great works as the basis for a feminist aesthetic leaves a number of important questions unanswered. For example, where do the criteria for distinguishing great from not-so-great women's art come from? Not, presumably, from the existing tradition of writing about art. Battersby paints such a gloomy picture of the quintessentially patriarchal nature of art history and criticism that it is hard to see how she could disentangle woman-centered criteria of value from what she depicts as a totally compromised tradition. Yet she does not offer any other criteria. Nor does she really engage with arguments against the creation of canons. Some feminists, at least, would argue that the very idea of a "masterpiece" betrays the legacy of phallocentrism. In a secular society, art takes on the status of a sacred artifact and source of truth. It becomes a new religion, promising an experience of transcendence in the encounter with the authentic aura of the artwork. In this context, while Battersby makes the case for a countertradition of great female artists, she does not stand back far enough from her argument to explain why feminism needs great art at all.

There is a second common approach to feminist aesthetics, in which feminism takes precedence over aesthetics. Any appeal to artistic value is viewed with mistrust, as a sign of elitism and a residual attachment to a patriarchal worldview. Instead, critics celebrate diverse forms of creativity as part of their general affirmation of a woman-centered culture. The diary or letter is now deemed as important as the sonnet or tragedy. Needlework or flower arranging are as valid as the paintings of the "great masters." In reality, this stance often leads to a reversal of traditional hierarchies of value rather than a leveling of all values. Artworks that appear spontaneous and uncrafted are praised for expressing the process-oriented nature of female creativity. By contrast, works that rely on structure, symmetry, and the controlled organization of artistic material may be accused of copying the questionable traits of a masculine, product-oriented aesthetic. The overriding desire is to reverse the artness of art, its autonomy and separation from everyday life, and to integrate it back into daily experience.

In my view, neither of these positions offers a plausible basis for a feminist aesthetic. In spite of their obvious differences, both draw on Romantic ideas about creativity in seeing art as a translucent expression of the psyche of its creator. Not only is female experience evoked as a universal category, but it is assumed that such experience will be legible in any particular work of art. This belief strikes me as unpersuasive. A few years ago, for example, I visited the National Museum of Women in the Arts in Washington, D.C. It was hard to find any common attributes among the artworks on display. Women paint flowers, but also construct monumental metal sculptures. They create postmodern collages of female bodies, but they also paint traditional, technically accomplished, realist portraits.

If this formal and thematic diversity can be found in a relatively small sample of contemporary Western women's art, how do we have any hope of finding a common basis in works by women that span centuries and cultures? Appealing to experience as the basis for a feminist aesthetic does not take us very far, simply because artistic creation passes through conventions of imagery, language, and representation that are social and intersubjective, not just personal. (In other words, the assumption that art should reflect personal experience is itself a socially inculcated belief, a historically specific way of thinking about art.) It is one thing to argue for a separate artistic space for women as a way of campaigning against institutionalized forms of sexism. It is quite another to claim that women's art bears witness—or should bear witness—to some shared essence of femaleness.

Part of the difficulty here comes from the frequent conflation of female and feminist, the assumption that all women, given the choice, will make feminist art. Nothing, of course, could be further from the truth. Some artists do see their art and their feminism as integrally and essentially linked. Other female artists do not see themselves as feminists at all. Yet another group of artists identify with feminist ideas but defend the value of their art on aesthetic, rather than political grounds, as linked to the works of other artists rather than the lives of other women. Jeanette Winterson, for example, has expressed her irritation at the repeated reading of her work in terms of autobiographical and lesbian themes. Expressing her admiration for the great modernist writers and poets, she insists that the "strange, prismatic worlds" of art have little to do with the gender or sexual identity of those who create them.[7]

Equating women with feminism encourages critics to believe that any work by a female writer or artist must be subversive, and to hunt for hidden signs of insurrection and antipatriarchal protest. Yet femaleness does not spring spontaneous and unbidden from women's psyches; women, like men, acquire their ideas about gender from the society in which they live. Female artists may hold and express highly traditional views about men and women. There is nothing inherently critical or subversive about women describing female experience, although there may be under certain social conditions. But an aesthetic theory grounded in the female psyche cannot specify what such conditions might be.

WHY FEMINISM DOESN'T NEED AN AESTHETIC

Finally, neither of the abovementioned approaches really comes to grips with the question of the aesthetic. Those who argue for female canons and female genius do not reflect on how such ideas link up to education- and class-based hierarchies of taste and prestige. Do all women enthuse over the works of Artemisia Gentileschi? Is Virginia Woolf on every woman's bookshelf? Clearly not. What does having Frida Kahlo or Barbara Kruger on one's wall say about an allegiance to a specific taste culture? The social role of art, according to Pierre Bourdieu, is closely tied to the game of distinction. Art is one of the ways by which particular classes and class factions display the superiority of their taste. Feminist discourse about art is obviously not free of such acts of distinction.[8]

Yet denying the aesthetic as elitist or irrelevant is not a plausible solution. Feminists cannot easily discard or dismiss the autonomy of art, an autonomy that is created in the act of reception as well as in the act of production. When an everyday object is given a signature and placed in an art gallery, it acquires a very different set of meanings. Visitors to the gallery now read it as a commentary on the history of art rather than as a functional object. A quilt displayed on a gallery wall is making a feminist statement, but it is also making an aesthetic statement. It is in conversation with other works of art.

Of course, those who frequent art galleries and can make connections between quilts and Marcel Duchamp come from a specific section of the population. They are differentiated to some extent by class origins, but even more by education. Feminist critics who are hostile to aesthetics see this as a problem. They dislike difficult, avant-garde, or experimental art because it is not immediately understandable by a wide audience. In a recent feminist anthology, for example, two writers criticize Mary Kelly's influential installation *Post-Partum Document* for being mystifying and inaccessible. Another contributor argues that avant-garde art is elitist and patriarchal because of its distance from everyday life.[9] The assumption here seems to be that feminist art should speak to everyone. But of course, no form of art can reach everyone. If a piece of performance art intimidates a factory worker with no knowledge of art, a conventional realist painting may bore the pants off a Soho software designer with a degree in art history. Such feminist accusations of elitism reveal an unexamined nostalgia for an art that would speak to all women simultaneously (nostalgia is perhaps the wrong word, for this art has never existed). There is little attempt to come to grips with the major differences in education, cultural background, and lifestyle among women. Such differences may have a greater impact on their attitudes to art and the aesthetic than the more commonly cited divisions of race, class, and sexuality.

## PARAESTHETICS

How, then, can feminism come to grips with the aesthetic instead of either hoping it will go away or resorting to traditional ideas about the canon? David Carroll has opened up another way of thinking about aesthetics. His term "paraesthetics" is an attempt to explain the importance of literature and art in the work of contemporary philosophers such as Derrida, Lyotard, and Foucault. For these thinkers, Carroll suggests, the value of art lies in resisting abstraction, dogmatism, and claims to truth. A line of poetry or a painting demands our attention in a specific way, inviting us to dwell on the particular and the nonidentical, on that which resists systematic thinking and confounds conceptual mastery. Yet poststructuralist thinkers are also at odds with traditional aesthetic theory. They reject any notion of the artwork as an organic, unified whole or of art as an autonomous, self-contained, transcendental sphere.

Here Carroll coins the term paraesthetics, meaning "an aesthetics turned against itself, pushed beyond or beside itself, a faulty, irregular, disordered improper aesthetic."[10] Poststructuralist theory draws on the heritage of aesthetics because it directs our attention to the metaphoric, self-reflexive, and polysemic aspects of literature and art rather than trying to extract a political message or evaluating a work in terms of its practical value. It is interested in art as a form of resistance to meaning and use. However, while classical aesthetics speaks of the harmony, totality, and integrity of the artwork, paraesthetics prefers the language of contradiction and undecidability. Art is important because it crystallizes and comments self-consciously on a general cultural condition: the end of metaphysics, the lack of foundations, and the slippery and indeterminate nature of language and communication.

Feminist critics influenced by poststructuralism draw on similar ideas to tackle the relations between art and gender. They begin by stressing the importance of language and representation in defining who we are as men or women. Language and culture go all the way down, shaping our most intimate sense of self. It is not that female experience comes to self-knowledge and then strives to express itself in language. Rather, our experiential reality at the most primal and instinctual level is always already soaked in culture. Our sense of what it means to be a woman, of how women look, talk, think, and feel, comes from the books we read, the films we watch, and the invisible ether of everyday assumptions and cultural beliefs in which we are suspended. Rather than subjects producing texts, in other words, texts produce subjects. Thus language and culture play a crucial part in reproducing the unequal relations between women and men. Patriarchal power pervades verbal and visual systems of meaning. Within such systems, woman is always connected to and inseparable from man. Men's ability to symbolize the universal, the absolute, and the transcendental depends on the continuing association of femaleness with difference, otherness, and inferiority.

These arguments lead us to a very different feminist aesthetic, or perhaps more accurately "textual politics." Clearly, we can no longer appeal to female experience as a ground for female creativity. The very idea of a single, common femaleness is a metaphysical illusion produced by a phallocentric culture. The goal of feminist criticism is not to affirm universal woman as counterpart to universal man. This is not only because of the many empirical differences of race, class, sexuality, and age that render notions of shared female experience untenable. It is also because all such visions of woman are contaminated by male-defined notions of the truth of femininity. This is true not only of the negative cultural images of women (prostitute, demon, medusa, bluestocking, vagina dentata) but also of positive ones (woman as nature, woman as nurturing mother, or innocent virgin, or heroic amazon . . .). Woman is always a metaphor, dense with sedimented meanings.

Rather than expressing the truth of female identity, then, art becomes a means of questioning identity. Art has the power to be uncanny and unsettling, to estrange us from the everyday and challenge our routine assumptions. For example, Jacqueline Rose questions the view of women's writing as a reflection of women's experience and suggests that "writing undermines, even as it rehearses at its most glaring, the very model of sexual difference itself."[11] Instead of subordinating aesthetic experience to feminist goals, we should recognize the power of literature and art to subvert taken-for-granted truths, including the truths of gender.

This strangeness and uncanniness, according to some critics, can be found in all significant art. Shoshana Felman, for example, suggests that works of literature are great to the extent that "they are self-transgressive with respect to the conscious ideologies that inform them."[12] Here, it is not the gender of the author that dictates how feminist scholars should value art. Rather, it is the formal elements of the work itself, the extent to which these elements come together to question our everyday assumptions about the reality, coherence, and separateness of male and female identity. This feminist approach has obvious parallels to Marxist aesthetics, which has also argued that great art can cast a critical light on the work of ideology.

Marxist critics were often divided on which forms and styles of writing were most radical. Was realism or modernism the most appropriate form for capturing the complex social and psychological realities of modern life? Similar debates have afflicted feminist criticism. Some feminist critics sympathetic to poststructuralist ideas have concluded that an experimental poetics is the best way of unsettling norms of femininity. The appeal of *écriture féminine* and Julia Kristeva's theories of poetic language to many feminist critics in the 1980s stemmed from the belief that subverting syntax, eschewing narrative, and using avant-garde strategies to question reality would help to shatter conventional ideas about gender.

Feminist visual artists also turned to a negative aesthetics of rupture, fragmentation, and disidentification. In her abovementioned *Post-Partum Document*, for example, Mary Kelly explored the experience of motherhood by juxtaposing her child's dirty diapers with psychoanalytic accounts of maternal fantasy and women's fetishistic desire for children in patriarchal culture. Kelly's work flatly refuses to offer the viewer an iconic representation of motherhood and to gratify feminist desires for positive images of women. How, after all, could any image of the maternal ever transcend the suffocating weight of the endless madonnas and pietàs that have over the centuries rendered women such easily consumable objects of the male gaze?[13]

The "paraesthetic" turn within feminist theory thus leads to a more serious and substantial engagement with the aesthetic as both a negative and a positive phenomenon. Negative because male-defined images, metaphors, and narratives are powerful and all-pervasive. We cannot simply cast off these false representations to uncover an unblemished and authentic female reality. Any attempt by women to depict women's perspective is enmeshed within rhetoric, narrative, and figure, shaped by the symbols and conventions of a phallocentric culture. Feminism cannot, in this sense, exist outside the male-defined heritage of aesthetic representation.

But the aesthetic also acquires a positive value. Given the importance of language and culture in shaping reality, questioning representation can become a powerful means of questioning the social world. In the twentieth century, art has often been another name for this questioning. Much modern art has sought to estrange us from everyday reality, to shatter the fiction of a unified, stable ego and to explore the opaque, enigmatic qualities of language. Art is not just a means to truth, but also a way of questioning the desire for truth. There are thus obvious affinities between avant-garde art and a feminist poststructuralism that seeks to undermine phallocentric norms. Ingrid Richardson writes, "feminism has embraced the aesthetic as that one final realm which has not been and cannot be subsumed into reason, as that place which sidesteps-undercuts preoccupations with identity, boundaries and norms, as the space where female desire can finally be written into discourse and spill out new matrices of subjectivity and experience."[14]

Aesthetics, in other words, can be a space of resistance as well as conformism. Feminist attacks on art as a bastion of male authority and linchpin of the status quo are too simple and reductive. Within modernity, at least, the role of the artist has often been that of dissident and outsider. Aesthetic experience has a complicated and often conflict-ridden relationship to a social order whose primary values are those of efficiency, rationality, and profit. This is not to suggest that male artists have always been friends and allies of feminism. If anything, the opposite has been true. But modern art does contain a rich and complex history of experimenting with differing styles and techniques of representation, with questioning everyday realities and imagining alternative worlds. As feminist critics and artists struggle to rethink the meaning of gender, they have found aspects of that history inspiring.

From the standpoint of paraesthetics, then, gender and the aesthetic are intertwined in a manner quite unlike conventional feminist aesthetics. Art is not subordinated to a feminist demand for a fixed and coherent female identity. Rather, art is the place where identity fails, where the fictions of separate, unitary and complementary male and female selves are revealed as fictions. This art is "feminine" in a metaphorical sense, in embracing everything that is elided and repressed by the binary logic of a patriarchal culture. Femininity is thus the space of non-identity rather than identity, heterogeneity and otherness rather than the will to truth. In this sense, there would appear to be no necessary relationship between the (female) gender of the author and the (feminine) gender of art. Some feminist critics, however, have insisted that the two are linked, and that the fragmented, chaotic, polysemic forms of experimental art have a close affinity with women's bodies and women's psyches. Feminine sexuality engenders feminine textuality.

This perspective in turn raises new questions about social meanings and effects of art. How revolutionary, after all, is poetic language? Does the shattering of form reach out beyond the aesthetic sphere? Art may offer new ways of seeing, but do these new ways translate into social change? Should they? Who are the audiences of experimental and avant-garde art and how does this fact affect claims about the subversive nature of feminine writing or antirepresentational art? Feminist critics sometime use the language of transgression too glibly, without thinking about the specific contexts in which literature and art are interpreted. Art may no longer offer positive truth, but it can easily slide into a form of negative truth or negative theology, whose subversive effects are assumed rather than demonstrated.

## ART AS INSTITUTION AND THE DEATH OF THE AVANT-GARDE

Some recent discussions of the state of art in a postmodern era zero in on precisely this issue. Discussions of postmodernism and art have splintered off in a hundred directions. Here I want to focus on two specific ideas: the idea of art as an institution, and the claim that the avant-garde is dead. Both of these ideas have been developed much more extensively in art criticism than in literary theory, perhaps because art criticism retains much closer ties to art institutions and the art market. They can, however, help to throw light on the politics of contemporary art in a wide range of media and contexts.

Drawing loosely on Victor Burgin's essay "The End of Art Theory," I define the institution of art as consisting of diverse sites such as publishing houses, galleries, literature and art departments, academic journals, museums, libraries, and so on. These sites are linked together by a cluster of common languages and vocabularies that they repeat and replenish through teaching, reviewing, writing, and research. This loose nexus of institutions and discourses plays a preeminent role in defining what counts as art.[15]

Looking at aesthetics this way obviously differs from the traditional view of art as a self-evident body of masterpieces. It draws attention to the specific practices and mechanisms by which social attitudes to art are created and reproduced over time. But it also differs from a political perspective that sees art and aesthetics as merely a veil for bourgeois and patriarchal oppression. Art has its own distinct logic, history, and cultural reality. It must be situated, in Griselda Pollock's words, in terms of its own distinctive "materials, resources, conditions, constituencies, modes of training, competence, expertise, forms of consumption and related discourses, as well as its own codes and rhetorics."[16] The politics of the art institution is a site-specific politics rather than a simple reflection of what is happening elsewhere in the economic and political system.

There are several important themes that come out of the idea of art as an institution. First, artists alone do not make art; rather, it is the institution that makes art. It is a commonplace of postmodern theory that we can only define art tautologically: art is what the art institution decides is art. At a time when artists can turn dead cows and dog turds into art, it is clear that artness is not inherent in the work itself, but in the way it is framed, perceived, and interpreted. What follows from this, however, is that no individual work of art can hope to do away with the institution of art. However radical it may be in form or content, such a work can be assimilated into the art institution, which thrives on challenges to its sovereignty. This is, of course, the lesson of the historical avant-garde. Dadaists and surrealists created iconoclastic works of anti-art only to find these works immortalized in art galleries as great works of art.[17]

Yet mourning the intransigent reality of art as institution may be misplaced. The aim of the historical avant-garde movements was to tear down museums as mausoleums of dead art and monuments to the bourgeoisie. They wanted to destroy the autonomy of art and to return art to everyday life. Contemporary critics and artists, including some feminists, often repeat these invectives

WHY FEMINISM DOESN'T NEED AN AESTHETIC

against the museum. As Llewellyn Negrin points out, what these diatribes ignore is that while contemporary art often opposes the museum, it is also dependent on it. "To dismiss museums simply as sepulchres of art is a one-sided appraisal of their role which neglects the fact that art only 'dies' in the museum so that it can be 'reborn' in another sense."[18]

In other words, while museums alienate artworks from their original use and social context, they place them in alternative contexts and new frames of reference, in dialogue with other works of art. They become meaningful in new ways and for new audiences far beyond the specific place and time in which they were created. Furthermore, much contemporary art does not *have* an original context. It is produced in M.F.A. programs or created to be displayed in museums and would not exist were it not for art galleries and the support of the art institution.[19] Postmodern art, in particular, draws on an acute self-consciousness about its relationship to a prior aesthetic tradition that is heavily dependent on encountering art in the museum. Rather than decrying museums as oppressive institutions that siphon off art from more authentic contexts, we may find it more accurate to think of museums as playing a key role in the creation, promotion, and preservation of art and in bringing it to a wider public.[20]

This brings us to the related theme of the death of the avant-garde. If the historical avant-garde movements showed that it was impossible to destroy the institution of art, then contemporary artists who claim to be shocking and outrageous could be accused of acting in bad faith. Even as they denounce the evils of bourgeois culture, they do so with an eye on the publicity machine and the hope that their work will be bought by curators and dealers. One strand of Marxist aesthetics originally placed a high value on avant-garde art as a mode of resistance to the mindless pablum of mass culture and the tyranny of the market. This distinction no longer carries much weight. There is no longer any obvious connection between symbolic transgression and political transgression, between stylistic rupture and processes of social change. Even the most outrageous work of art can be turned into a commodity, as the shock of the new drives the inflationary spiral of a New York art market that is fueled by media hype and controlled by a managerial elite of dealers and curators. The death of the avant-garde, in other words, is a paradoxical result of the success of the avant-garde.[21]

Moreover, the art institution reaches beyond the walls of the gallery to embrace an entire knowledge industry of catalogues, books of criticism and theory, journals, and numerous other discourses about art. In this way, contemporary art is translated and interpreted for specific publics. The transgressive gestures of radical art form part of the cultural capital of educated and professional elites in Western urban societies. A cynic could argue that, rather than transforming

WHY FEMINISM DOESN'T NEED AN AESTHETIC

the status quo, this radical art is simply one of the cogs that keep the high culture industry turning over smoothly. In the gloomiest version of this scenario, the compromised social position of art means that it can no longer have any effect or bring about social change.

How are these insights helpful for feminist critics and how do they need to be modified? They are useful, I think, in making it clear that the politics of art is not simply a question internal to the artwork—a question of expressing the right feminist content or espousing an authentically subversive feminine form. It also involves thinking about how art is produced, disseminated, and interpreted. It is here that postmodern theories of art differ from the Romantic ideal of art as authentic self-expression, embodied in the feminist call for an aesthetic of women's experience, and also from the modernist belief in formal radicalism, echoed in some versions of feminist poststructuralism that retain avant-garde affinities. Instead, these theories draw our attention to the specific institutional contexts and power relations that shape the meaning and effects of art.

Yet a feminist critic might plausibly argue that the discussions of these contexts is often not specific enough. Claims about the end of political art in the postmodern era do not usually pay much attention to the differing positions of male and female artists. The Guerilla Girls have drawn attention to the minimal representation of women in major galleries and exhibitions and their often precarious position in the art institution. In fact, there are no women whose work attracts the same price tags, institutional prestige, or media coverage as the creations of male artists such as Warhol, Johns, Schnabel, Hockney, Kiefer, and others. Thus the meanings and associations accruing to women's art will differ, not because of a uniquely feminine aesthetic but simply because of the different conditions under which such work is produced and interpreted. Women's increasing presence in high art is charged with significance. The signature of the female artist does not carry the same meaning as that of the male.

When we couple this fact with the feminist concerns that motivate many, though by no means all, contemporary female artists, the narrative of the end of political art loses much of its power. For example, Zygmunt Bauman ends his lucid summary of the dilemmas of postmodern art by noting that "the present-day arts, on the contrary, care nothing about the shape of social reality."[22] By contrast, one might argue that for women art is in the process of being re- rather than depoliticized. The unprecedented explosion of women's art in the last twenty years, often exploring issues of gender and sexuality, female bodies and women's desire, seems at odds with postmodern notions of exhaustion and ennui. In this sense, feminism could provide a model for a politically conscious yet post–avant-garde art theory and practice. In other words, the death of the avant-garde does not mean an end to political art, but rather the end of a political aesthetic that allows only two alternatives: radical change outside institutions or total co-option and death inside them. The museum, the gallery, and the seminar room do not destroy the potential social resonance of art.

However, feminist critics have not always been willing to face up to their involvement in bureaucratic and commercial structures: "institution" is often a dirty word. Yet feminist art and writing do not take place in a mysterious feminine wild zone; they are often funded by grants, produced by women who work in colleges and universities, or otherwise linked to art institutions. More generally, feminist artists and critics who contest the male-dominated history of art also draw on the language, skills, and techniques of that same history. They are not outside the power relations that accrue to certain forms of art, culture, and knowledge production. For example, artists who subvert hierarchy at a textual level by creating fluid, multi-perspectival artworks may also reinforce hierarchy at a social level, in creating difficult art that presumes specialized skills in interpretation. As I noted in my earlier discussion of feminist intellectuals, women thus find themselves in contradictory positions as professionals in institutions. If they are not "insiders," neither are they simply "outsiders."[23]

Feminist theory, of course, is not only interested in the gender politics of the art institution. Rather, it also looks at large-scale structures of gender inequality that cut across specific sites. From this vantage point, it is clear that contemporary gallery art or experimental fiction speaks only to specific subgroups of women. To note this is not, I should stress, to dismiss their value. I have already noted the flaws of a feminist aesthetic that claims to include all women. Rather, it is to recognize that any art form will resonate only in a specific milieu. Feminist critics need to connect aesthetic strategies to the needs and interests of specific female audiences, rather than opposing masculine and feminine, conservative and radical forms.

For example, theories of art as institution often exaggerate its autonomy and deny its permeability and openness to external social forces. While feminism cannot do away with the art institution, it has helped to open up art to a wider variety of perspectives and alternative locations. Through such initiatives as adult education, community art projects, alternative publishers, and arts festivals, feminists have modified some of the rules of the game of distinction and brought both women's and feminist art to the attention of wider audiences. Obviously, those involved in public outreach need to gauge the specific interests, needs, and vocabularies of their targeted viewers or readers. As a result, they often draw on popular and accessible forms of feminist imagery. While feminist scholars committed to a paraesthetics of subversion often disdain such conventional images or even dismiss them as phallocentric, they can play an important role in communicating feminist ideas to a broader public. Chastising popular feminist art for an insufficient grasp of deconstructive theory is beside the point.[24]

Similarly, feminism cannot afford to ignore the pull of television and popular film. Even the most accessible feminist novel or painting, after all, will reach only one section of the population. While popular culture has not traditionally been part of the subject matter of aesthetics, cultural studies has paid considerable attention to the symbolic richness and formal complexity of much contemporary media culture. As I noted in chapter 7, it has little patience with vanguard aesthetic theories, including those of Marxism and feminism, that dismiss mass culture as an inauthentic realm of false needs and mindless gratification. Aesthetics can no longer define itself in opposition to popular culture; rather, popular culture in the era of MTV is often aesthetically sophisticated and highly self-conscious. Here again, feminism cannot afford to align itself with a single aesthetic strategy. The audience of mass-media forms is not monolithic or homogeneous, but widely diversified according to affiliations, tastes and cultural reference points.[25]

I hope to have shown, in conclusion, why trying to unite aesthetics and feminist politics in a single phrase is not a particularly good idea. Such a forced reconciliation does not do justice to the real tensions and conflicts, as well as the interconnections, between these two fields. In one common scenario, feminist aesthetics leads to art being assigned a secondary and supportive role as the handmaiden of feminist politics. Art, it is assumed, will obediently reflect the truths of female identity and experience. The aesthetic is effectively canceled out in being reduced to an instrumental role as the vehicle of feminist ideology.

Alternatively, feminist aesthetics can mean that art and politics become one and that one is art. The feminist turn to paraesthetics recognizes the value of ambiguity, contradiction, and non-identity. Art can help to complicate and cast new light on our perceptions of maleness and femaleness, gender and sexuality. But this aesthetic principle of non-identity does not accord with the more concrete and goal-directed concerns of feminist politics. Women's novels and films, paintings and sculptures, poetry and videos have immeasurably enriched our culture in the last twenty years. But this creativity does not translate neatly into specific political outcomes, nor should its value be measured in such terms. In this regard, as I have suggested, feminist critics sometimes place too much hope in the subversive effects of formal innovation and do not come to terms with the social and institutional frameworks of contemporary art.

Of course, one could argue that a feminist aesthetics, properly conceived, would retain a delicate balance between the competing demands of art and politics rather than simply subsuming one within the other. Yet the welding of feminism and aesthetics into a single phrase still leaves me uncomfortable,

WHY FEMINISM DOESN'T NEED AN AESTHETIC

because it deflects attention away from the real tensions that exist between art and politics as well as the important connections. Furthermore, feminist aesthetics is a singular noun, suggesting a specific art practice deriving from a specific politics. I have argued, in contrast, that it is impossible to define in general terms what a feminist aesthetic might be, that feminist approaches to art must be plural, not singular. The putative community of women fragments into diverse publics that are familiar with particular aesthetic traditions, vocabularies, and frameworks of interpretation. There is no single form of feminist art that can encompass and reach all these audiences. Here I agree with Mary Kelly's observation: "One very important point which applies to all so-called politically engaged art is that there's no such thing as a homogeneous mass audience. You can't make art for everyone."[26]

## NOTES

This essay was originally published in *Feminism and Tradition in Aesthetics*, ed. Peggy Brand and Carolyn Korsmeyer (University Park: The Pennsylvania State University Press, 1994). Copyright 1994 by The Pennsylvania State University. Reproduced by permission of the publisher. I have significantly expanded and clarified the latter half of the argument. Thanks to Janet Lyon for her reading of the manuscript.

1. The best overview of debates in Marxist aesthetics remains *Aesthetics and Politics*, ed. Fredric Jameson (London: New Left Books, 1977). Recent criticisms of the project of a Marxist aesthetic include Peter Bürger, *Theory of the Avant-Garde*, trans. Michael Shaw (Minneapolis: University of Minnesota Press, 1984); and Tony Bennett, *Formalism and Marxism* (London: Methuen, 1979).

2. See Rita Felski, *Beyond Feminist Aesthetics: Feminist Literature and Social Change* (Cambridge: Harvard University Press, 1989).

3. The following list is necessarily selective. In the fine arts, see, for example, Christine Battersby, *Gender and Genius: Towards a Feminist Aesthetic* (Bloomington: Indiana University Press, 1989); Rozsika Parker and Griselda Pollock, *Old Mistresses: Women, Art and Ideology* (New York: Pantheon, 1985); Linda Nochlin, *Women, Art, and Power and Other Essays* (New York: Harper and Row, 1988); Whitney Chadwick, *Women, Art and Society* (London: Thames and Hudson, 1990). Feminist accounts of gender bias in literary criticism and history include Mary Ellman, *Thinking About Women* (New York: Harcourt Brace Jovanovich, 1968); Joanna Russ, *How to Suppress Women's Writing* (London: Women's Press, 1984); Gaye Tuchman with Nina E. Fortin, *Edging Women Out: Victorian Novelists, Publishers and Social Change* (New Haven: Yale University Press, 1989).

4. See Parker and Pollock, *Old Mistresses*.

5. Battersby, *Gender and Genius*, 4.

6. Ian Watt, *The Rise of the Novel: Studies in Defoe, Richardson and Fielding* (New York: Chatto and Windus, 1957).

7. Jeanette Winterson, *Art Objects: Essays on Ecstasy and Effrontery* (New York: Knopf, 1996).

8. Pierre Bourdieu, *Distinction: A Social Critique of the Judgment of Taste* (Cambridge: Harvard University Press, 1984).

9. Margot Waddell and Michele Wandor, "Mystifying Theory," and Angela Partington, "Art and Avant-Gardism," in *Visibly Female: Feminism and Art Today*, ed. Hilary Robinson (London: Camden, 1987).

10. David Carroll, *Paraesthetics: Foucault, Lyotard, Derrida* (New York: Methuen, 1987), xiv.

11. Jacqueline Rose, *Sexuality in the Field of Vision* (London: Verso, 1986), 121.

12. Shoshana Felman, *Reading and Sexual Difference* (Baltimore: Johns Hopkins University Press, 1993), 6.

13. For an overview of *écriture féminine* and the work of Julia Kristeva, see Toril Moi, *Sexual/Textual Politics* (London: Methuen, 1985). Griselda Pollock discusses an aesthetics of disidentification in "Screening the Seventies: Sexuality and Representation in Feminist Practice—A Brechtian Perspective," in *Vision and Difference: Femininity, Feminism, and Histories of Art* (London: Routledge, 1988).

14. Ingrid Richardson, "Feminism and Critical Theory," unpublished manuscript.

15. Victor Burgin, "The End of Art Theory," in *The End of Art Theory: Criticism and Postmodernity* (London: Macmillan, 1986).

16. Griselda Pollock, "Feminist Interventions in the History of Art," in *Vision and Difference*, 9.

17. On this point, see Bürger, *Theory of the Avant-Garde*.

18. Llewellyn Negrin, "On the Museum's Ruins: A Critical Appraisal," *Theory, Culture and Society* 10, 1 (1993): 116.

19. See Howard Singerman, *Art Subjects: Making Artists in the American University* (Berkeley: University of California Press, 1999) for a detailed analysis of the close ties between university art departments and the creation of art.

20. In making this point, I do not deny the historical links between the museum and colonialism and the important part played by museums in the objectification of other cultures. The question remains, however, of how intrinsic these aspects of museums are to the museum as institution. For a scathing critique of the museum along these lines, see Deborah Root, "Art as Taxidermy," in *Cannibal Culture: Art, Appropriation and the Commodification of Difference* (Boulder: Westview, 1996).

21. See Suzi Gablik, *Has Modernism Failed?* (New York: Thames and Hudson, 1984). Gablik's questionable nostalgia for tradition and a consensus of values does not prevent her from making some very pertinent observations on the current aporias of the avant-garde.

22. Zygmunt Bauman, "Postmodern Art, or The Impossibility of the Avant-Garde," in *Postmodernity and Its Discontents* (New York: New York University Press, 1997), 101.

23. Griselda Pollock expresses this contradictory position well. She notes that the feminist "desire for political effectivity for art cannot be realised exclusively in terms of the art world. Yet art practices have to maintain a relation to the art world in order to be accredited as art, to be effective as that specific form of social operation. There has to be an intervention generated from a *social* space." Griselda Pollock, "Feminism and Modernism," in *Framing Feminism*, ed. Roszika Parker and Griselda Pollock (London: Pandora, 1987), 106.

24. See, for example, Judith Barry and Sandy Flitterman Lewis, "Textual Strategies: The Politics of Art-Making," in Robinson, *Visibly Female*. In criticizing popular forms of feminist art and claiming that only a more "theoretically informed art can prove capable of producing enduring changes," the authors overestimate the political effects of theory, as well as the potential audience for such theoretically informed art.

25. For one attempt to integrate the findings of cultural studies into traditional aesthetic theory, see Richard Schusterman, *Pragmatist Aesthetics: Living Beauty, Rethinking Art* (Cambridge: Basil Blackwell, 1992).

26. Mary Kelly, interview, in Robinson, *Visibly Female*.

WHY FEMINISM DOESN'T NEED AN AESTHETIC

# 9

# FEMINISM, POSTMODERNISM, AND THE CRITIQUE OF MODERNITY

In this chapter, I look at some points of connection and contradiction between contemporary feminism and the influential if elusive concept of the postmodern. This is a revised version of the first essay I wrote on this subject and covers some important groundwork, though some of the terrain is now relatively familiar. I do not try to survey the vast body of writing on postmodernism or deliver a conclusive judgment on the value of the term. Instead, I consider some common hypotheses about a "postmodern condition" from the standpoint of feminist theory. I suggest that feminism cannot simply sidestep the political and epistemological issues posed by recent debates, but that discussions of postmodernism often blur together differing and nonsynchronous political positions. As a result, they do not help us come to grips with feminism's specific relationship to the ideas and institutions of modernity.

Writing in 1983, Craig Owens maintained that while feminism's engagement with postmodernism had been minimal, women's insistence on difference and incommensurability was not only compatible with postmodern thought, but a clear instance of it.[1] Subsequently, feminist theorists began to tackle this question. In *Gynesis*, for example, Alice Jardine explores the points of intersection between feminism and the writings of Derrida, Lacan, and Deleuze, whom she describes as theorists of modernity. In Jardine's French-inspired usage, "modernity" denotes the cluster of issues more often linked to postmodernism in the United States: the loss of faith in history and the dialectic, the crisis of truth and representation, the disappearance of the subject. Jardine reads the crisis of modernity as closely linked to the feminine, defined as the space of desire, the maternal body, the mystical, the repressed Other of reason. Yet she concedes that this admiration for the feminine in recent French theory usually occurs at the expense of women. Feminism is dismissed as anachronistic because of its continuing reliance on reason, truth, and similar elements of a supposedly discredited metaphysical tradition.

The paradox is noted, but not resolved. In fact, Jardine's juxtaposition of feminist and poststructuralist thought presents the latter as the master discourse, feminism as the lagging partner, doomed to anachronism and "conservative and outdated polemic" if it doesn't quickly get up to speed.[2] Yet she does not explain how exactly feminist concerns are supposed to jell with a deconstructive questioning of all norms and values. As Barbara Creed argues in her own discussion of feminism and postmodernism, "The paradox in which we feminists find ourselves is that while we regard patriarchal discourses as fictions, we nevertheless proceed as if our position, based on a belief in the oppression of women, were somehow closer to the truth."[3] How, then, can feminism justify its own critique of patriarchy, once it faces up to a pervasive legitimation crisis that corrodes the authority of all forms of knowledge and reveals truth as nothing more than the ruse of power?

One possible response is simply to dismiss postmodern and poststructuralist theory as an unwarranted generalization from a limited set of experiences. Some scholars have suggested that the language of meaninglessness, instability, and apocalypse reveals more about the standpoint of a disaffected and marginal Western intelligentsia than about a general cultural condition.[4] Pursuing a similar line of thought, some feminists see postmodernism as the symptom of a crisis in male authority that has no relevance for women. Nancy Hartsock, for example, makes what is now a familiar claim: it is no coincidence that subjectivity, history, and truth are under attack by white men at the very moment that these ideas are inspiring the culture and politics of disenfranchised groups.[5] Similarly, Barbara Christian notes that the academic prestige of poststructuralism, along with its notorious claims about the death of the author, is undermining the authority of literary criticism devoted to interpretations of black female writers. Perhaps, she suggests, it is the flourishing culture of African American and postcolonial peoples that is causing this Paris- and Yale-inspired retreat from reality, history, and subjectivity.[6] The most forceful case for postmodernism (or more accurately, poststructuralism) as a ruse of patriarchy has been made by Somer Brodribb. She writes, "the law of postmodernism is Father Knows Best and the phallus is its symbol. Feminism is the Devil, staked out and variously pilloried as bourgeois deviation, biological determinism, foundationalism and determinism. . . . Postmodernism is the cultural capital of late patriarchy. It is the art of self-display, the conceit of masculine self."[7]

My own sense is that the questions raised in the language game of postmodernism cannot be dismissed so easily. First, the skepticism toward epistemological and ethical norms that is commonly associated with postmodernism echoes, yet also undermines, the feminist critique. If we want to persuade others of the value of feminist claims, we need to engage with these questions rather than simply retrenching and insisting on a self-evident female identity or reality. Second, postmodern (though not necessarily poststructuralist) theories deal with social transformations that are clearly relevant to the position of women, even if male postmodern theorists rarely pause to think about how gender might enrich or complicate their analysis.

Whether we defer to the concept of the postmodern or read the present as continuing the crisis-laden development of modernity, we need to think through certain important mutations in the fabric of Western societies. While the implications of such changes and the interrelations between them are blurred and unclear, there are a number of often cited factors that contribute to a "postmodern problematic."[8] These include the proliferation of information technologies and the gradual shift toward a postindustrial (although not postcapitalist) society, the declining authority of liberalism and Marxism, the visibility of feminism and other social movements that place cultural difference on the agenda and condemn the patriarchal, heterosexist, and ethnocentric nature of many Western ideals, a growing aestheticization of everyday life in the mass dissemination of signs and images and a simultaneous questioning of the art/life opposition inherent in high modernism, and a shift in philosophy and social theory toward linguistic frameworks accompanied by a sustained critique of foundationalist thought.

Any such list is necessarily partial. It is also clear that these disparate phenomena are open to very diverse readings. Baudrillard, for example, seizes on the influence of the mass media in order to proclaim the end of politics, with the ironic silence of the masses offering the only remaining point of resistance to an all-encompassing simulation. John Keane, by contrast, argues that contemporary forms of capitalist development and bureaucratic rationalization continually incite opposition and resistance in the emergence of autonomous public spheres.[9] Still, most theorists of postmodernism, including Jean-François Lyotard, Jürgen Habermas, Gianni Vattimo, Fredric Jameson, Ihab Hassan, and Andreas Huyssen, agree that the Enlightenment ideals enshrined in both liberalism and Marxism are under siege. Their responses to this legitimation crisis differ, of course: some seek to reproduce this crisis of meaning in their own writing, others to explain and account for it through a unifying framework.

We can see immediately that feminism's relationship to this shift in sensibility is ambiguous. In recent years feminist scholars have crafted a sustained and influential critique of the Western philosophical and cultural tradition. They have explored the patriarchal foundations of its ethical and epistemological assumptions and its claims to objective authority. Scholars such as Luce Irigaray, Genevieve Lloyd, and Susan Okin have exposed the masculinity of the universal subject of Western philosophy and political theory, which deflects its anxieties about material embodiment by projecting them onto an irrational, natural, feminine Other.[10] More generally, diverse fields of intellectual inquiry in the sciences and humanities have come under critical scrutiny from feminists who have argued that women's marginal position is a question not simply of gender-biased content, but also of the methodologies and assumptions underpinning the disciplines. As a result, there are obvious connections between the postmodern sense of a crisis of truth and the feminist challenge to patriarchal truth.[11] It is also clear, however, that a legitimation crisis knows no boundaries, and that the critique of knowledge claims can just as easily be turned against feminism itself. Can feminism claim to be more true than the positions it criticizes, and if not, how is it to defend its own claims?

## FEMINIST EPISTEMOLOGIES

It is this difficulty that has inspired attempts to create a feminist epistemology that can account for not just the specific but also the superior nature of women's standpoint. One important source has been Nancy Chodorow's work on the acquisition of gender identity in early childhood. Chodorow describes how girls learn to be female by identifying with a caretaker of the same gender, whereas boys learn that maleness means separating from the mother. This early experience "creates an 'objectifying' sense of self in men and a 'relational' sense of self in women."[12] This psychological differentiation is in turn responsible for the difference between a "masculine" knowledge based on abstraction and objectification and a "feminine" knowledge that relies on empathy and relationships with others.

Such polarities may appeal to our intuitive biases about gender differences. However, they have been thoroughly criticized by feminist scholars who view them as abstract and ahistorical, inattentive to the many cultural, social, and economic differences between women. Jane Flax, for example, who originally sought to ground a feminist epistemology in the work of Chodorow, later distanced herself from monocausal explanations of gender.[13] Furthermore, it is not immediately obvious how object relations can provide a solid foundation for feminist theory. Even if we can show empirically that women are, on average, more empathic and other-directed than men, this can only generate more questions rather than provide hard-and-fast answers. Feminism involves, after all, a questioning of existing gender relations and identities rather than a simple endorsement of them.

A second argument in feminist epistemology suggests that women's distinctive perspective on the world has less to do with distinctive psychosexual characteristics than with their social experience of subordination. Sandra Harding and Nancy Hartsock both make use of the Hegelian master/slave schema. The female slave will invariably know more than the master, whose vision is "partial and perverse."[14] Whereas the master only needs to know about his own reality, the slave, by dint of her subjugated position, must know both her reality and that of the master. Similarly, Hilary Rose finds a basis for a distinctive feminist science and epistemology in the caring labor of women, as the only hope of overcoming female alienation in a male-dominated social world.[15] There are obvious parallels here to the Marxist belief that the proletariat has a superior grasp of the social structure thanks to its unique position in the relations of production. The obvious failure of this prediction that the working class would create itself as a revolutionary historical subject points to the flaw of assuming a necessary link between a structural position of subordination and an oppositional consciousness.

Again, we see in this version of feminist standpoint theory the crucial slippage between female and feminist. We have no grounds for assuming that all women are in essence feminist, and that it is only the mystifying veil of male ideology that prevents them from recognizing their true interests. Against the master/slave thesis, for example, we can weigh the equally plausible Nietzschean theme of *ressentiment*. If the master is blinded by power, the slave may be blinded by the soul-destroying experience of powerlessness. She may be driven by hatred, fear, and envy of the master, an internalized sense of inferiority, and a compulsive and jealous dwelling upon the master's privilege. Being exploited is no guarantee of clarity of vision or possession of truth.

Furthermore, gender is hardly the only axis of oppression, and mainstream feminism has been forced in recent years to confront extensive criticisms of its race- and class-blindness. In this regard, there is a certain tactlessness in the feminist use of Hegel's master/slave metaphor: were the wife of the plantation owner and her black maid really sisters in slavery? The claim that women's superior knowledge of the world derives from their practical immersion in dishes and diapers ignores the fact that until recently, class and race decreed which women occupied themselves with such mundane routines. Again, it is hard to see how we can retrieve from such arguments a core of feminist truth that can succeed a deposed patriarchal wisdom.

Finally, another common defense of feminist epistemology is to argue that it is better, not because it is more true, but because it frankly admits its partiality and does not pretend to offer definitive wisdom and objective truth. I would agree that being conscious of one's biases and limited vision is better than claiming to have a God's-eye view of the world. Still, there is no simple correlation between such a view and gender difference. On the one hand, there are plenty of dogmatic feminists around; on the other, there are various traditions of philosophy—negative dialectics, deconstruction, pragmatism, and the like— that thrive on skepticism and a wariness of absolutes. The claim that contextualist positions are unique to women or feminists usually sets up a straw man of positivism as the epitome of "masculine" thought. This is, however, to skim over some very important countertendencies to the dogmatic worship of reason in Western thought.[16]

Trying to ground a feminist standpoint in the epistemology of women is, in my view, a dead end. I agree with Margareta Halberg that feminist epistemology is "an impossible project."[17] Female subordination does not lead automatically to superior knowledge and feminist resistance; indeed, for most of human history, it has spectacularly failed to do so. There is no *a priori* antagonism between patriarchy and women's values through which women are constituted as political subjects. To think of being a woman as a problematic condition is an insight that emerges only under specific historical circumstances. Thanks to the upheavals of modernity, including the growth of capitalism and the consequent emergence of individualist and egalitarian ways of thought, feminism becomes possible. The various philosophical assumptions, rhetorical figures, and narrative modes of feminist thought have continued to change over time. In other words, political identities are created in the flux of ideology and practice. They are not natural extensions of particular kinds of psyches or bodies.

## RETHINKING RATIONALITY: INTERSUBJECTIVITY AND COUNTER-PUBLIC SPHERES

At this point, however, we need to confront the political implications of this critique of feminist epistemology. Feminism cannot remain oblivious to an intellectual history that has dismantled a correspondence theory of truth and a philosophy of consciousness. Feminist scholars sympathetic to poststructuralism stress that any apprehension of reality is mediated by culture and language and that we can never shake knowledge free of ideological interests. Yet to conclude at this point by condemning feminist essentialism is hardly sufficient. This is merely to give the last word to a long-standing history of intellectual skepticism. Skepticism has an important role to play, but it also has its limits. The relentless questioning of fixed truths that goes on in the seminar room may not be much use in other cultural or political arenas.

Moreover, it is too simple to assume that because truth cannot be guaranteed, the whole question of epistemology can be jettisoned. Truth *claims* are indispensable; a political standpoint always asserts the cogency of a particular view of reality, even if only implicitly.[18] To argue a case for women's subordinate status is to commit oneself to discriminating between different descriptions of gender relations on the basis of their explanatory power. Critiques of the class, race, and heterosexist biases of mainstream feminism have made it clear that a single metanarrative cannot encompass women's diverse experiences and lives. But feminism is equally incompatible with a stance that denies the possibility of generalizing about anything and hence sanctions each and any perspective on the world as equally legitimate. As a result, feminism needs what Seyla Benhabib describes as "an epistemology and politics which recognizes the lack of metanarratives and foundational guarantees, but which nonetheless insists upon formulating minimal criteria of validity for our discursive and political practices."[19]

Some feminist scholars have chosen to respond to deconstructive skepticism by claiming the need for a "strategic essentialism" that affirms the provisional coherence of woman as a category. Such an argument, however, shifts us to a different terrain. We are no longer thinking about the superior knowledge afforded the female subject, but the value of certain ways of talking and arguing in trying to bring about social change. We have shifted from the terrain of the subjective to the intersubjective. This way of thinking offers, in my view, a plausible alternative to either a transcendental, universal model of rationality or a position that denies the possibility of distinguishing between truth claims and collapses all distinctions between truth and power. Seyla Benhabib offers a helpful discussion of this shift away from "the epistemic subject and the private contents of its consciousness" to the anchoring of truth claims in the "public signifying activities of a collection of subjects."[20] Language is conceptualized as a messy field of intersubjective symbolic practices linked to changing forms of life. Meaning does not spring from a private consciousness, nor is it embedded in the objective world. Rather, it derives from the communicative norms, models of interpretation, and narrative traditions generated by different social groups.

Similarly, Nancy Fraser speaks of a discourse ethic of solidarity grounded in an appeal to shared commitments that needs to be struggled for rather than simply assumed, and that draws on culturally specific vocabularies, interpretative resources, and forms of life.[21] Thus while women may have a potential greater sensitivity to the unequal dimensions of familial and social relations, female experience emerges as a meaningful category only within a framework. Even if this framework is feminist, it will, of course, be fractured by other social allegiances and identities. It is this status of feminism as a public network of cultural and political activities seeking to transform existing social relations that distinguishes it from the various forms of covert and tacit resistance that women have employed throughout history.

Thus we cannot establish the nature of feminist knowledge *a priori* by appealing to what we think a female self is or should be. We will know this knowledge only when it comes to expression in feminist interpretative communities. This does not mean that the content of feminist discourse is completely arbitrary. There are certain themes and preoccupations that recur (sexuality, reproduction, the gender division of labor), even though perspectives on these questions are shaped by the differing social positions of women and their degree of access to particular vocabularies and modes of public discourse.

The concept of a feminist public sphere is one useful model for thinking about the ideological features and institutional locations of feminist discourse in late capitalism.[22] I should emphasize that "public" in this context does not mean neutral impartiality and abstract equivalence. Rather, feminism has relocated difference squarely in the public domain. It has also helped to expand our definition of rationality. Instead of seeing reason purely in cognitive and instrumental terms and endorsing strict boundaries between reason and desire, feminists have argued that emotions, subjective response, and aesthetic expression can be legitimate ways of knowing and understanding the world.

The model of a feminist counter–public sphere dramatizes the contingent and changing forms of feminist discourse. These forms of discourse are embedded in a wide array of conditions, from socioeconomic changes in the role of women in late capitalism to the influence of other vocabularies, philosophies, and styles of thought on the development of feminist ideas. Clearly, gender is not an isolated variable; it is informed by differences of race, class, sexuality, and culture, which inspire various and sometimes contradictory accounts of

FEMINISM, POSTMODERNISM, AND THE CRITIQUE OF MODERNITY

women's experience. Rather than a homogeneous or unified grouping, the feminist public sphere is composed of loose and contingent coalitions of diverse groups. Equally clearly, some women—the white, educated, heterosexual middle class—have had a much greater power to set the agenda for feminist debate than other women. A sociological perspective that anchors feminist culture and politics in the power-laden practices of a counter–public sphere can look more carefully and realistically at the conflict and dissent among women. Yet such a perspective can also concede the historical importance of appeals to common goals, the strategic value of reclaiming repressed traditions, and the potential value of narratives and symbols of female identity as enabling fictions. In contrast to a deconstructive skepticism that revels in dismantling identities and undermining commonalities, public sphere theory sees the fashioning of imagined communities as an essential part of social change.

Anchoring feminist knowledge in the practices of a feminist public sphere thus does not require us to assume that such knowledge is free of ideology or power relations, or that it can anchor itself in an essential feminist truth. Rather, feminist discourse simply is the unending process of generating questions and critical interpretations of gender. The emergence of a counter–public sphere allows women's increased (if unequally distributed) access to networks of communication and interpretation. It allows them to reflect explicitly on what their desires and needs might be. Anchoring feminist knowledge in the practices of a counter–public sphere makes it clear that the question of what femaleness is or might be cannot be conclusively resolved. Rather, it is a permanent question posed by feminism; any answer will be partial and open to critique, contestation, and reformulation.

Looking at feminist practice in this way moves us beyond the impasse of universality versus particularity, of trying to decide whether feminism is a form of subjective or objective knowledge. Anchoring truth claims in the practices of discursive communities makes it clear that such communities rely on specific norms, values, and background assumptions that will shape the way they think. Yet the feminist public sphere is not unified but rather differentiated and fractured by the locations and specific contexts within which feminist activity takes place: women's groups, universities, health centers, bureaucracies, and so on. Moreover, it does not just exist alongside other forms of language and knowledge, but shapes and is shaped by them (see my discussion of hybridity in chapter 5). Rather than a radical incommensurability of paradigms, of "male" and "female" discourses that can only speak past each other, we can more accurately speak of degrees of family resemblance between sets of norms and assumptions that both overlap and diverge. As a porous public discourse, feminism is messy, conflicted, and impure.[23]

## FEMINISM AND MODERNITY

This linking of feminist theory to a counter–public sphere offers a perspective from which to consider feminism's relationship to modernity, and hence the question of whether or not it constitutes a postmodern politics. Modernity, almost as inchoate a term as postmodernism, usually refers to a diverse cluster of phenomena. These include not only socioeconomic changes such as industrialization, urban expansion, and a growing division of labor, but also an epistemic shift toward a secular worldview and the proclamation of universal ideals of reason, freedom, and equality. Rather than breaking completely with the past or simply continuing the Enlightenment tradition, feminism's relationship to modernity is dialectical and ambivalent, both dialogic and confrontational.

The feminist reconstruction of women's past has eloquently refuted narratives of universal progress, revealing often radical disjunctures between men's and women's history. Periods of supposedly progressive change have often coincided with a loss of power and status for women and occurred at their expense.[24] Thus bourgeois Enlightenment, for liberals and Marxists a crucial stage in the story of human emancipation, is seen by some feminist scholars as leading to a deterioration in women's condition as a result of the ever stricter separation of private and public spheres.From this perspective, the logic of modernity is essentially hostile to women's interests. The domination of instrumental reason, diagnosed in Adorno and Horkheimer's account of the pathologies of Enlightenment, fuses with the feminist critique of a patriarchal scientific tradition that has seen nature as a malleable feminine object to be dominated and subjugated. In the most pessimistic feminist reading, the modern era involves the escalating domination of a fundamentally irrational phallocentric reason, with catastrophic consequences.[25]

This view of the negative legacy of the Enlightenment leads to a global condemnation of modernity. Here feminism has often turned to Romanticism; the narrative of progress is reflected in inverted form in the myth of the fall, the nostalgia for lost innocence. This myth is clearly espoused in works of cultural feminism and ecofeminism such as Susan Griffin's *Woman and Nature*.[26] It also lies behind those forms of feminist psychoanalysis that celebrate the pre-Oedipal, the sensuous bliss of the mother's body before we are pulled remorselessly into the sphere of language and alienated subjectivity. Nostalgia is a powerful and perhaps ineradicable emotion that saturates visions of femaleness among feminists and nonfeminists alike.[27]

Nostalgia becomes a problem, however, if it sees all forms of social change as deleterious to women's interests. Feminism is, after all, profoundly implicated in the rapid transformations of cultural and social life that accompany modernity. For example, Joan Scott points to the contradictory legacy of the French

Revolution, which allowed some women to claim their rights as active citizens, while also cementing the link between citizenship and the white, male, bourgeois subject.[28] Christine Buci-Glucksmann argues that the growth of urban and industrial culture helped to disrupt traditional gender roles by depriving them of their natural and God-given quality, even as the doctrine of separate spheres sought to rein in and stabilize this ambiguity.[29] More recently, as Nancy Fraser points out, the large-scale movement of women into the workforce has brought new experiences of subordination but has also made possible a degree of economic independence, increased political participation, and an identity located outside the private sphere.[30] It is precisely the disjunctures and contradictions created by women's movement into the public world that provided the fertile terrain for feminism to reemerge as a force for social change. Angie McRobbie, for example, argues that feminism is a quintessentially modern movement in its gesturing toward the future and its insistence on access to the public sphere.[31]

What all this suggests is that the effects of modernization and modernity are ambiguous and complicated, and that we need to weigh the value of particular modern ideas and institutions. For example, struggles for equal representation in the workplace, government, or public sphere are not even partially resolved for women. Hence, as I indicated in chapter 5, egalitarian values rooted in an Enlightenment tradition are still relevant, even as feminists have pointed to the problems of an abstract and formal notion of equality that does not pay attention to differing contexts and needs. It is, moreover, in the contradictory spaces of such quintessentially modern institutions as bureaucracies and universities that feminism has made influential gains. The trend toward dismantling welfare structures, abolishing free or subsidized education, and placing further restrictions on abortion and other reproductive rights means that such basic rights cannot be taken for granted.

Of course, feminist scholars have also been highly critical of modern institutional frameworks, suggesting that such frameworks may free women from traditional forms of patriarchal authority only to enmesh them in more anonymous and insidious networks of domination and control. For example, the traditional nuclear family based on female dependence on a male breadwinner has been replaced by a feminization of poverty and a welfare clientele subject to processes of surveillance and regulation. Wendy Brown has expressed one of the most forceful feminist critiques of the state, arguing that "critical theory turned its gaze away from the state at the moment when a distinctively late modern form of state domination was being consolidated."[32]

There is a similar feminist ambivalence about capitalism. Feminists have often been less hasty than Marxists to condemn all aspects of capitalism, arguing that

FEMINISM, POSTMODERNISM, AND THE CRITIQUE OF MODERNITY

the experience of urban culture and consumerism allowed women to experience new forms of freedom and pleasure denied them by patriarchal constraints. Against the puritanical strands of certain forms of left cultural pessimism, for example, Elizabeth Wilson argues that certain features of modernity—constant change, urban anonymity, increased individualism, and the pursuit of pleasure, crystallized in the emblematic status of fashion—have been exhilarating and liberating for many women.[33] Scholars of sexuality have also explored the close links between modern urban capitalism and the crystallization of homosexual and lesbian identities.[34] Yet Stuart Ewan and Elizabeth Ewan echo the views of many feminist scholars when they point out that new pleasures and possibilities are intertwined with new forms of regimentation. "As women moved from the constricted family-dominated culture to the more individualized values of modern urban society, the form and content of domination changed, but new authorities replaced the old. In the name of freedom from tradition, women were trapped anew in fresh forms of sexual objectification and bound to the consumerized and sexualized household."[35]

One of feminism's main concerns has been to diagnose these repressive dimensions of modernization. Feminist critics have been acutely sensitive to the multiple levels at which power operates, showing how structures of domination may permeate the most mundane activities irrespective of the conscious intentions of individuals. In this sense, feminism differs from both liberalism and Marxism in its attention to what Habermas calls the "grammar of forms of life."[36] It looks at the politics of gender difference as they are embedded in language, clothing, movements and gesture, and the expression of emotional and sexual needs. If feminism's view of power is more diversified than that of its ideological predecessors, so is its view of agency. Women's resistance takes many forms and crops up in different places: it is not limited to either working within, or the revolutionary transformation of, state institutions.

## CONCLUSION

I have only touched briefly on the question of feminism's relationship to modernity, a question that obviously requires much more detailed investigation.[37] But I am not convinced that we can learn much from scholarly writing that counterposes a subversive postmodernity against an oppressive modernity. I confess to being particularly irritated by tables that draw up oppositions between the modern (hierarchy, reason, identity, depth) and the postmodern (anarchy, desire, difference, surface), while claiming in the same breath that postmodernism overcomes dualistic thinking. Such a view of the postmodern subsumes and simplifies the many political, cultural, and aesthetic strands of modernity. It betrays an exaggerated hope in the subversive power of postmodern ideas, often based, as Habermas suggests, on a denial of the contradictory and crisis-laden nature of modernity itself.[38] Furthermore, as I have noted at several points in this book, the apocalyptic appeal to deaths and endings obediently repeats one of the most enduring topoi of modernity, the radical negation of the past.

The terminological debate over whether feminism is modern or postmodern is ultimately of less interest than the actual task of thinking through feminism's complicated relationship to modernity. Drawing on an egalitarian social imaginary that derives from the democratic aspirations of the Enlightenment, feminists have also radicalized this tradition by turning it against itself, showing how the attempt to realize these ideals has created new forms of gender inequality. Rather than proclaiming the death of reason, subjectivity, and history, many feminists have suggested that these terms need to be thought differently in relation to the interests and struggles of gender politics.

I would also suggest that capitalism is a term missing from many discussions of feminism and postmodernism (Haraway's cyborg manifesto is one important exception). Instead, postmodernism is often seen as a phenomenon of thought, a crisis of truth and representation that is either beneficial or harmful to feminism. Yet ideas about language, identity, and reality are not purely autonomous and self-propelled; they connect in complicated ways to social and economic systems. Teresa Ebert has recently tackled this question, insisting that only a return to the truths of Marxism can save us from the errors of poststructuralist feminism. Yet Ebert's Marxism is singularly un-Marxist in the radical power it attributes to ideas. She claims that revolutionary theory can transform the structures of patriarchal capitalism, but without explaining how academic discourse connects to the broader social world or which class or group will be the agent of revolution. There is almost no engagement with the material historical conditions that have rendered the classic Marxist narrative of liberation obsolete, including the dramatic decline of the traditional working class.[39]

Unlike Ebert, I do not believe that "late capitalism" is a monolithic system of seamless domination, or that the interests of patriarchy and capitalism are automatically in synchrony. The relations between different levels of the social structure are neither automatic nor unidirectional, but need to be pinpointed in analysis. For example, early Marxist-feminist theory sometimes assumed that one could graft feminism onto classic Marxism by combining the category of reproduction with production to create a dual systems theory. Rather, the emergence of feminism and other social movements should be seen as a challenge to the ontology of labor and narrative of class conflict underpinning Marxist thought.

Still, the relative autonomy and differentiation of spheres should not prevent us from looking at widespread mechanisms of gender inequality, including the separation of paid work and privatized child rearing, the status of housework as invisible labor, and the assignment of many women, particularly women of color, to low-status and badly paid jobs. Donna Haraway, for example, presents a dazzling overview of new forms of gender inequality that result from the expansion of high-tech culture and new communication technologies. The model of the counter–public sphere as a critical forum reveals its obvious limitations at this point. If the validity claims of contemporary feminism are voiced through various forms of public debate, women's access to this public arena is clearly stratified by race, class, and education. Not all groups possess even potential access to frameworks through which difference can be expressed, so that otherness can simply trail off into voicelessness.[40] The linguistic turn in social theory gives us little help in understanding the structural inequalities of late capitalism as they affect women's desire or freedom to participate in critical discourse. Thus economic conditions, even though they do not simply cause or explain other levels of the social formation, nevertheless set brutal and real limits to the choices available to many women.

The relationship between postmodern ideas and late capitalism has important implications for feminist theory. Scholars sometimes celebrate a decentered, fragmented, "feminine" subjectivity as a bold resistance to the tyranny of a phallic unified self. As I noted in my discussion of Judith Krantz, however, such traditional gender distinctions may no longer make much sense in a consumer culture that feeds on dispersed subjectivity and the stimulation of desire. Terry Eagleton has made the most forceful case for the complicity of poststructuralist theory with late capitalist ideology.[41] We need not endorse his entire thesis in order to recognize the importance of situating linguistic, cultural, and psychic changes in socioeconomic contexts.

Feminist engagement with the inchoate cluster of ideas associated with the postmodern thus requires multitasking. It means paying attention to diverse and often contradictory strands of cultural expression and affiliation without losing sight of broader social determinants of inequality. It also means realizing that power and inequality do not simply reside in language, even though we can make sense of them only through language. I have already noted that the doxa of difference takes us only so far in this project. On the one hand, the idea of pluralism has freed itself from the Marxist sneer of "bourgeois." There is a general recognition that diversity is a good thing and that the current range of attitudes, affiliations, and perspectives cannot be encompassed and synthesized within a single vision. On the other hand, the celebration of difference does not address questions of power and control over language games, over who has ac-

FEMINISM, POSTMODERNISM, AND THE CRITIQUE OF MODERNITY

cess to modes of communication and interpretation. To think of feminism as merely one more localized strategy of subversion in a postmodern era trivializes and neutralizes the force of the feminist critique, reducing it to merely one more voice in the "happy polytheism" of language games.[42]

## NOTES

This essay was first published in *Cultural Critique* 13 (1989). Reprinted by permission of the publisher, University of Minnesota Press. A fellowship at Cornell University's Society for the Humanities allowed me to complete it. I am grateful to colleagues at Cornell and Murdoch University who provided helpful criticism on earlier drafts. Special thanks to Paula Treichler for detailed and perceptive comments. I have revised aspects of the original essay and updated some of the references.

1. Craig Owens, "The Discourse of Others: Feminists and Postmodernism," in *Postmodern Culture*, ed. Hal Foster (London: Pluto Press, 1985), 61-62.
2. Alice Jardine, *Gynesis: Configurations of Women and Modernity* (Ithaca: Cornell University Press, 1985), 155.
3. Barbara Creed, "From Here to Modernity: Feminism and Postmodernism," *Screen*, 28, 2 (1987): 68.
4. See, e.g., Alex Callinicos, "Postmodernism, Post-Structuralism, Post-Marxism?" *Theory, Culture and Society* 2, 3 (1985): 99; Zygmunt Bauman, "Is There a Postmodern Sociology?" *Theory, Culture and Society* 5, 2–3 (1988): 217-38.
5. Nancy Hartsock, "Rethinking Modernism: Minority vs. Majority Theories," *Cultural Critique* 7 (1987): 196.
6. Barbara Christian, "The Race for Theory," in *The Nature and Context of Minority Discourse*, ed. Abdul JanMohammed and David Lloyd (Oxford: Oxford University Press, 1990).
7. Somer Brodribb, *Nothing Mat(t)ers: A Feminist Critique of Postmodernism* (Melbourne: Spinifex, 1992), 20-21.
8. I borrow the term "postmodern problematic" from Stephen K. White, "Justice and the Postmodern Problematic," *Praxis International* 7, 3–4 (1987–88): 306-19.
9. Jean Baudrillard, *Simulations*, trans. Paul Foss et al. (New York: Semiotext(e), 1983); John Keane, *Public Life and Late Capitalism: Towards a Socialist Theory of Democracy* (Cambridge: Cambridge University Press, 1984).
10. Luce Irigaray, *Speculum of the Other Woman*, trans. Gillian C. Gill (Ithaca: Cornell University Press, 1985); Genevieve Lloyd, *The Man of Reason: "Male" and "Female" in Western Philosophy* (London: Methuen, 1984); Susan Mollin Okin, *Women in Western Political Thought* (Princeton: Princeton University Press, 1979).
11. See, e.g., Susan Hekman, "The Feminization of Epistemology: Gender and

the Social Sciences," *Women and Politics* 7, 3 (1987): 65-83. Hekman's discussion is, however, marred by its complete rejection of the Enlightenment tradition and a failure to recognize its self-critical dimensions.

12. Sandra Harding, "Is Gender a Variable in Conceptions of Rationality?" in *Beyond Domination: New Perspectives on Women and Philosophy*, ed. Carol Gould (Totowa, NJ: Rowman and Allanheld, 1984), 50. For uses of Chodorow's work, see also Nancy Hartsock, "The Feminist Standpoint: Developing the Ground for a Specifically Feminist Historical Materialism," and Jane Flax, "Political Philosophy and the Patriarchal Unconscious: A Psychoanalytical Perspective on Epistemology and Metaphysics," both in *Discovering Reality: Feminist Perspectives on Epistemology, Metaphysics, Methodology and Philosophy of Science*, ed. Sandra Harding and Merrill B. Hintikka (Dordrecht: D. Reider, 1983).

13. Jane Flax, "Postmodernism and Gender Relations in Feminist Theory," *Signs: Journal of Women in Culture and Society* 12, 4 (1987): 621-43.

14. Hartsock, "The Feminist Standpoint"; and Harding, "Is Gender a Variable in Conceptions of Rationality?" 44-45. Like Flax, Harding has become critical of feminist standpoint epistemologies, while also remaining wary of the "postmodernist" position that Flax has embraced. See Sandra Harding, "The Instability of the Analytical Categories of Feminist Theory," *Signs: Journal of Women in Culture and Society* 11, 4 (1986): 645-64.

15. Hilary Rose, "Hand, Brain and Heart: A Feminist Epistemology for the Natural Sciences," *Signs: Journal of Women in Culture and Society* 9, 1 (1983): 73-90.

16. See, for example, Ellen Messer-Davidow, "The Philosophical Bases of Feminist Literary Criticism," *New Literary History*, 19 1 (1987), and the response by Gerald Graff in the same volume.

17. Margareta Halberg, "Feminist Epistemology: An Impossible Project?" *Radical Philosophy* 53 (1989): 3-7. See also Mary E. Hawkesworth, "Knowers, Knowing, Known: Feminist Theory and Claims of Truth," *Signs: Journal of Women in Culture and Society* 14, 3 (1989): 533-57. For an argument that feminist epistemology does have a future, see Jane Duran, *Toward a Feminist Epistemology* (New York: Rowman and Littlefield, 1991).

18. Terry Eagleton has stressed this point. See "Two Approaches in the Sociology of Literature," *Critical Inquiry* 14, 3 (1988): 471.

19. Seyla Benhabib, "Epistemologies of Postmodernism: A Rejoinder to Jean-François Lyotard," *New German Critique*, no. 33 (1984): 126.

20. Benhabib, "Epistemologies of Postmodernism," 110.

21. Nancy Fraser, "Towards a Discourse Ethic of Solidarity," *Praxis International* 4 (1986): 425-29.

22. See, among others, Rita Felski, *Beyond Feminist Aesthetics: Feminist Literature and Social Change* (Cambridge: Harvard University Press, 1989), esp. 164-74; Nancy Fraser, "Rethinking the Public Sphere: A Contribution to the Cri-

tique of Actually Existing Democracy," in *Justice Interruptus: Critical Reflections on the "Postsocialist" Condition* (New York: Routledge, 1997). For a useful overview of recent public sphere theory, see G. Thomas Goodnight and David B. Hingstman, "Studies in the Public Sphere," *Quarterly Journal of Speech* 83 (1997): 351-70.

23. This argument draws on Helen Longino, "Feminist Critiques of Rationality" (paper delivered at the annual conference of the Australian Philosophy Association, Perth, March 1988). Longino's argument drew on her book, *Science as Social Knowledge: Value and Objectivity in Scientific Inquiry* (Princeton: Princeton University Press, 1990).

24. See Joan Kelly-Gadol, "The Social Relations of the Sexes: Methodological Implications of Women's History," *Signs: Journal of Women in Culture and Society* 1, 4 (1976) for an early discussion of this question. For a specific analysis of women's loss of status in revolutionary France, see Joan B. Landes, *Women and the Public Sphere in the Age of the French Revolution* (Ithaca: Cornell University Press, 1988).

25. Theodor Adorno and Max Horkheimer, *The Dialectic of Enlightenment* (London: Verso, 1979); Evelyn Fox Keller, *Reflections on Gender and Science* (New Haven: Yale University Press, 1985).

26. Susan Griffin, *Woman and Nature: The Roaring inside Her* (New York: Harper and Row, 1978).

27. For a detailed analysis of gender and nostalgia, see Rita Felski, "On Nostalgia," in *The Gender of Modernity* (Cambridge: Harvard University Press, 1995).

28. Joan Wallach Scott, *Only Paradoxes to Offer: French Feminists and the Rights of Man* (Cambridge: Harvard University Press, 1996).

29. Christine Buci-Glucksmann, *Baroque Reason: The Aesthetics of Modernity*, trans. Patrick Camiller (London: Sage, 1994).

30. Nancy Fraser, "What's Critical about Critical Theory? The Case of Habermas and Gender," in *Unruly Practices: Power, Discourse and Gender in Contemporary Social Theory* (Minneapolis: University of Minnesota Press, 1989).

31. Angie McRobbie, review of Marshall Berman's *All That Is Solid Melts into Air: The Experience of Modernity*, *Feminist Review* 18 (1984): 129-33.

32. Wendy Brown, *States of Injury: Power and Freedom in Late Modernity* (Princeton: Princeton University Press, 1995), 18.

33. Elizabeth Wilson, *Adorned in Dreams: Fashion and Modernity* (Berkeley: University of California Press, 1985).

34. John D'Emilio, "Capitalism and Gay Identity," in *Making Trouble: Essays on Gay History, Politics and the University* (New York: Routledge, 1992).

35. Elizabeth Ewan and Stewart Ewan, *Channels of Desire: Mass Images and the Shaping of American Consciousness* (New York: McGraw-Hill, 1982), 105.

36. Jürgen Habermas, "New Social Movements," *Telos* 49 (1981): 33.

37. For the detailed analysis that grew out of the original version of this chapter,

FEMINISM, POSTMODERNISM, AND THE CRITIQUE OF MODERNITY

see Felski, *The Gender of Modernity,* in particular "Myths of the Modern" and "Feminism and Modernity." See also Barbara Marshall, *Engendering Modernity: Feminism, Social Theory and Social Change* (Cambridge: Polity Press, 1994).

38. Jürgen Habermas, *The Philosophical Discourse of Modernity* (Cambridge: MIT Press, 1987). See also Peter Dews, *Post-Structuralist Thought and the Claims of Critical Theory* (London: Verso, 1987).

39. Teresa Ebert, *Ludic Feminism and After: Postmodernism, Desire, and Labor in Late Capitalism* (Ann Arbor: University of Michigan Press, 1996). Ebert's failure to engage the work of such important, Marxist-influenced feminist scholars as Nancy Fraser and Seyla Benhabib is also puzzling.

40. White, "Justice and the Postmodern Problematic," 310.

41. Terry Eagleton, "Capitalism, Modernism, and Postmodernism," in *Against the Grain: Selected Essays* (London: Verso, 1986). See also *The Illusions of Postmodernism* (Oxford: Basil Blackwell, 1996).

42. Benhabib, "Epistemologies of Postmodernism," 124. Nancy Fraser and Linda Nicholson comment on the limitations of Lyotard's account of language games in "Social Criticism without Philosophy: An Encounter between Feminism and Postmodernism," in *Feminism/Postmodernism,* ed. Linda Nicholson (New York: Routledge, 1990).

# INDEX

Acker, Kathy, 5
Adams, Barbara, 17, 19–20
Adorno, Theodor, 66, 68, 86, 102, 162, 202
Althusser, Louis, 90
Ang, Ien, 8, 125–26, 127–29, 169
Angel, Maria, 106
Anzaldúa, Gloria, 8
Appadurai, Arjun, 56, 63–64, 66, 67, 69, 73, 76n. 33
Aristotle, 157
Armstrong, Nancy, 26

Bakhtin, Mikhail, 35
Balzac, Honoré de, 107, 100, 108, 110

Banks, William M., 174n. 39
Barkan, Elazar, 47
Barrett, Michèle, 118
Barry, Judith, 192n. 24
Barthes, Roland, 90
Battersby, Christine, 176, 177–78
Baudrillard, Jean, 7, 9, 103, 113, 138, 139–42, 146, 147, 148, 149, 151
Bauman, Zygmunt, 156, 187
Benhabib, Seyla, 199
Bech, Henning, 56, 59, 65, 67, 68–69
Beckett, Samuel, 90
Benjamin, Walter, 59, 70
Bennett, Tony, 167

# ABOUT THE AUTHOR

**RITA FELSKI** was born in Birmingham, England. She studied French and German at Cambridge University and went on to do graduate study in Australia. After gaining her M.A. and Ph.D. at Monash University, she taught English and Comparative Literature for several years at Murdoch University in Western Australia. Since 1994 she is Professor of English at the University of Virginia.

Rita Felski is also the author of *Beyond Feminist Aesthetics: Feminist Literature and Social Change* (1989) and *The Gender of Modernity* (1995), both published by Harvard University Press. In 2000 she was a visiting fellow at the Institute for Human Sciences in Vienna.